Boxing Is...

BOOKS BY THOMAS HAUSER
GENERAL NON-FICTION
Missing
The Trial of Patrolman Thomas Shea
For Our Children (with Frank Macchiarola)
The Family Legal Companion
Final Warning: The Legacy of Chernobyl (with Dr. Robert Gale)
Arnold Palmer: A Personal Journey
Confronting America's Moral Crisis (with Frank Macchiarola)
Healing: A Journal of Tolerance and Understanding
Miscellaneous
With This Ring (with Frank Macchiarola)
A God To Hope For

ABOUT BOXING
The Black Lights: Inside the World of Professional Boxing
Muhammad Ali: His Life and Times
Muhammad Ali: Memories
Muhammad Ali: In Perspective
Muhammad Ali & Company
A Beautiful Sickness
A Year At The Fights
Brutal Artistry
The View From Ringside
Chaos, Corruption, Courage, and Glory
The Lost Legacy of Muhammad Ali
I Don't Believe It, But It's True
Knockout (with Vikki LaMotta)
The Greatest Sport of All
The Boxing Scene
An Unforgiving Sport
Waiting For Carver Boyd
Boxing Is . . .

FICTION
Ashworth & Palmer
Agatha's Friends
The Beethoven Conspiracy
Hanneman's War
The Fantasy
Dear Hannah
The Hawthorne Group
Martin Bear & Friends
Mark Twain Remembers
Finding The Princess

Boxing Is . . .

Reflections on the Sweet Science

Thomas Hauser

The University of Arkansas Press
Fayetteville
2010

ISBN-10: 1–55728–942–5
ISBN-13: 978–1–55728–942–1

14   13   12   11   10   5   4   3   2   1

⊗ The paper used in this publication meets the minimum requirements of the
American National Standard for Permanence of Paper for Printed Library Materials
Z39.48–1984.

Library of Congress Cataloging-in-Publication Data

Hauser, Thomas.
  Boxing is— : reflections on the sweet science / Thomas Hauser.
      p. cm.
  Includes bibliographical references.
  ISBN 978-1-55728-942-1 (pbk. : alk. paper)
  1. Boxing—United States. 2. Boxers (Sports)—United States—Anecdotes. I. Title.
  GV1125.H29 2010
  796.83—dc22

                                                                2010015354

*For Larry Malley and the rest of the staff
at the University of Arkansas Press,
for giving me a home*

Contents

Round 4: Non-Combatants

Author's Note

Boxing Is . . . contains the articles about professional boxing that I authored in 2009. The articles I wrote about the sweet science prior to that date have been published in *Muhammad Ali & Company; A Beautiful Sickness; A Year at the Fights; The View From Ringside; Chaos, Corruption, Courage, and Glory; The Lost Legacy of Muhammad Ali; I Don't Believe It, But It's True; The Greatest Sport of All, The Boxing Scene,* and *An Unforgiving Sport.*

Special thanks are due to Secondsout.com, under whose aegis most of the articles in this book first appeared.

Round 1
Fights and Fighters

Each year, I look forward to writing a historical retrospective about one of the alltime greats. In 2009, it was Sugar Ray Robinson.

Sugar Ray Robinson Revisited

Sugar Ray Robinson is the gold standard against which all fighters are judged.

"He had everything," legendary trainer Eddie Futch said after Robinson died. "Boxing skills, punching power, a great chin, mental strength. There was nothing he couldn't do. He knew almost everything there was to know about how to box. When Ray was in his prime, he owned the ring like no fighter before or since."

Robinson was a natural welterweight who knocked out middleweights with one punch. In his first 131 professional fights, he lost once. During that time, he beat Henry Armstrong, Sammy Angott (twice), Fritzie Zivic (twice), Tommy Bell (twice), Kid Gavilan (twice), and Jake LaMotta (five times).

In 201 fights spanning twenty-five years (a career that began before Pearl Harbor and ended at the height of the war in Vietnam), Robinson suffered a single "KO by." That came when he challenged Joey Maxim for the light-heavyweight championship and collapsed from heat prostration after controlling the fight for thirteen rounds.

Sixty years after Robinson was in his prime, he's still thought of as the greatest fighter to ever lace on a pair of gloves.

Boxing has the most distinguished written history of any sport, but the literature on Robinson is surprisingly thin. His 1969 autobiography (ghostwritten by Dave Anderson) is typical of its time, offering a cleaned-up version of a multi-faceted life. The other biographies currently in print range from ordinary to dreadful. This autumn, Alfred A. Knopf will publish *Sweet Thunder: The Life and Times of Sugar Ray Robinson* by Wil Haygood. Haygood researches thoroughly and writes well. He comes closer than any of his predecessors to explaining Robinson's legacy, both in and out of the ring.

Two film documentaries are also worthy of mention. *Sugar Ray Robinson: Pound For Pound* was produced by Bill Cayton in 1970 and presents the best of the existing Robinson fight footage. *Sugar Ray Robinson: The Bright Lights and Dark Shadows of a Champion* (an HBO *Sports of the 20th Century* documentary) gives Robinson his due as a fighter and reveals many of his personal flaws.

Putting the pieces of the puzzle together, a remarkable portrait emerges.

In 1920, a man named Walker Smith moved from rural Georgia to Detroit and took a job as a construction worker. Several months later, his wife (Leila) and two daughters joined him. On May 3, 1921, Walker Smith Jr (known to the world as "Sugar Ray Robinson") was born.

Eventually, Leila Smith separated from her husband because of his abusive behavior and philandering ways. She took her children to Georgia, left them with her mother, and returned to Detroit, where she worked as a maid at the Statler Hotel. Eventually, she saved enough money to bring her son and daughters back to Detroit. In 1932, they moved to New York. She rented an apartment in an area of the city known as Hell's Kitchen and found a job as a seamstress. At night, her son went to Times Square, where theater patrons gathered on the sidewalk during intermission. He danced for them as they tossed coins his way. In 1933, the family moved to Harlem.

Walker Jr quit school in ninth grade. Thereafter, he hustled on the streets and seemed destined for bad things. His life was saved by boxing. In 1928, when he was seven years old, his mother had set aside twenty-five cents a month so he could spend time at the Brewster Recreation Center in Detroit, where he was introduced to the rudiments of boxing. He enjoyed the sport. But as he'd grown older, discipline was a problem.

Eddie Futch (who worked with amateurs in Detroit in the early 1930s) later recalled, "There was an eleven-year-old who would come to the gym. He wasn't there to train; just hang out with his friends and make noise. One day, he made so much noise that I chased him out of the gym and told him not to come back until he was ready to behave himself."

Smith never came back. After his family moved to New York, he was introduced to George Gainford, who coached the boxing team for the Salem Crescent Athletic Club (located in the basement of the Salem Methodist Church in Harlem).

"At first, he didn't look like much of a fighter," Gainford said of the man who would later become the greatest fighter of all time. "All he did was hit and run. But he had one thing; he wanted to learn. He was the first kid in the gym and the last one to leave. He'd say to me, 'Suppose I do this; what do the other guy do?' I'd tell him, and then he'd say, 'And suppose I do this and this. Then what happens?'"

Dates blur when Walker Smith Jr's early years are discussed. What's clear is that there came a time when Gainford took a team from the Salem Crescent Athletic Club to a fight card in Kingston, New York. A club member who was slated to box in a flyweight bout that night failed to appear. Smith had made the trip with the team as a spectator and asked to take his place. But he'd never fought in an authorized bout and didn't have the requisite Amateur Athletic Union card.

Gainford shuffled through a stack of AAU cards that he carried with him and chose one with the name "Ray Robinson" (a fighter who had stopped coming to the gym). "That's you," he told Smith.

"Ray Robinson" won a unanimous decision. A week later, he returned to Kingston, fought again under the same name, and emerged victorious for the second time.

On January 5, 1939, Gainford and his team traveled to Watertown, New York, where "Ray Robinson" triumphed over a highly regarded amateur named Dom Perfetti. After the fight, Jack Case (sports editor for the *Watertown Daily Times*) told the coach, "That's a sweet fighter you've got there."

Some versions of the story say that what came next emanated from Gainford's lips. Others attribute it to a woman who was standing nearby and overheard the conversation. Everyone agrees that the next three words spoken were, "Sweet as Sugar."

The following day, Case's article in the *Watertown Daily Times* referenced "Sugar Ray Robinson."

A legend had been born.

Years later, Gainford would boast, "I'm the greatest trainer who ever lived. I trained Sugar Ray Robinson." The response he heard was, "George, you've had hundreds of fighters. Why weren't they all as good as Sugar Ray?"

Robinson had an unblemished record of 85 wins with 69 knockouts in 85 amateur fights. Forty of those knockouts were in the first round. He won the New York City Golden Gloves featherweight championship in

1939 and the lightweight title in 1940 at a time when New York was the center of the boxing world and amateur boxing mattered.

On September 19, 1940, he filed an application for a professional boxer's license with the New York State Athletic Commission. He listed his address as 215 West 116th Street in New York and his previous occupation as "tap dancer." The "name" entered on the application was "Walker Smith." The "ring name" was "Ray Robinson." He signed the application "Raymond Robinson."

On October 4th, Robinson made his professional debut at Madison Square Garden and knocked out Joe Echeverria in the second round. Four nights later, he scored another second-round stoppage on a card in Savannah, Georgia.

On September 19, 1941, after 23 consecutive victories, Robinson was matched against Maxie Shapiro in his first Garden main event.

"I moved out in the first round and went into a crouch," Shapiro said years later. "All of a sudden—whsst! This blur went past my head. Then—whsst! Another blur. It must have been something like that in the foxholes. The second round, I didn't get low enough. It felt like I got hit in the forehead with a baseball bat. I was on the floor twice. In the third round, I was being careful, but he was too fast. Whsst! Here it comes, and I'm on the floor again."

Robinson knocked Shapiro out in the third round. Six weeks later, he fought the first of two consecutive fights against Fritzie Zivic. "I boxed Sugar Ray Robinson a couple of times," Zivic would reminisce. "Real tough; and everything I done, he done better. His hands went off automatic."

By the end of September 1942, Robinson was undefeated in 35 fights and had been on the cover of *Ring Magazine*. On October 2nd, he entered the ring at Madison Square Garden for the first of six wars that he would wage against Jake LaMotta.

LaMotta (fourteen months younger than Robinson) had turned pro five months after his more celebrated rival. Ray's debut had been on the undercard of a welterweight championship fight at Madison Square Garden. Jake's maiden voyage (for which he'd been paid twenty-five dollars) was at St. Nicholas Arena. Both men were products of the streets of New York. Robinson was Harlem; LaMotta, the Bronx.

Robinson was tall for a welterweight; an inch shy of six feet; slender with great punching power. LaMotta was a natural middleweight; short and stocky with good ring skills and an otherworldly ability to withstand punishment. One commentator later likened him in appearance to a hairy-chested garbage collector.

LaMotta was to Robinson as Joe Frazier was to Muhammad Ali; the less physically-skilled, equally tough, indomitable foe.

LaMotta entered the ring for his first fight against Robinson with a thirteen-pound weight advantage. "He hurt me a couple of times," Ray acknowledged afterward. "I never fought a fighter as strong as he is." But Robinson emerged with a unanimous ten-round decision.

On February 5, 1943, in Detroit, they fought again. *Ring Magazine* had just named Robinson its 1942 "Fighter of the Year." His record was now 40-and-0, and he was a 3-to-1 betting favorite. This time, there was a sixteen-pound weight differential between the two men. LaMotta knocked Robinson down in the eighth round and won a unanimous verdict.

The following day, a headline in the *New York Times* blared, "End of Robinson Streak Shocks Ring World."

Two weeks later, Robinson decisioned Jackie Wilson at Madison Square Garden. One week after that, he returned to Detroit for his second fight in three weeks against LaMotta. This time, despite being knocked down in round seven, Sugar Ray prevailed on all three scorecards.

Several days after beating LaMotta for the second time, Robinson was inducted into the United States Army. World War II was raging. In August 1943, he and Joe Louis began a tour of military bases in the United States, giving boxing exhibitions for soldiers who were about to be sent overseas. Louis was the big name; Robinson the up-and-coming star. There were some ugly moments on segregated bases in southern states. Both men stood their ground.

Then Louis and Robinson were sent to Fort Hamilton in Brooklyn, preparatory to continuing their tour abroad to boost the morale of American troops who were fighting in Europe. Robinson indicated that he had no interest in leaving the United States. The penalty for desertion was explained to him. At that point, depending on one's version of events, either Robinson went AWOL or suffered a medical crisis. Either way, on March 29, 1944, he disappeared.

Shortly after midnight on April 1st, Robinson was "found" by a stranger on a street in Manhattan. He was taken to a hospital on Staten Island, where he told Army investigators that he had no memory of what had happened during the preceding three days but believed that he had tripped over a duffel bag in the barracks and fallen down a flight of stairs, banging his head and incurring a severe case of amnesia.

The examining physicians found no credible evidence of brain trauma. On April 7th, Robinson was detained by military police and held for court-martial. Then, for reasons that are unclear, on June 3, 1944 (three days before D-Day), he was discharged from the Army on "medical" grounds.

Years later, Robinson asked noted sportswriter W. C. Heinz to ghost-write his autobiography. Heinz declined because Robinson failed to explain his military history with what the writer thought was sufficient candor. The fact that Robinson never again suffered from "amnesia" and, in 201 professional fights, was never knocked unconscious casts further doubt on his conduct with regard to the Army.

Robinson resumed his ring career in October 1944 and ran off eight victories in a row. On February 23, 1945, he fought LaMotta for the fourth time and won a unanimous decision. On September 26, 1945, they battled again. Sugar Ray prevailed on a split verdict that was poorly received in some circles. Afterward, he acknowledged, "LaMotta is the toughest man I've ever fought. I've fought him five times and hit him with everything I know how to throw, but he still stands up."

They had now fought five times. Robinson was twenty-four years old. LaMotta was twenty-three.

"All the fights I had with him were very close," Jake said after both men had retired. "That's why we fought six times. You don't fight six times unless it's very very close."

Fighters were fashioned from rough cloth in those days. They fought with cuts that hadn't healed. They fought with faces that were bruised before the bell rang for round one. To be considered a contender, a man had to beat more than a few world-class fighters.

Robinson had done all that was asked of him. As 1946 began, the injustice in his not having had a title fight was obvious. Former welterweight champion Freddie Cochrane had ducked him. Then Marty Servo seized the crown from Cochrane. But Servo had lost to Robinson twice in the early 1940s and wanted nothing more to do with him.

Sportswriters and fans began referring to Sugar Ray as "the uncrowned champion." He fought twelve times in the first nine months of 1946, winning on each occasion. He'd now had seventy-two fights with a single loss.

On September 25, 1946, Servo announced his retirement from boxing. Finally, a championship fight was within reach. Robinson defeated a club fighter named Ossie Harris; knocked out Cecil Hudson; and five days after beating Hudson, journeyed to Cleveland to fight Artie Levine.

In the fourth round, Levine knocked Robinson down. Sugar Ray later said that it was the hardest he was ever hit. After walking Levine to a neutral corner, the referee returned to Robinson and picked up the count at "one"—a quintessential "long count." Robinson struggled to his feet at "nine" and barely survived the round. He knocked Levine out in the tenth stanza.

On December 20, 1946, in his seventy-sixth professional fight, Sugar Ray Robinson fought Tommy Bell at Madison Square Garden for the vacant welterweight championship of the world. Joe Louis, Jack Dempsey, and Gene Tunney were at ringside. In the second round, Bell knocked Robinson down with a sharp left hook. But as the bout progressed, Robinson took control, staggering his foe several times and dropping him once. There was little doubt as to the outcome after fifteen hard-fought rounds.

In his autobiography, Robinson recalled, "The ring announcer was holding a microphone and blaring 'The new world welterweight champion . . .' And even though he was only a few feet away, I could hardly hear him. My ears were almost bursting with the noise. The most noise seemed to come down out of the balcony; a steady roar, like a waterfall splashing all over me. Unless you've been in that ring when the noise is for you, there's no way you'll ever know what it's like. The sound wasn't the same as it had been at my other pro fights or when I won my Golden Gloves titles. I always had the feeling that the spectators were saying, 'Good for you, kid, but let's see the rest of the bouts.' This time, there were no more bouts. They were cheering for me, the world champion."

There's no such thing as perfection in boxing. But Sugar Ray Robinson as welterweight champion of the world came close. He had prodigious physical gifts and a disciplined work ethic. He was always in condition and all business in the gym.

"When Ray went to the gym," says Don Turner, "he wasn't there to party. He didn't play to the crowd. All he cared about was getting ready for the fight. There was no radio, no entourage. If someone was talking loud, Ray threw him out. He shadow-boxed like there was a guy in front of him. When he punched the heavy bag, it was five-punch combinations. Every punch meant something and it sounded like he was shooting guns. No fighter worked harder, and everyone else in the gym worked harder because he was there."

"Ray had his own music in the gym," says Angelo Dundee. "It was the slap of the jump-rope against the floor and the whappity-whack of his fists hitting the speed-bag. He put on a show. It was like going to the opera. You didn't talk. You just watched and listened."

"The great layer of muscle on the back of Robinson's neck," A. J. Liebling observed, "is the outward indication of his persistence. It is the kind that can be developed only by endless years of exercise."

But Robinson had more than a rigid work ethic and great physical gifts. He had courage, heart, the pride of a champion, and an unyielding will to win.

"Also," Don Turner adds, "to be a great fighter, it helps if part of you is a mean arrogant nobody-likes-you prick. And Robinson had that. That's for sure. He was a nasty guy in the ring. And lots of times, he was a nasty guy outside it."

Watching Robinson in combat was like watching a graceful deadly tiger. Most fighters can hurt an opponent with a straight righthand, an uppercut, or left hook, but not with all three punches. Most fighters can disable a foe with the first or last punch in a combination, but not with every punch in a sequence. Robinson threw combinations all the time with both hands to every part of the body and could knock an opponent out with any punch at any time. If he missed the first two punches in a combination, he'd land the third.

"To get physically and mentally prepared to fight a dozen or more times a year is extraordinary in itself," Emanuel Steward observes. "Ray did that. And when he was in the ring, there was nobody like him. He was a smart fighter and a tough vicious competitor. Nobody punched harder to the head or body, and nobody had a better chin. He never lay back. He never eased up. He applied constant pressure, round after round; fighting, fighting, fighting; always trying to knock the other guy out. And he didn't just knock guys out. He knocked guys out cold."

"Ray was so superior to everyone else," Steward continues. "He could do everything. And the most amazing thing was, he made mistakes—all fighters make mistakes—but he had no technical flaws. The top three fighters of all time are Sugar Ray Robinson, Sugar Ray Robinson, and Sugar Ray Robinson."

Declining to match one of his fighters against Robinson, Irving Cohen declared, "I'm a manager, not an undertaker."

Lightweight champion Ike Williams voiced similar reservations and later acknowledged, "I wouldn't fight Sugar Ray Robinson because I never could have beaten him. When I mentioned the possibility of such a fight to my wife, she said, 'Ike; that's one fight I don't want to see.' I didn't either."

Harry Markson (director of boxing for Madison Square Garden), observed, "With all due respect to all the good fighters who were before my time, I can't conceive of a better fighter than Ray Robinson. To be better than Robinson, you'd have to improve on perfection."

And W. C. Heinz wrote, "When I was young, I used to hear the old men talk of Joe Gans, Terry McGovern, and Kid McCoy. They told me of Sam Langford, Stanley Ketchel, and Benny Leonard. When I am old, I shall tell them about Sugar Ray Robinson."

In addition to being a great fighter, Robinson had style and more flair in the ring than any fighter who had come before him. "The thing that gets you is the way he moves," A. J. Liebling wrote. "He is such a combination of skill and grace."

"When Ray walked into the ring," Angelo Dundee recalls, "it was like he was going to a ballroom dance. He had a walk that no one could copy. Smooth, like he was gliding on ice skates. The first thing he'd do was shake hands with the referee. His robe and trunks were always pressed just right. Ray dressed well just to go to a weigh-in."

That style was also evident away from boxing. Robinson went to great lengths to groom his public image. He had jet-black processed pompadour hair and neatly manicured nails. Once he became champion, his wardrobe, by his count, consisted of "about twenty-five suits, a dozen sports jackets, a couple dozen pairs of slacks, a couple dozen pairs of shoes, three tuxedos, and drawers full of shirts and sweaters."

"He had that look," Jerry Izenberg says. "There was an aura about him. He carried himself like a champion and he carried himself like a star. Even if you didn't know who he was, if you were in the room when he came in, you knew he was special. In and out of the ring, people were happy just to look at him."

Robinson hung around with the movie stars and popular singers of his era. There was also the matter of his car; a fuchsia-colored Cadillac convertible with white-walled tires. Robinson called it "the Hope Diamond of Harlem" and "the symbol of my reputation."

"When people think they recognize a celebrity," he said in his auto-biography, "they hesitate a moment. But when they saw me in that car, they knew. There was only one like it; Sugar Ray's pink Cadillac. Most people called it pink. But to me, it was always more than pink."

And there was the beautiful wife. Robinson met Edna Mae Holly at an outdoor swimming pool in 1941. She came from a middle-class family and had taken courses at Hunter College in New York before becoming a professional dancer. She'd worked at fashionable venues like the famed Cotton Club in Harlem and performed behind stars like Lena Horne.

Robinson pursued Edna Mae with flowers and increasingly luxurious gifts. She started attending his fights. They were married in 1943. He was twenty-two years old; she was twenty-seven. In 1945, they bought a house in the upscale Riverdale section of the Bronx.

Edna Mae had her own charisma. Husband and wife looked like a fairy-tale prince and princess when they were out on the town together.

"Robinson was a superstar personality in the age of print," Larry Merchant observes. "God knows how big he would have been if he'd come along during the explosion of sports on television. A few athletes before him had developed their own public persona. But Sugar Ray was unlike any black athlete that America had seen before."

Robinson also broke the mold in that he was the first black fighter (and one of the few fighters of any color up until his time) to successfully control his own ring career.

"In the fight game," W. C. Heinz wrote, "they like fighters who will fight anybody anywhere at any time and leave the business end to their managers."

Robinson was the antithesis of that. Curt Horrmann was his manager when he turned pro. Horrmann came from a wealthy New York family and was looking for a good time. He could afford to pay for sparring partners and give Robinson enough of a stipend that the fighter wouldn't have to work outside the ring.

Horrmann was entitled by contract to receive one-third of Robinson's earnings. George Gainford took 10 percent. Robinson received the rest. Once Ray's career was launched, he forced Horrmann out (ultimately paying a settlement of $10,000). From then on, he was self-managed.

Robinson's fights attracted the moneyed black elite (both legitimate businessmen and hustlers) in a way that wasn't duplicated until Muhammad Ali in the 1970s. He sold tickets. He knew it. And he demanded his due from promoters; sometimes more.

"Robinson," Red Smith wrote, "is the only man in the world who can unbutton a promoter's shirt from behind while wearing boxing gloves and remove the victim's pants and bankroll."

In other words, he wanted to be properly compensated.

"If I had to get punched," Robinson reflected when his career was over, "I was going to get as much money as I could for it. If I was due a dollar, I wanted that dollar. And if I could help a man make a dollar, I thought I deserved part of it."

"Why do you put up with Robinson?" James Norris (president of the International Boxing Club, which controlled Madison Square Garden and most of boxing in the 1940s) asked Harry Markson. "You don't need him."

"I know," Markson answered. "But he's such a good fighter."

A fighter who constantly dreamed of more.

Prior to Robinson's appearance on the boxing scene, there had been popular champions (particularly heavyweights) who were well-paid for stage appearances during their ring career. Some (most notably, Jack Dempsey) opened restaurants when their fighting days were done.

Robinson sought to create a business empire while he was an active fighter. Within weeks of winning the welterweight championship, he opened Sugar Ray's Café in Harlem. "My café had a good reputation," he noted in his autobiography. "Women enjoyed coming because it had rules. There were always fancy people arriving."

Fancy people like Frank Sinatra, Jackie Gleason, Nat King Cole,

Dorothy Dandridge, and Eartha Kitt; not to mention sports heroes like Joe Louis, Joe DiMaggio, and Jackie Robinson.

The café was a magnet for "beautiful people" before anyone thought to label them as such. Soon, the west side of Seventh Avenue between 123rd and 124th Streets in Harlem was dominated by Ray Robinson Enterprises (his business office), the Golden Gloves Barber Shop, Sugar Ray's Quality Cleaners, and Edna Mae's Lingerie Shop.

Robinson had become the standard bearer for a new kind of athlete; although where the media was concerned, much of his importance slipped between the cracks. The sportswriters of that day were largely disinterested in what happened beyond the playing field. And in a way, that was a blessing for Ray because it shielded the uglier aspects of his personal life from scrutiny.

Robinson's first entanglement of note with a woman had come at age seventeen, when he impregnated a girl named Marjie.

Marjie was underage. According to Robinson's autobiography, his mother told him, "If you don't marry her, you'll go to prison and that will be on your record for the rest of your life. You have to get married."

The autobiography then recounts, "We had a quiet ceremony at a little red-brick church in the neighborhood. After the wedding, I never even kissed my bride. She walked away with her father and mother. I went back to our apartment with Mom. We were like two criminals being led away to different cells."

Ronnie Smith was born on September 25, 1939. Later that year, his parents' marriage was annulled. For the rest of his life, he had little contact with his father.

Nor did Robinson's only child by Edna Mae fare much better. "What kind of father was my dad?" Ray Robinson Jr asked rhetorically after Sugar Ray's death. Then he answered his own question with one word: "Horrible."

A lot of women lusted after Robinson from a distance during his marriage to Edna Mae. There were quite a few up close, too. He was a profligate womanizer.

"There were so many of them," Edna Mae later said. "And just one me."

But it was worse than that.

"Dad would have three or four rooms in the Hotel Theresa [in Harlem] where he kept his girls," Ray Robinson Jr recalled. "And when he got caught, it precipitated violence. I think one of the reasons my mother had so many miscarriages [five] was because of the abuse she suffered from my father. I can recall him hitting her on several occasions for no reason at all."

"He had a hell of a temper," Edna Mae acknowledged. "If he got angry, everybody stayed out of his way. He'd give me a slap if he thought I deserved one."

One of the few writers who didn't shy away from comment on Robinson's character flaws was Sam Lacy (a leading sportswriter in the black community, now enshrined in the writers wing of the Major League Baseball Hall of Fame). Swimming against the tide, Lacy wrote, "I have said many times that Sugar Ray Robinson was the greatest athlete in a given field I have had the pleasure of observing. I have also said many times that he can be one of the most disgusting figures one is compelled to meet in his business."

After Robinson won the welterweight championship, he fought four non-title bouts against soft competition. Then, on June 24, 1947, he returned to Cleveland (the site of his near-defeat at the hands of Artie Levine) for the first defense of his crown.

The opponent was Jimmy Doyle. It was a bad fight for Doyle to take. Fifteen months earlier, he had been knocked out by Levine and rendered unconscious for fifteen minutes. He was carried from the ring on a stretcher and hospitalized for observation. The doctors who tended to him recommended that he not fight again. He was a disaster waiting to happen.

Robinson dominated Doyle throughout. A left hook in round eight ended matters. Lewis Burton of the *New York Journal-American* wrote, "Doyle fell back rigidly, pivoting on his heels as if they were hinged to the canvas. He cracked against the floor in three parts, his seat, his shoulders, and finally, like the snapping end of a whip, the back of his head."

The beaten fighter was rushed to St. Vincent's Charity Hospital, where surgery was performed to relieve pressure on his brain caused by a cerebral hemorrhage. He died the following afternoon. He was twenty-two years old.

Robinson fought five more times in 1947, five times in 1948, thirteen times in 1949, and eight times in the first six months of 1950. On August 9, 1950, against a clearly overmatched Charlie Fusari, he defended his welterweight championship for the final time.

By all accounts, Robinson refused to do business with the mob throughout his ring career. The Fusari fight might have been an exception. On the surface, Ray took the fight as a favor to Walter Winchell for a one-dollar purse with the proceeds going to the Damon Runyon Cancer Fund. But a substantial bet is said to have been placed on his behalf at 5-to-1 odds that the bout would go the distance.

Robinson-Fusari lasted for fifteen stultifying rounds. In his autobiography, Robinson acknowledged, "I occasionally agreed to carry an opponent. I never considered it morally wrong. As long as I was winning the fight, I saw no reason why I had to punish a lesser opponent. I'm sure guys in the know made some money betting on an opponent going the distance with me, but I never bet on any of my fights." Then he added, "I agreed to carry Fusari."

In late 1950, Robinson traveled to Europe and fought five times (in Paris twice, Brussels, Geneva, and Frankfort) between Thanksgiving and Christmas Day. He'd now engaged in 123 professional fights, losing once.

In February 1951, *Ring Magazine* announced its "Annual Ranking of World Fighters." Reviewing the previous year, Nat Fleischer coined the phrase that would be attached to Robinson's name forevermore. Sugar Ray, Fleischer wrote, was "the greatest all-around fighter pound-for-pound in any division."

But there was the nagging matter of Jake LaMotta. Robinson was the better fighter. But in five bouts, he had never truly dominated the Bronx Bull. There were even those who argued that, with different judges, LaMotta would have won three of their five encounters. And the loss stuck in Robinson's craw.

On February 14, 1951, in a fight known in boxing lore as the St. Valentine's Day Massacre, Robinson established his ring supremacy over LaMotta beyond a shadow of a doubt.

Robinson-LaMotta VI differed from its predecessors in several notable respects. First, it was a championship fight. Neither man had won a world title at the time of their previous contests. Now Robinson was the reigning welterweight king, and LaMotta had defeated Marcel Cerdan in June 1949 to annex the middleweight crown.

Second, Robinson had never demanded that LaMotta fight at a "catch-weight." And LaMotta was the naturally bigger man. In their first five fights, he'd outweighed Robinson by an average of thirteen pounds.

Now, weighing in on the day of their championship fight, LaMotta was constrained by the 160-pound middleweight limit. Robinson had grown to 155 pounds.

And last; Robinson-LaMotta VI was seen live throughout the nation on a new medium known as television. Thirty million people (one-fifth the population of the United States) watched it.

Robinson (a 17-to-5 favorite) entered the ring at Chicago Stadium wearing white trunks, his lithe frame wrapped in a black silk robe. LaMotta wore black trunks beneath a leopard-patterned robe.

For eight rounds, Sugar Ray dazzled the crowd with his speed and footwork. And for eight rounds, Jake trudged forward, forcing the fight, battling from a low coiled crouch as the bull and matador fought on even terms.

In the ninth round, the fight changed. "I couldn't match strength with LaMotta," Robinson said afterward. "But he was slower than he had been six years earlier. That made him an easier target. My jab had puffed up his face and I had hit him with quite a few body shots. His punches had lost their zing."

Over the next four rounds, LaMotta was battered as brutally as any man has ever been battered in a boxing ring without going down. His eyes were closing; his lips were swollen. He was bleeding badly, staggering blindly. His championship was gone, but he wouldn't fall. Finally, in the thirteenth round with Jake draped helplessly against the ropes, referee Frank Sikora called a halt to the carnage.

Sugar Ray Robinson had scaled Mt. Everest and staked his claim as the greatest fighter of all time.

Robinson's knockout victory over LaMotta captured the imagination of America. Baseball and boxing were the country's two national sports. Ray had now entered the ring for 124 fights, losing once. This was his fifth victory over the man who'd defeated him. And thanks to television, thirty million people had witnessed him in his prime. He was handsome, telegenic, and lethal.

After vanquishing LaMotta for the middleweight crown, Robinson appeared on the cover of *Time Magazine*. Joe Louis and Louis Armstrong were the only black Americans to have previously received that honor.

The comparison with Louis was significant. During the early years of his career, Robinson had fought in the shadow of the Brown Bomber.

The two men had vastly different personalities. Louis was passive and plainspoken. Robinson was assertive and had an easy way with words. As Jesse Abramson wrote in the *New York Herald-Tribune,* "Everyone likes Joe Louis. Not everyone likes Ray Robinson." Robinson would tell people what was on his mind whether they liked what he had to say or not. Louis wouldn't.

Louis, of course, had become an American icon by defeating Max Schmeling in their 1938 rematch at a time when the nation needed him most. But by Valentine's Day 1951, his time had come and gone. He'd retired, come out of retirement, and lost to Ezzard Charles. Only a brutal beating at the hands of Rocky Marciano later that year lay ahead. He was still a hero, but Robinson was boxing's brightest star.

In April 1951, after two non-title fights in the United States, Robinson returned to Europe. Having refined the art of the entourage, he was accompanied by his trainer, barber, masseuse, golf instructor, various playmates, and a four-foot-four-inch dwarf. The group brought fifteen suitcases and thirty-two trunks. Robinson's personal luggage included twelve suits, five overcoats, dozens of neckties, and 140 jazz albums.

"The symbol of my reputation" (Robinson's fuchsia Cadillac convertible) also made the trip.

The first stop on the tour was Paris, where Robinson was treated like a conquering hero. He had defeated the hated Jake LaMotta, who'd beaten France's beloved Marcel Cerdan (Cerdan's loss being all the more bitter because he died in a plane crash before it could be avenged).

Robinson fought non-title bouts in Paris, Zurich, Antwerp, Liege, Berlin, and Turin within the course of six weeks. He'd become an international star; something that no non-heavyweight before him had ever done. On July 10th, he entered the ring in London against Randy Turpin for the first defense of his middleweight crown.

In his autobiography, Robinson later observed "All your training is timed so that, on the night of the fight, you are at your best. Not the night before; not the night after. The night. And not near your best; your very best."

Against Turpin, Robinson broke that rule. The European tour, and particularly his time in Paris, had taken him out of a serious training mode. In the days leading up to the Turpin fight, he'd trained sporadically; playing golf during the day and partying in clubs at night.

Turpin was an untested challenger. Still, at twenty-three, he was seven years younger than the champion. And like LaMotta, he was a naturally bigger man. Robinson fought like a tired out-of-shape fighter, which is what he was that night. In round seven, an accidental head butt opened an ugly cut above his left eye. Ten stitches would be required to close the wound. Turpin won a unanimous decision.

For only the second time in 132 fights, Sugar Ray Robinson had been defeated. Less than five months after beating Jake LaMotta in the greatest victory of his career, he'd been toppled from the middleweight throne.

"It hit me [when I was waiting to be stitched up in the dressing room after the fight]," Robinson later recalled. "I hadn't quite realized that Randy Turpin was the new middleweight champion and I was the former champion. Until that moment, it had seemed like another stop on my grand tour of Europe. But suddenly it hit me that this had not been an appearance."

Time Magazine labeled the bout "boxing's biggest upset since 1936, when Max Schmeling knocked out Joe Louis."

An immediate rematch followed; this time in New York. A crowd of 61,370 jammed the Polo Grounds, paying a live gate of $767,626 (a record at that time for a non-heavyweight bout). General Douglas MacArthur was at ringside. So were Joe DiMaggio, Joe Louis, Ezzard Charles, Jersey Joe Walcott, and myriad celebrities from the entertainment world.

Early in round ten, as was the case in their first fight, an accidental head butt opened a gash above Robinson's left eye. That same round, he knocked Turpin out.

Six months passed before Robinson's next fight; his longest period of inactivity since 1943–1944 when he was sidelined by the military. On March 13, 1952, he returned to the ring with a victory over Carl "Bobo" Olson. Five weeks later, he defended his championship against Rocky Graziano.

"He must be good," Graziano said afterward, "because he knocked me out in three rounds."

Then Robinson undertook his greatest ring challenge. At Yankee Stadium on June 23, 1952, he sought to wrest the light-heavyweight championship from Joey Maxim. A victory would give him a title in his third weight division at a time when the phrase "world champion" really meant something. Only Henry Armstrong and Bob Fitzsimmons had accomplished that feat before.

Maxim was a shade younger than Robinson and, more significantly, outweighed him by fifteen pounds. Robinson was a 7-to-5 favorite because of his extraordinary skills. But fighting for the 175-pound championship was a tremendous reach for a fighter who'd begun his career at 135 pounds.

"How are your legs?" Robinson was asked several days before the bout.

"I hope they're all right," he answered. "This would sure be a bad time for them to go wrong."

The temperature in the ring on fight night was 104 degrees. It was the hottest June 25th in the history of New York. "A miasma of cigarette smoke hung over the ringside seats on the baseball diamond," A. J. Liebling wrote. "There was no breeze to dispel it, and the American flags on the four posts at the corners of the ring drooped straight down."

"I thought I was being roasted to death," referee Ruby Goldstein said afterward.

The first ten rounds were slow-paced, with Robinson piling up a lead on the scorecards. Later, he recalled, "Maxim was an easy target. In the seventh, I stunned him with a right hand to the jaw. But the heat was beginning to get to me. After the ninth, I plopped on my stool. 'I don't know what's the matter,' I said. 'I'm getting sleepy.' That is the last memory I have of anything that happened that night."

At the end of round ten, Goldstein collapsed from the heat and was replaced by Ray Miller. The new third man in the ring broke clinches more quickly than his predecessor and the pace of the fight quickened a bit.

"In the eleventh round," Dave Anderson recounted in the *New York Times,* "Robinson jolted Maxim with another right hand to the jaw. But when the bell rang, he wandered aimlessly toward a neutral corner."

In round twelve, Robinson forced himself onto the attack again, scoring repeatedly but at the expense of the little strength left in his reserve. Then he hit the proverbial wall.

"When Robinson came out for the thirteenth," Liebling wrote, "he walked as if he had the gout in both feet and dreaded putting them down.

When he punched, which was infrequently, he was as late and wild as an amateur; and when he wasn't punching, his arms hung at his sides. Maxim, at first apparently unable to believe his good fortune, began after a period of ratiocination to hit after him. Then Robinson, the almost flawless boxer, the epitome of ring grace, swung wildly like a child, missed his man completely, and fell on his face."

Robinson rose and finished the round. When it ended, he hung onto the ropes in a neutral corner. His cornermen dragged him to his stool, held smelling salts beneath his nose, and pressed ice against the back of his neck.

A commission doctor asked Robinson if he could stand up. The two judges had him leading Maxim 10–3 and 9-3-1 in rounds. The composite score of the two referees had him ahead 7-4-3. In other words, under the round scoring system then in effect in New York, all he had to do was finish the fight to win.

Robinson shook his head. He was physically unable to rise from his stool.

The bell rang. Maxim was declared the winner by knockout at the start of the fourteenth round.

After the fight, Robinson suffered from delirium in his dressing room. His body was covered with blisters and he had lost twelve pounds. He refused to go to the hospital and was taken to his mother's home.

Two months later, Robinson announced his retirement from boxing. He was thirty-one years old. "I do not feel I can any longer give the public my best as it has come to recognize it," he said. "I know better than anyone else how good I am and what my limitations are. I find I can't move in the ring with the same speed, dispatch, and accuracy. My instinct used to guide my hands and feet. I could see the opening in a flash and, in the same twinkle, handle the situation. The coordination isn't there anymore. No one knows that better than I do."

Then Robinson set out in pursuit of the next stage of his dream. Great fighters of the past had made good money on the vaudeville circuit. Ray had more ambitious plans. He wasn't just a great fighter. He could dance and sing, and he was convinced that people would pay to see him do it. He was an entertainer, a star.

"I'm a celebrity's celebrity," he said with pride. "Other celebrities come to see me."

On November 7, 1952, Robinson made his debut as an entertainer at the French Casino in the Paramount Hotel in New York. Joe Louis was in the audience. So were Milton Berle, Delores Parker, Hazel Scott, and Adam Clayton Powell Jr.

During the course of the evening, Robinson wore six different outfits: a yellow-and-black plaid tuxedo, a cream-colored suit, a dark-brown suit, a dusty-rose jacket with cerise slacks, a white suit, and midnight-blue tails with a top hat. He danced with a chorus line of beautiful women behind him, told jokes, and sang a bit. The event was covered in both the entertainment and sports sections of New York's newspapers. The audience was enthusiastic. The sportswriters were kind in their reviews.

Then Robinson went on tour with the Count Basie Orchestra. A national television audience saw him on *The Ed Sullivan Show*. He played the Sahara Hotel in Las Vegas and the Apollo Theatre in New York.

But there were problems. And the biggest problem was that, as a singer and dancer, Robinson wasn't very good. As Wil Haygood notes in his forthcoming biography, "Robinson's act seemed to be in a state of continuous flux. The machinery never seemed well-oiled. Cues were missed. It lacked the authority of movement and precision that the best acts had down cold. Audiences that saw Robinson had also seen the likes of the Step Brothers and the Will Mastin Trio starring Sammy Davis Jr, just two of the acts soaring during that golden age of tap. But those other groups had honed their dance routines over years and years of being on the road. They were masters at the ad lib and improvisation, but that came in large part from hard work and practice. Though Robinson's name secured him a position with marquee-name traveling acts—Louis Armstrong, Count Basie—it also gave audiences a chance to compare him to those performers, and he paled next to them. Edna Mae would watch her husband perform and sometimes shake her head. She had danced at the Cotton Club. She knew timing and movement."

Frank Sinatra could punch people out in bars; particularly when he got off first and had a bodyguard standing beside him. But he wasn't a professional fighter; only the greatest popular singer of his time and maybe all time. Sugar Ray Robinson could carry a tune. But he wasn't a professional singer or dancer; not really.

Time Magazine labeled Robinson "a second-rate song and dance man." A review in *The Chicago Defender* (one of America's most prominent black newspapers) said that he was "out of character in a nightclub as an entertainer" and "just an average dancer."

"Robinson thought he could sing and dance," Jimmy Breslin later recalled. "I went to a thing one night, a kind of audition. It was in an apartment on Seventh Avenue. Robinson played the piano and sang. He did this to let the agents see him for the first time. It was okay, but it was street stuff. It wasn't professional."

As the novelty of Robinson's act wore thin, the paychecks got slimmer. He performed four times in Pittsburgh. The shows cost $20,000 to produce. The receipts were $5,000. He took his show to Paris, where as a fighter, he'd been a star. "My first night there, the show was bad," he acknowledged in his autobiography. "So were the reviews. The show got better after that, but critics don't come back."

Empty tables became the norm. "I had made more money in my debut than Fred Astaire or Gene Kelly," Robinson noted. "But I wasn't making it now. My agent told me that he could book me for at least $25,000 a year. But that wasn't enough."

Things went from bad to worse. Robinson was a big spender where his personal life was concerned. Taxes had gone unpaid and his business judgment was often unwise. After he retired from boxing in 1952, there was no longer a constant flow of cash from his fights to keep things running smoothly. His business empire started to fall apart. Real estate properties were in danger of being foreclosed upon. And his name drew increasingly fewer customers.

On October 20, 1954, Robinson announced that he was returning to the ring. "I need a buck as well as anyone else," he said.

The comeback began against a journeyman named Joe Rindone on January 5, 1955, in Detroit. Rindone was at the end of his career and winless in his previous four fights. Robinson knocked him out in six rounds. Two weeks later, Ray was in Chicago to fight Ralph "Tiger" Jones. Jones was a seasoned professional. But he'd lost five fights in a row and was on a downward slide that would see him win only twenty of his last forty-seven outings. Robinson was a 3-to-1 favorite. And he embarrassed himself. Jones dominated from beginning to end, winning by scores of 100–88, 98–89, and 99–94. "It was humiliating," Ray said afterward.

Former ring great Henry Armstrong, who was at ringside, concurred. Twelve years earlier, Robinson had charitably carried Armstrong (one of his boyhood heroes) for ten rounds in the twilight of Armstrong's career. Now, speaking of himself and Robinson, Armstrong noted, "When you get old, you don't get young again. When you're through, you're through."

Several days later in the *New York Journal-American,* Jimmy Cannon summed up his feelings regarding Robinson's performance. "This is one I don't like to do," Cannon wrote. "It may seem cruel, but I don't intend it to be that way. There is no language spoken on the face of the earth in which you can be kind when you tell a man he is old and should stop pretending he is young. What he had is gone. The pride isn't; the gameness isn't. The insolent faith in himself is still there. But the pride and the gameness and that insolent faith get in his way. He was marvelous, but he isn't anymore. He must know how bad he was with Jones because there were nights when he was perfect. He knows and he's kidding no one."

Robinson's next three fights were victories over mediocre opponents. Then, on July 22, 1955, he was matched against Rocky Castellani (a contender with 60 wins, 8 losses, and 4 draws) and told that, if he defeated Castellani, he'd get a title shot.

Castellani entered the ring a 9-to-5 favorite. In round six, a barrage of punches put Robinson on the canvas. He rose shakily at the count of nine and hung on to win a ten-round decision.

On December 9, 1955, for the third time in his life, Robinson entered the ring as a challenger for the middleweight championship of the world. The champion was Carl "Bobo" Olson (seven years Ray's junior), who Robinson had beaten twice before. After Ray's retirement, Olson had defeated Randy Turpin to seize the vacant throne. He'd defended the title successfully against Kid Gavilan, Castellani, and Pierre Langlois.

Robinson was a decided underdog. The assumption was that he was shot. He knocked Olson out in the second round. Five months later, there was a rematch. This time, Olson lasted four rounds.

"He was the greatest boxer to ever step into the ring," Olson said years later. "I tried to copy his style a few times, but I couldn't do it. He was too good."

In truth, Robinson was no longer the greatest fighter in the world. Age and the wear-and-tear of 144 professional fights had caught up with him. After beating Olson for the second time, he took the rest of 1956 off, save for a meaningless non-title fight against Bob Provizzi that was a tune-up for a January 2, 1957, date against Gene Fullmer.

Fullmer was a rough tough brawler from Utah with a 37-and-3 record; twenty-five years old, compared to Robinson's thirty-five. He had a granite chin and lacked a big punch but wore opponents down through attrition. In other words, he was the sort of fighter that Robinson would have carved to pieces in his prime.

"Robinson was tough on the contract negotiations," Fullmer said when the last of what would be four fights between them was done. "He wanted all the money and everything else in his favor. He wanted everything his way."

But in their first encounter, once the bell rang, everything went Fullmer's way. "I was in charge," he said afterward. "Just cut the ring off and put pressure on him, move in close before he started doing much punching."

"There's nothing I can say," Robinson acknowledged after the unanimous decision against him was announced. "The better man won tonight."

Gene Fullmer was the new middleweight champion of the world.

Four months later, they fought again. Fullmer was a 3-to-1 favorite. After four rounds, he was in control. Robinson seemed to be tiring, and the assumption was that he'd wilt further as the night wore on.

"Up to that time, it wasn't a tough fight," Fullmer later recalled. "I was winning on everybody's card. I was working on his body a lot and he was hurting. Never seen the punch coming. I don't know anything about the punch except I've watched it on movies a number of times. I didn't know anything about being hit. I didn't know anything about being down. The first thing I knew, I was standing up. Robinson was in the other corner. I thought he was in great condition, doing exercises between rounds. My manager crawled in the ring. I said, 'What happened?' He said, 'They counted ten.' Up to then, I didn't know."

Sugar Ray Robinson, two days shy of his thirty-sixth birthday, had landed the ultimate highlight-reel punch of alltime; a short compact left-hook that exploded flush on Fullmer's jaw. It was possibly his greatest single moment as a fighter and also his last moment of true ring greatness. Later, he called the blow "the most perfect punch of my career."

On September 23, 1957, Robinson defended his newly reacquired middleweight title against Carmen Basilio, the welterweight champion of the world.

When Robinson was a welterweight, he'd enjoyed a decided advantage in height and reach over virtually all of his opponents. Against Basilio, he had a five-inch edge in height and outweighed his foe by seven pounds.

Basilio was a blood-and-guts fighter who would take two punches to land one. "When people buy a fight ticket," he said, "they're paying to see blood and knockdowns." He was also fueled by a hatred of Robinson, who he called "an egotistical son of a bitch." Three decades after they fought, Basilio said of Sugar Ray, "Don't talk about that bastard to me. I got no use for him. I didn't like him then, and I don't like him now. Call me a jerk, fine. But that's the way I feel. When he died, I said, 'I don't give a shit.'"

Basilio worked Robinson's body for fifteen rounds and took the championship from him on a split decision.

On March 25, 1958, they fought again. This time, the split decision went Robinson's way.

"I got stupid that night," Basilio said of his second fight with Robinson. "He kept throwing a right uppercut at me. He never quit. He threw it at me five times. He knew that I bobbed and weaved, and he tried to catch me going down in a bob and weave. He'd throw it; I'd go down; I'd catch his right uppercut with my right hand; and I'd counter him with a left hook because he was wide open for it. I did it four times. The fifth time he threw it at me, I missed it with my hand and it hit me right in the eyebrow and blew my eyelid up. My eye shut. This was the middle of the sixth round, and I fought the next nine rounds with one eye."

Robinson didn't fight again for the rest of the year. In 1959, he entered the ring just once (against a club fighter named Bob Young, who he knocked out in two rounds). On May 4, 1959, the National Boxing Association stripped him of his title for failing to fight a return bout against Basilio. Now only the state athletic commissions in New York and Massachusetts recognized him as the middleweight champion.

On January 22, 1960, Robinson defended what was left of his crown against Paul Pender in Boston. He wasn't a great fighter anymore, but he had no intention of going quietly into the night.

Don Turner, then a twenty-year-old middleweight, was hired as a sparring partner preparatory to Robinson fighting Pender.

"The man was thirty-nine years old," Turner recalls. "First sparring partner gets in the ring. Robinson knocks him down in the first round and hurts him bad enough that he can't go on. Second sparring partner gets in the ring. Robinson knocks him down in the first round and hurts him bad enough that he can't go on. Now it's my turn. I'd had two pro fights and they want me to spar three rounds. I was a little nervous but I was getting paid. And to be in the ring with Sugar Ray Robinson. Wow! First round, he hit me with a left hook that knocked my headgear off, clear out of the ring. I don't know if I'd strapped it on wrong or what. But I figured, better the headgear than my head. I lasted the three rounds, but it wasn't easy."

Pender won a decision over Robinson. Afterward, the new middle-weight champion of Massachusetts and New York declared, "My strategy, knowing that Robinson is so old, was the only intelligent one. Wear him out and then break him down."

Five months later, they fought again. Dick Schaap wrote in advance of the fight, "Nothing dulls the impact of a powerful play so surely as an anticlimax. And all Sugar Ray has left are anticlimaxes."

Once again, Pender won a decision.

After losing twice to Pender, Robinson had two more fights against Fullmer (who by then, had beaten Basilio twice to lay claim to the legit-imate middleweight crown). The first was declared a draw, with Fullmer retaining his title. In the second, Robinson lost a unanimous decision.

He wasn't Sugar Ray Robinson anymore; not as a fighter. "When you're younger, you can take it better," he said.

Meanwhile, Robinson's world away from the ring was falling apart. Sugar Ray's Café and his other businesses shut down in 1962. Later that year, Edna Mae was granted a divorce. Immediately thereafter, Robinson became engaged to Millie Bruce, who he'd met in the early 1950s while performing on tour in Los Angeles.

Edna Mae had encountered Millie by chance years earlier, when the latter was in a supermarket with Robinson's mother during a visit to New York. "I thought she was lovely, as so many others that had preceded her were," Edna Mae recalled.

And he kept fighting. "That's what happens when the money runs out," Robinson said. "You always say, 'I'll quit when I start to slide.' Then, one morning, you wake up and you've done slid. You can't choose your ending in boxing."

The end game was ugly. "It was hard to watch Robinson in decline,"

Larry Merchant recalls. "Seeing him fight when he got old was like watching Fred Astaire trip and fall on the dance floor or the desecration of a great painting."

In the last fifty fights of his career, many of them against ordinary opposition, Robinson lost thirteen times and had four draws. "Ray had problems at the end with guys who could jab," Emanuel Steward recounts. "And they kept him away from punchers. But he never complained about losing a fight. When he lost, no matter how close the decision, he'd go across the ring and congratulate the other guy. That's just the way he was."

Don Chargin journeyed to a bullring in Tijuana in 1965, the last year of Robinson's career, to watch him fight Memo Ayon.

"It was pathetic," Chargin remembers. "Ray was in this terrible-looking dressing room before the fight, all alone, wrapping his own hands. Not another soul was there except for myself. He lost the fight. But for a few seconds, as shot as he was, I thought I saw flashes of what he'd once been. Since then, I've often wondered if that was something I really saw or just something I wanted to see."

The day after losing to Ayon, Robinson flew with Millie to Las Vegas, where they were married by a justice of the peace. The cab driver who picked them up at the airport was their witness at the ceremony.

"I knew Millie loved me because there wasn't anything else for her to love," Robinson said several years later. "My flamingo Continental [that Ed Sullivan had given him at the behest of a sponsor to replace the fuchsia Cadillac] had been sold. My café had closed. The symbols of my success had disappeared. Only me was left."

The Robinsons "honeymooned" in Honolulu, where (six days after they were married) Ray lost a ten-round decision to Stan Harrington.

On September 23, 1965, he was taken the ten-round distance in a victory over Harvey McCullough (who'd won only three of thirty-one fights in the preceding eight years).

Eight days later, Robinson won again but was extended the full ten rounds by Peter Schmidt (who retired soon after, having won just one of his final eleven fights).

On October 20th, Ray knocked out Rudolf Bent (who was in the midst of a thirteen-fight losing streak). His purse for the Bent fight was five hundred dollars.

On November 10, 1965, Sugar Ray Robinson entered the ring as an active fighter for the last time. The opponent was Joey Archer, a stylish boxer with a 44-and-1 record and a powder-puff punch. Ray had been told that, if he beat Archer, he might get another title shot. And he needed the money. Besides, as Robinson noted in his autobiography, "Archer hadn't knocked down anybody in five years."

In round four, Archer put Robinson on the canvas. When Ray was young, on those rare occasions when he was decked, he'd spring to his feet immediately. When Archer knocked him down, he took an eight-count. The need for a few more seconds outweighed his shame at finding himself on the canvas.

Archer won a unanimous decision. By most accounts, he won every round.

One month later, Robinson formally retired from boxing at an elaborate farewell ceremony just prior to Emile Griffith's welterweight title defense against Emanuel Gonzalez at Madison Square Garden. A sell-out crowd of 12,146 jammed the arena to pay tribute. The ceremony started at 9:30 PM, a half-hour before television coverage of the night's main event began. Robinson had refused to be on camera because he wasn't being paid for his presence.

In retirement, Robinson was revered by the boxing public. When he was introduced at fights, he had a way of tilting his head a little to the side and reaching out with both hands as he moved across the ring, as if he were embracing the crowd.

Money remained an issue. To make ends meet, Millie took a job as a receptionist. Frank Sinatra got Robinson a part in a 1968 film (starring Sinatra) called *The Detective*. In 1969, Viking paid a $50,000 advance for Ray's autobiography. A national tour highlighted by an appearance on *The Tonight Show* with Johnny Carson was planned to promote the book. But Robinson refused to participate unless he was paid for the appearances. The tour was cancelled.

Bob Arum recalls that, when the Las Vegas casinos started hosting big fights, Robinson was invited to sit ringside for a mega-event at Caesars. He asked for a five-thousand-dollar appearance fee on the theory that his presence on television would be a marketing plus for the casino. Caesars refused, so Ray asked Arum for a hundred-dollar ticket and sat in the nosebleed seats.

Robinson's final years were spent in Los Angeles, where he and Millie lived on the top floor of a two-story lime-green duplex. His once-stylish wardrobe had been replaced by Hawaiian shirts that hung loosely over his expanding middle-age frame. Asked by a reporter if he still owned a Cadillac convertible, Ray answered, "No more. The car I drive now is a little red Pinto. But I've been there."

In 1984, he was diagnosed with Alzheimer's disease. That year, when a writer inquired about his status as the greatest fighter of all time, Robinson fumbled for words before saying, "It's the most wonderful feeling in the world. I can't say any more. I loved boxing, and every time I hear someone say 'pound for pound' . . ." His voice trailed off, then picked up again. "It's the most wonderful feeling in the world."

Arteriosclerosis, diabetes, and hypertension left him further debilitated. Don Chargin recalls, "A year or two before Ray died, Lorraine [Chargin's wife] and I were with him and Millie at the Forum Shops in Caesars. Lorraine and Millie went into a dress shop. I was standing outside with Ray, talking. And he panicked. 'Where's Millie? Where's Millie?' He got very upset that she wasn't there. By then, he needed her around to protect him all the time."

On April 12, 1989, Walker Smith Jr (known to the world as Sugar Ray Robinson) died. At his funeral, Jesse Jackson eulogized him as "an original art form." The United States Postal Service would print one hundred million postage stamps bearing his likeness. The only other boxer so honored was Joe Louis.

Most of us tend to be loyal to the sports heroes we worshipped and the music we listened to when we were young. But respect for Robinson transcends time and fondness for any given era.

Indeed, Robinson's legacy arguably would have been even greater than it is but for the absence of film footage of his fights from the 1940s. People who watch films of Ray as a middleweight (particularly his final victory over Jake LaMotta and one-punch knockout of Gene Fullmer) have seen Sugar Ray Robinson. But they haven't seen him at his best and never will.

Virtually no film footage of Robinson in action prior to 1950 exists. There are home-movie snippets from seven fights in the 1940s (three Golden Gloves bouts and four professional contests against lesser foes), but that's all. The first professionally filmed footage of a Robinson fight is of his lackluster title defense against Charlie Fusari in mid-1950.

That's like a Frank Sinatra songbook without the young Sinatra.

Robinson's final ring record was 175 wins against 19 losses with 109 knockouts and 6 draws. There was one "no contest." He was never knocked out. Once, he collapsed from the heat. As a pro, he boxed 1,403 rounds.

By way of comparison, Sugar Ray Leonard boxed a total of forty pro fights. Leonard's record after the age of thirty-two was 1 win, 2 losses, and 1 draw. Robinson, on his thirty-second birthday, had retired from boxing after losing to Joey Maxim and had been defeated just three times in 136 fights. After he returned, he had 66 more fights and won the middle-weight championship three more times.

"With some fighters," Jerry Izenberg observes, "the longer they're away from the game, the better they get. But Ray was as good as people say he was. He did things that were beyond the imagination of other fighters."

"The great ones are pioneers in some way," adds Teddy Atlas. "That's what Ray was. He took speed and combination-punching and a certain smoothness when it wasn't all connected, and he connected it. Everything he did, he did with meaning and accuracy. He took away the waste. He didn't just throw flurries. He threw tighter harder combinations that were all meaningful. He had more than talent. He had genius."

Consider the phenomenon of being the best ever; a man who defines his craft. Shakespeare . . . Michelangelo . . .

In recent decades, Tiger Woods, Roger Federer, and Michael Jordan have been called "the greatest ever" in their respective sports. But Sugar Ray Robinson required that the language of boxing be changed as a way of codifying his greatness. "Pound for pound" belongs to him. Only Babe Ruth (think "Ruthian blasts") had a similar impact on the language of his game.

Don Dunphy was the premier blow-by-blow announcer of the Robinson era. He called more than two thousand fights in a career that began during the golden age of radio and ended after the glory years of Muhammad Ali. Reflecting on a half-century behind the microphone, Dunphy declared, "Any ingredient that any champion ever had, Ray Robinson had them all."

Joe Louis was in accord, saying, "Sugar Ray Robinson was the greatest of anyone who stepped in the ring. I saw him at his best. He was the best fighter that ever lived."

2009 brought the beginnings of change insofar as boxing's economic model is concerned.

February 21, 2009:
Top Rank Goes It Alone

Don't get carried away by the title of this article. It would be a stretch to liken Bob Arum to Gary Cooper in *High Noon*. But in recent weeks, there has been talk of a new economic model in boxing. And Arum, in tandem with Todd DuBoef (his stepson and the president of Top Rank) might be charting a path out of the wilderness that the sweet science has wandered through in recent years.

Arum is an old-time promoter who is adapting to today's economic and technological realities. "I don't look back," he says. "I'm seventy-eight years old. If I look back, I'd stumble and fall, so I just look forward." Then he adds, "Boxing needs to move into a new era. We have to face realistically what's going on in the world and present our product in different ways."

That thinking was evident on February 21st, when Top Rank promoted separate bouts featuring Kelly Pavlik and Miguel Cotto held at separate sites linked by an independently produced pay-per-view telecast.

The move was born of necessity. Last July, Cotto suffered a brutal beating and the first loss of his career when he was knocked out by Antonio Margarito. Three months later, Pavlik was outboxed by Bernard Hopkins over twelve one-sided rounds and defeated for the first time. Kelly retained his WBC and WBO middleweight belts because Pavlik-Hopkins was contested at 170 pounds. Cotto lost his WBA welterweight crown.

But the titles were of secondary importance. More significantly, two undefeated fighters who were being groomed for super-stardom by Top Rank lost in an era when a single defeat often sends a fighter's commercial viability spiraling downward. Pavlik and Cotto had to be rehabilitated in the public eye.

The world sanctioning organizations (for a sanctioning fee, of course) provided the "get well" tonic for Arum's fighters. The WBC offered up mandatory challenger Marco Antonio Rubio for what ailed Pavlik, while the WBO approved a match between Cotto and Englishman Michael Jennings for its vacant 147-pound throne. Neither Rubio or Jennings was given a serious chance to win.

"When a fighter loses," DuBoef said, stating the obvious, "there are steps that have to be taken to get him to the top again. Not every fight can be Cotto-Margarito, Cotto-Mosley, Pavlik-Taylor, or Pavlik-Hopkins."

Besides; Pavlik and Cotto were entitled to a breather. Pavlik's opponents in his previous five bouts (Jermain Taylor twice, Edison Miranda, Gary Lockett, and Bernard Hopkins) had a 160-8-3 composite record. Cotto's previous ten opponents included Margarito and the likes of Shane Mosley, Zab Judah, Ricardo Torres, and Carlos Quintana (who, let's not forget, beat Paul Williams).

Rubio and Jennings had faced "no-chance" opponents themselves to get to where they were in boxing's food chain, so they knew the odds. So did HBO, which declined to bid on the fights. If that was done to punish Arum for his recent public criticism of HBO's boxing programming, then it was poor form. If it was done as part of a new network policy to televise more competitive fights in the future, then hats off to HBO.

The idea of holding the title fights at two different sites originated when Top Rank was trying to sell the bouts to HBO. Todd DuBoef explained, "It was an effort on our part to make the deal work in the face of the relatively low license fee that HBO seemed willing to pay. Then HBO passed and we decided to do it on our own. This way, we get two live gates. The whole thing is labor intensive and requires a huge amount of coordination. We're putting all the pieces together times two, but we think it will be worth our while."

The other major piece in the puzzle was Arum's decision to distribute the telecast as an independent pay-per-view show. "We've been doing it for Julio Cesar Chavez Jr," the promoter elaborated. "We did it for Erik Morales early in his career and for Manny Pacquiao not long ago. What else are we supposed to do? Tell Pavlik and Cotto that they can't fight because HBO isn't interested? That's not the way we do things at Top Rank. If we have to, we move our fighters on our own. For a mega-fight, we'd probably still need HBO's marketing power. But for a card like this, we think we can do it as well as they can and save the ten-percent distribution charge. Thank God, my life doesn't depend on whether or not I make [HBO Sports president] Ross Greenburg happy."

The fights took place in New York and Youngstown, Ohio. Boxing belongs in both of those cities, and each one has a boxing tradition of its own.

Cotto-Jennings marked Miguel's return to Madison Square Garden, where he'd drawn well in the past. Pavlik versus Rubio was slated for the Chevrolet Center in Youngstown, where Kelly's hometown fans were expected to turn out in force. There would be a live undercard at each venue. The first three bouts on the pay-per-view telecast would originate from New York. Pavlik-Rubio would follow. At each location, the off-site pay-per-view bouts would be seen on giant screens in the arena.

On fight night, Arum was in Youngstown, while DuBoef spearheaded operations in New York. Ring announcing honors went to Jimmy Lennon in Ohio and Michael Buffer at Madison Square Garden.

Youngstown was the easier sell where on-site tickets were concerned. Arum greased the skids with pronouncements like, "The people in Youngstown are throwback people. They realize that, when boxing was boxing, a loss wasn't the end of the world for fighters . . . The great fighters lost fights . . . Kelly's fans traveled to Atlantic City and Las Vegas for Kelly. Now Kelly is fighting at home for them."

Tickets for Pavlik-Rubio went on sale on January 10th. Thirty minutes later, 5,500 of them had been sold. The remaining 1,700 were gone by fight night.

"I was really surprised when I saw how fast everybody lined up," Kelly said. "It made me feel pretty good. The support helps and it gives me another motivation. Naturally after a loss, you'll have people that turn away or jump off the bandwagon. You're always going to have guys that say, 'Oh, he was overrated; he fought bums; he ain't this, he ain't that.' But when you have people that are still your fans, that makes a big difference."

As for the loss to Hopkins, Pavlik observed, "Losing sucks, but I've gotten past it. The only thing I can take from that fight is to say mentally, 'Hey, I lost; screw it; let's move on.' That's what I've done. In my head, I said, 'It's not worth it. I'm going to beat myself up over what? Shit happens; especially in boxing. Your greatest fighters have four, five, six, seven losses in their careers. It took about a week to get over it. Then I realized that I had to put my concentration on the next fight; not the one that was done. My job is to bounce back and dominate and show that it was a fluke. I still feel like a champion, but I also feel like I have a lot of proving to do."

Meanwhile, Cotto was on a more difficult emotional journey. Kelly had lost by decision to Bernard Hopkins and taken a bit of a beating. Miguel was knocked out by Antonio Margarito and badly beaten up.

At the January 13th kick-off press conference in New York, Cotto seemed dispirited and acknowledged that he'd been walking around at 178 pounds (31 pounds over his fighting weight). Arum opined, "I think the loss affected Miguel psychologically more than it did Kelly because that's the kind of guy he is."

Then the Margarito hand-wrap scandal broke. In the dressing room prior to Antonio's January 24th fight against Shane Mosley, it was determined that trainer Javier Capetillo had improperly wrapped his fighter's hands, inserting an illegal hardened pad over the knuckles in each glove. The pads were removed and Margarito re-wrapped. Mosley knocked him out in the ninth round.

Thereafter, Margarito's license was revoked by the California State Athletic Commission. He is precluded from fighting in the United States for at least one year.

It's well within reason to surmise that Margarito-Mosley wasn't the first time that Antonio's hands were improperly wrapped. That meant Miguel could put his mind at ease by telling himself that the damage Antonio inflicted upon him wasn't dealt in a fair manner and that he'd been a victim of foul play. Moreover, Mosley's stock was sky-high after his dominant performance against Margarito. And in November 2007, Cotto had scored a unanimous-decision victory over Mosley.

When February 21st arrived, Pavlik-Rubio and Cotto-Jennings went pretty much as expected.

In Youngstown, Pavlik went after Rubio from the opening bell, while the challenger simply tried to survive. There weren't ten seconds in the first five rounds when it appeared as though Marco Antonio was trying to win the fight. In the sixth stanza, the challenger decided to challenge a bit, opened up, and landed a few solid blows. But that meant he took more punishment in return. In round eight, the beating got ugly. Rubio retired on his stool after round nine.

In New York, Jennings found out that the trouble with fighting Cotto is that you're fighting Cotto. The Brit's record was 34-and-1; but he'd never fought, let alone beaten, a world-class opponent. The fact that he'd lost to Young Mutley three years ago didn't enhance his credentials.

Against Cotto, Jennings fought as well as he could, which wasn't nearly well enough. Earlier, when asked how he planned to beat Miguel, Michael had responded, "I've got to use my jab a lot and use the whole ring and keep moving."

That sounded a lot like he planned to stay away from Cotto for as long as he could and then . . .

Class told, and rather quickly. In round four, Jennings was staggered by a left hook upstairs, took a knee after a hook to the body, and was downed a second time by another body shot. Cotto ended matters in round five with a right to the jaw that put the Brit on the canvas for the third time. Jennings rose but referee Benjy Esteves appropriately stopped the fight.

The next day's newspapers had headlines like, "Youngstown Fight Brings Celebration to the Valley . . . Pavlik Thrills His Hometown Fans with TKO . . . Cotto Roars Back at the Garden . . ."

In truth, Pavlik and Cotto had beaten seriously overmatched opponents. Nonetheless, Arum had the story-line that he wanted, and each fighter had taken an important step on the road back to where he'd been before.

Most likely, Pavlik's next fight will be in June or July. Cleveland Browns Stadium and Progressive Field (home of the Cleveland Indians) beckon. But Arum says, "I'm not doing outdoor stadiums unless they're covered; not at my age." The loss to Bernard Hopkins still stings. But it should be remembered that Kelly is only twenty-six years old. At age twenty-six, Hopkins was fighting in six-round preliminary bouts and had just beaten a guy named Mike Sapp in Fort Myers, Florida.

Cotto is likely to be in action again at Madison Square Garden on June 13th (the night before the annual Puerto Rican Day Parade). At the moment, there's tension between Miguel and his promoter. Arum has mounted a spirited defense of Antonio Margarito (also a Top Rank fighter), saying that Margarito should not be held accountable for the misdeeds of his trainer.

"All I know," Cotto says in response, "is, when we get our hands wrapped, every boxer knows what is in them. I'm very angry [with Top

Rank]. In the name of boxing, Margarito and his group have to comply with the penalty. Everyone in his group was aware. You go in the ring thinking you are on the same level. This is a sport. This is not a slaughter-house."

Meanwhile, Evangelista Cotto (Miguel's uncle and trainer) says of Cotto-Jennings, "This was a very important fight psychologically. Miguel had to get back in the ring, and he looked very decisive. I was very pleased."

But the greater significance of February 21st lies in the changing economic landscape of boxing. As previously noted, the venture gave Top Rank two live gates.

Take note of the phrase "live gate." Arum didn't simply act as a middle-man dependent upon a license fee from a television network and a site fee from a casino. He actually PROMOTED the fights. The crowd at Madison Square Garden was a bit disappointing. The paid attendance was 9,903 with live gate receipts of $969,424. But the Chevrolet Center in Youngstown sold out.

Now put that in context with the sell-out crowd of 20,820 at the Staples Center in Los Angeles on January 24th for Margarito-Mosley (the arena's largest crowd ever) and another sell-out crowd at the Toyota Center in Houston for the February 28th match-up between Juan Diaz and Juan Manuel Marquez and one can see a trend. To wit; match-ups between elite fighters can succeed financially without a casino subsidy.

The first key to success is to have a fighter with a strong local fan base in the main event.

Would the University of Michigan football team (stadium capacity 107,000) sell out all of its home games if the games were played in Norman, Oklahoma? Obviously not.

Why not?

Answer: Because football fans in Norman want to see the University of Oklahoma.

Duh !

Thus, Arum posits, "This is the year when boxing realized what all sports know; that if you have a Philadelphia Eagles–Arizona Cardinals game, you'll sell-out in the stadium in Arizona. But if you put that same game in the Meadowlands, you couldn't get 25-percent of your seats filled. So you put the event where the fighters are popular. You put the fight in a place where there's going to be some connection and it's going to draw."

Second key to success: Give the fans entertaining competitive match-ups. Pavlik-Rubio succeeded locally despite violating this rule because Kelly has been loyal to Youngstown and the fans there figured they owed him one. But Margarito-Mosley and Diaz-Marquez were great fights going in.

Third key: Tickets should be affordable for the average fan. Prices for Diaz-Marquez ran as low as twenty-five dollars. Margarito-Mosley, Pavlik-Rubio, and Cotto-Jennings could each be seen live for as little as fifty dollars.

Too often, boxing treats its live fans as though they don't matter. Television cameramen stand on the ring apron blocking their view. There are long waits between fights. Many arenas don't even have a round clock. But on-site fans are important for many reasons. They generate revenue. And a passionate crowd also enhances the experience of watching a fight on television. The excitement is contagious.

Here, the thoughts of Sylvester Stallone are instructive. Stallone wrote and starred in *Rocky* without ever having been to a professional fight. Years later, he recalled the first fight he actually went to (Larry Holmes versus Ken Norton).

"What a great fight," Stallone reminisced. "If I'd seen that fight before writing *Rocky*, the movie might have been a little different because one of the things that struck me about Holmes-Norton was the audience participation. In the fight scenes in *Rocky*, we focused on the fighters and their corners. But at Holmes-Norton, I realized that the crowd is a character in itself."

Contrast that thinking with the upcoming rematch between Chad Dawson and Antonio Tarver.

Dawson is from New Haven; Tarver is from Tampa.

"So why the fuck are they fighting in Vegas?" Arum queries. "I know that's the easy way to do it. But if you're a real promoter and you think that maybe Dawson can be a star, you build a fan base for him in Connecticut. You fight him in Hartford and at Foxwoods and Mohegan Sun. These two guys already fought once at The Palms and sold something like three hundred tickets. Were those three hundred people who bought tickets so happy that maybe you'll sell three hundred tickets again?"

Only one of Dawson's last eight fights has been in Connecticut.

Frank Warren didn't develop Ricky Hatton as a mega-attraction by putting him in casinos. Joe Mesi became a box-office star fighting in and around Buffalo.

Get the point?

HBO and Showtime offer lifelines from time to time. But the few television dates available today are distributed to a select group of individuals. Given the current economic climate, it's now more important than ever that a fighter be able to sell tickets. And that's particularly true of mid-level fighters who have yet to attract significant television dollars but can command respectable purses if they put asses in seats.

At present, there's virtually no middle class in boxing. A renewed emphasis on fighters who sell tickets might create one. That, in turn, could lead to less emphasis on mega-fights and more emphasis on entertaining match-ups featuring mid-level fighters with strong local support.

That would make boxing healthier in the long run. Pyramids are built from the bottom up; not from the top down.

★   ★   ★

(A note on Miguel Cotto's next fight)

The June 13th match-up between Miguel Cotto and Joshua Clottey was the sixth time that Cotto had headlined in the main arena at Madison Square Garden and his fourth appearance there on the eve of New York's Puerto Rican Day Parade.

Miguel is one of boxing's elite fighters. His only loss was a now-suspect eleventh-round stoppage at the hands of Antonio Margarito in July 2008.

Clottey (born and raised in Ghana, now living in New York) won the IBF welterweight title last August with a decision over Zab Judah. Then he gave it up for a big payday against Cotto rather than fight a meaningless defense for minimal compensation against a mandatory challenger.

Prior to facing Cotto, Clottey had suffered two losses. The first came against Carlos Baldomir in 1999, when he was disqualified in the eleventh round for repeated head butts. The second was a decision setback at the hands of Antonio Margarito in 2006; a fight in which Clottey says he suffered a broken hand in the fourth round.

Cotto was a 3-to-1 favorite over Clottey. But everyone understood going in that Joshua was a live underdog. Adding fuel to the fire, Clottey opined at the final pre-fight press conference that Cotto had lost the will to fight through pain and do the other things that a fighter must to do in combat to win.

Also, Cotto-Clottey was the first time in eighteen years that Miguel had trained for a fight with someone other than his uncle Evangelista. That happenstance was the result of long-simmering differences between the two men that boiled over in early April, when they came to blows twice in the same day and Evangelista threw a brick through the window of Miguel's 2009 Jaguar.

When fight night came, Cotto vs. Clottey lacked the Jerry Springer histrionics of Cotto vs. Cotto. But it did feature an exciting ebb and flow with action throughout.

The first dramatic highlight came when a sharp jab put Clottey on the canvas just before the bell ending round one.

In round three, an accidental clash of heads opened an ugly gash along Cotto's right eyebrow.

In the final minute of round five, referee Arthur Mercante Jr stumbled over a photographer's camera (boo on the photographer), and Cotto took advantage of the moment to throw his opponent to the canvas. That left Clottey writhing in pain for the better part of a minute and favoring his right knee when the action resumed.

After nine rounds, Cotto appeared to be outboxing Clottey, while Clottey was outfighting Cotto. At that point, judges Tom Miller and John McKaie had the fight even, while Miguel was ahead by two points on Don Trella's scorecard.

Then Clottey tired and Cotto hung tough, albeit largely in retreat. When it was over, the judges agreed that Miguel had won rounds one, six, and eleven, while five, seven, and eight belonged to Joshua. Beyond that, things got a bit dicey. Miller scored the fight 114–113 for Clottey, while McKaie (115–112) and Trella (116–111) gave the nod to Cotto. This writer scored it even at 114–114.

It wasn't the worst decision ever. But given the margin on Trella's scorecard, it was far from the best; especially since Clottey had a 222-to-179 advantage in punches landed with a 168-to-124 margin in power punches.

Meanwhile, in the aftermath of Cotto-Clottey, several things are clear:

(1) A frenzied pro-Cotto crowd of 17,734 made it fun to be at Madison Square Garden and also enhanced the television-viewing experience. A packed arena with a cheering crowd makes for good television. It reinforces the message to viewers that they're watching something exciting.

(2) Give Cotto credit for fighting someone his own size. And contrast that with Floyd Mayweather Jr (who, after besting Ricky Hatton, has contracted to fight Juan Manuel Marquez) and Andre Berto (last seen in title defenses against Stevie Forbes and Juan Urango with Luis Collazo sandwiched in between).

(3) True world championships rarely exist in boxing today. Winning a belt is akin to winning a conference title in college football. If you've won the SEC, you're entitled to bragging rights. If you finished on top in Conference USA, you're a big fish in a small pond. Cotto-Clottey was for a WBO belt, but very few people in attendance at Madison Square Garden seemed to care. The important thing is that it was a competitive fight between two very good fighters.

This was the first of several articles that I wrote in 2009 about New York City prospects.

Will Rosinsky: A Fighter with Options

There was a time when New York City was a breeding ground for elite fighters. Those days are long gone, but prospects still surface in the Big Apple. Will Rosinsky is one of them.

Rosinsky is the youngest of three sons and has spent his entire life in Queens (one of New York's five boroughs). His father was an automotive mechanic, who repaired large vehicles (think fire engines and eighteen-wheel trucks). In the early 1990s, Bill Rosinsky suffered crippling injuries from a fall off a scaffold and has been on disability ever since. Will's mother, now retired, was a customer representative for Verizon. His oldest brother is a tattoo artist. His other brother does janitorial work and hopes to become a New York City corrections officer.

At age twenty-four, Will still lives with his parents. "I'm the baby in the family," he says. "And I've lived in the same house for almost my whole life. I guess that's why it's hard for me to leave."

Rosinsky transitioned into boxing after practicing karate in junior high school. Thereafter, he won four New York Golden Gloves championships and a USA Amateur national crown; all at 178 pounds.

"I don't know my exact amateur record," he says. "It was something like 85 wins and twelve losses with a handful of knockouts." He was twenty-pointed once in a tournament in Russia (a stoppage based on points), but has never been knocked out.

Still, despite his accomplishments, it wasn't a foregone conclusion that Rosinsky would turn pro. As an amateur, he'd trained at the Starrett City Gym with Jaidon Codrington; a super-middleweight from Connecticut, who was once considered a "can't-miss" prospect.

On November 4, 2005, Codrington (then 9-and-0 with 9 knockouts) journeyed to Oklahoma to fight Allan Green. Seconds into the bout, Green landed a left hook to the temple. The blow landed in a freakish way that left Jaidon senseless but still standing with his arms frozen upright. Then Green landed several more blows and Codrington pitched forward face-first into the ropes where he was entangled on the bottom two strands. Several spectators pushed him back into the ring. His body looked lifeless and his neck was twisted grotesquely so that his head was tucked beneath his torso. He was carried from the ring on a stretcher.

"I thought he was dead," Showtime boxing analyst Steve Farhood who was at ringside later admitted.

"Coming up behind Jaidon and sparring with him in the gym," Rosinsky recalls, "I'd put him on a pedestal. I was in China at an amateur tournament when he got knocked out, so I heard about it before I saw the tape. Then Jaidon got knocked out again [by Sakio Bika in 2007]. Knowing how good he was, I questioned my own ability and had second thoughts about turning pro."

Rosinsky entered the ranks of professional fighters in August 2008. Since then, he has lost weight and plans to compete at 168 pounds. His record stands at 6-and-0 with six knockouts. But he acknowledges, "So far, we've been able to pick the opponents, so I've gone from fighting the best amateurs in the country to fighting guys who aren't so good. The first six guys I fought; three came to win, the other three just came for the paycheck. But I think we're doing it the right way. I started fighting guys who had losing records. Now I'm looking for guys who are at .500. Next, it will be guys with winning records."

Rosinsky is self-managed. His business advisors when it comes to boxing are the father-and-son team of Pat and Keith Connolly. Felipe Gomez (a New York City cop) is his trainer. "I keep a pretty tight circle," Will says. "Trust is important to me. I trust my family. I trust Felipe, Keith, and Pat. I don't need a lot of people hanging on."

As for his skills, Rosinsky says, "I'm not a good gym fighter. In the gym, I get hit with way too many stupid punches. But on the big stage, I rise to the occasion. My best punch is the hook to the body. I don't have one-punch knockout power. I'm more of a volume puncher, but I do have the power to hurt you. I've got good footwork and a good chin. I see myself making some noise as a fighter and being good enough to get a title shot. Will I win that night? Realistically, I know that all my hard work and skills and dedication might be matched by the other guy. So when that time comes, we'll see."

"The best thing about being a fighter," Will continues, "is feeling you're being rewarded for all the hard work you've put in. When I put my mind to something, I give it one hundred percent. That's the kind of person I am. I can't stop until it's perfect, and you need that in boxing. If you don't put in the work, you're disrespecting the sport. And if you disrespect boxing, it will disrespect you. I know I can be good. I don't know if I can become great. Time will tell."

As for the dangers in boxing, Rosinsky says, "It sucks to get hit. The punches hurt; I promise you that. I can take a punch. But I don't care how good your chin is, you don't want to get hit. And you can have a fight where the winner's brain gets hit just as much and just as hard as the loser's. You can win and walk out of the ring just as messed up as if you'd lost. I get hit too much, especially in the gym. I like boxing, but I don't want to do it forever. That's for sure."

Many fighters think that way. Will is simply more open about it than most. And unlike most young fighters, he has a career option that might be more attractive to him than boxing.

Rosinsky is a graduate of Queens College. As part of his bachelors degree program, he worked as a student teacher at St. Francis Prep and PS 207 (both in Queens). He's now certified by the New York State Board of Regents to teach in the New York City school system.

Teaching requires a blend of qualities that Rosinsky feels he has in abundance. Confidence, creativity, compassion, enthusiasm, and common sense. "It's a rewarding job," he says. "You get attached to the kids, and they get attached to you. Whatever happens to me in boxing, whether I'm a world champion or never get beyond eight-round fights, I'm going to teach when I'm done."

"St. Francis was very strict," Rosinsky recalls, reflecting on his time as a student teacher. "If you told the kids to be quiet, they were quiet. If you told them to get in line, they got in line. The public school kids were less disciplined and you've got fifty kids in a class. All you need is one clown, and the others follow. At one point, I would have said I want to teach high school. Now I'd go with elementary school. That's where you can see the most change and make the biggest difference in a child's life. It's easier to teach in the Catholic schools and there's less stress. The pay in the public schools is better. Probably, my boxing background would get me some respect up front from the kids in public school where other teachers might have to work harder to earn it. But at the end of the day, either you're a good teacher or you're not. I think I'd be good."

How will the pieces of Rosinsky's career fit together?

Promoter Lou DiBella has developed a number of New York City fighters. Rosinsky has fought on two of his "Broadway Boxing" cards and is likely to do so again.

"I'd love to sign Will," DiBella says. "First of all, I like him. He's a smart kid, somewhat circumspect, very aware of the dark side of boxing and the dangers that go with it. He has good boxing skills, probably better than he realizes. And he's a ticket seller with a good local following that will get bigger as his career progresses."

Then DiBella sounds a note of caution.

"Sometimes, I think that a lack of belief in himself as a fighter might hold Will back. But the biggest potential limitation in terms of his career is that the hunger might not be there. Most guys who are where he is right now in boxing are fighting to eat. Will has other options, and those options are attractive to him. At some point in his life, he wants to be a teacher. That shows character and a lot of other good things. But it also means that he might wake up one morning after a tough fight, maybe even a tough fight that he wins, and say, 'Screw this. I'd rather teach. No one will be hitting me in the head; the pay is good; and I'll be changing the lives of children.' I think he's a good guy. I have no idea what he'll do. But whatever he does, as long as he follows his heart, more power to him."

Rosinsky's father would like him to stop boxing. "He supports me in what I want to do," Will says. "But he's in my ear from time to time, saying, 'Just be a teacher.'" Meanwhile, his mother would like him to keep fighting. "She loves it, which is pretty weird," Will observes. "After each fight, she asks me, 'When's the next one?'"

So how long will Rosinsky keep fighting?

The question is put to him as he's eating a salad while those gathered around him in a restaurant are devouring pizza.

"I don't know," Will answers. "If you're a teacher, you don't have to make weight."

As 2009 progressed, Danny Jacobs was considered the best of New York's young fighters.

Danny Jacobs: "The Golden Child"

Danny Jacobs is being groomed for stardom.

Outside the ring, Jacobs is easy-going with a natural, almost disarming, quality about him. He likes to talk. "And I love to cook," he offers. "Chicken, pasta, different sauces. Bread pudding is my favorite. I make it well." He's also a talented young fighter, who says without false modesty, "I'm capable of being the best in the world. I can make a big mark in this game."

Jacobs was born in the Brownsville section of Brooklyn on February 3, 1987. His mother was a nurse. His father ("he was in and out of my life; I saw him every few months when I was growing up") is a building superintendent.

"It was a challenging childhood," Danny remembers. "I saw things on the streets that I'd have rather not seen. And I wasn't one of the smartest kids in school. Some of the other kids used to tease me. But right now, I'm probably one of the most successful of the people I went to school with."

Like many fighters, Jacobs found boxing by accident. He was just shy of fifteen years old.

"In school," he remembers, "you'd fight, be friends; fight, be friends. Some of the kids I knew had been going to the Howard Houses Gym, which was two blocks from where I lived. One time, I went with them. The first time I was in the ring, it was weird. The gloves were heavy; I'd never heard of headgear; the cup didn't fit; I got tired real quick."

But Jacobs was hooked.

"There had been times," he says, "when I'd sit in school, wondering what I'd do with my life. When I found boxing, I loved it from the first day. I learned early that I was good and that I had something special. The gym was someplace I needed to be. I even got used to getting hit. It comes with the territory; but getting punched in the nose still hurts."

Within a month, Jacobs was working with Victor Roundtree, who, with Andre Rozier, trains him today. Eventually, the Starrett City Gym became his home and the plaudits started pouring in.

Jacobs won National Golden Gloves titles in 2004 and 2005, National PAL titles in 2005, 2006, and 2007, and a USA Boxing National Championship in 2006. His overall amateur record was 137 wins against 7 losses. He was knocked down only three times in 144 fights and stopped once (by Matvey Korobov in a 2005 tournament in Russia). "I was eighteen years old and in over my head in that one," he admits.

The downside to Jacobs's ring success was that he dropped out of high school after tenth grade. "Boxing kept me behind," he says. "I was addicted to boxing. I was in the gym a lot and going to tournaments all the time. I'd found what I wanted to do with my life and put all my dedication into that."

It was widely assumed that Jacobs would represent the United States in the 165-pound division at the 2008 Olympics in Beijing. Then he lost to Shawn Estrada at the Olympic Trials and was forced to abandon that dream.

"Not making the Olympic team was heartbreaking," he acknowledges. "It hurt bad for about a month. But I knew there were still good things in my future and it wasn't the end for me. I'm a little ahead in my professional development of where I'd be now if I'd made the Olympic team." Then he adds, "I'd love to fight Estrada again someday. Korobov too."

Jacobs made his professional debut with a first-round knockout of Jose Jesus Hurtado on the undercard of the December 8, 2007, mega-fight between Floyd Mayweather Jr and Ricky Hatton in Las Vegas. His record now stands at 14-and-0 with 13 knockouts, but the opposition has been soft. His toughest test to date was a six-round decision over Emmanuel Gonzalez (who began his career with nine straight wins but has since been shopped as an opponent and lost four bouts in a row).

"I set goals and then I try to achieve them," Danny says. "I'm learning a lot and there's a lot more to learn. The route that I'm on, I'm doing just fine. Last year, I wanted to be one of the top prospects in boxing. This year, I want to be a contender; 20-and-0 by the end of the year and rated in the top ten. Next year, I want to be a champion."

But Jacobs wants to be more than a champion. He's focused on becoming a superstar. He's a high-profile prospect and he knows it. He isn't arrogant, but he does have a full appreciation of his boxing skills and where they might lead him.

"A lot of it is natural talent," Danny says. "I'm a very talented guy. The rest is dedication and hard work. I like attention. I like being in the spotlight. I'm used to people coming to see me fight and cheering me on. I like to read about myself. I go on the Internet every day to see what's written about me. My level of fame isn't high yet. I'm not a household name, but I'm getting to be famous. Sometimes people recognize me and come up to me and ask for my autograph or to have their picture taken with me, and I love it. I'd love to be someone like Derek Jeter and be appreciated for what I do and go to parties and have people know who I am. I can't see it ever being a bother."

The dream could come true. Jacobs has speed, power, good footwork, and a solid chin. His manager is the ubiquitous Al Haymon. Golden Boy has promoted most of his pro fights, although Danny says that he hasn't signed with them and is a promotional free agent.

From a commercial point of view, Team Jacobs has yet to capitalize on Danny's New York roots. He still lives in Brooklyn and unequivocally states, "I love New York. I don't ever want to leave. And if I do leave, I don't want to go far."

But he has fought in New York only once as a pro (on the undercard of Joe Calzaghe vs. Roy Jones Jr) and hasn't developed significant local media support. It wouldn't hurt if, from now on, he entered the ring to the accompaniment of Frank Sinatra singing *New York, New York*.

Still, whatever happens, Jacobs's connections are good. More than half of his fights have been on the undercard of major bouts like De La Hoya-Pacquiao, Calzaghe-Hopkins, and Pavlik-Taylor II. And he has charisma outside the ring, coupled with an exciting style in it.

Maybe too exciting.

"I'm very aware of the crowd," Danny says. "It's a big part of the experience for me. When you're going toe-to-toe in combat and people are cheering you on, that's the biggest high you can get. When I fight on the undercard of these big fights and there's only a few hundred people in the stands, I do what I have to do but it's not the same for me."

And suppose he were to fight someone like James Kirkland?

"We'll get in the ring and slug it out," Jacobs answers. "If I got hit too hard, I suppose I'd fight smart. If something's not working, you use an alternate route. But when your homeboys are there and the crowd is cheering for you, you want to do it the way they want you to."

"It's ego," Danny adds by way of further explanation. "I don't know anyone who would take a decision over a knockout. Knockouts are dramatic. They feel so good."

In sum, Danny Jacobs wants to be a superstar, make tens of millions of dollars, and, lest one think he's short-sighted, retire from boxing in perfect health at age thirty.

A lot of young men with dedication and prodigious physical gifts have that dream.

He has the potential to rise to the top. But it will be a hard road to fruition and some unanswered questions remain.

The last time Jacobs entered the ring as an underdog was against Matvey Korobov in 2005. That's due in part to his ring skills and also, during the past sixteen months, to one-sided matchmaking.

To be a superstar, Jacobs will have to go in tough and he won't always be favored to win. When crunch-time comes, will he rise to the occasion or crack and fold? Will he reign supreme or have the hope and optimism beaten out of him?

Time will tell.

There have been times, most notably with Joe Louis, where the hopes of a nation rested on a heavyweight. They have never been on the shoulders of a fighter as small as Manny Pacquiao.

Manny Pacquiao:
A Fighter for the Ages

On May 2, 2009, Manny Pacquiao and Ricky Hatton engaged in battle for the right to be called boxing's "pound-for-pound" champion.

Pacquiao and Hatton have aggressive relentless ring styles. They are two of the most exciting fighters in the world. Each man has stayed close to his roots, geographically and in terms of character. Both have special meaning to their constituents. No two fighters are more loved in their native lands.

Boxing has produced some of the most famous men who ever lived. John L. Sullivan, Joe Louis, and Muhammad Ali were known around the globe in their time.

The Philippines, with 96,000,000 people, is the twelfth most-populous nation on the planet. Another 10,000,000 Filipino expatriates live in countries around the world. Manny Pacquiao is the most idolized Filipino ever. All of his countrymen know who he is, and his story is familiar to them.

Pacquiao has lived virtually his entire life in a world surrounded by need. He ran away from home as a child, reportedly because his father ate a stray dog that Manny wanted to keep. Thereafter, he slept on the streets, often in a cardboard box. He began boxing for money at age fourteen.

To date, Pacquiao has won world championships at weights ranging from 112 to 140 pounds. Relying upon a devastating blend of speed and power, he has fought and beaten some of the best fighters in the world. Last December, he moved up in weight to 147 pounds and battered Oscar De La Hoya over eight one-sided rounds. That triumph elevated him from hero to icon. Hundreds of thousands of idolaters lined the streets of General Santos City in the Philippines for his victory parade. He was received with the joy and reverence normally accorded a conquering army.

Outside the ring, Pacquiao has a gentle quality about him. He's playful, almost childlike; polite with a shy smile. He speaks so softly that, at times, one has to lean close to hear him. Despite his accomplishments and celebrity status, there's a humility about him.

Pacquiao gives of himself the way Muhammad Ali used to give. He has a wave and a smile for everyone. He signs autographs, poses endlessly for photographs, and gives away money. A lot of money. Perhaps more than he should.

At any given time, 250 Filipinos are in school on scholarships paid for by Pacquiao. Each year on his birthday, he gives one-hundred-pound sacks of rice, other food supplies, and money to people who line up outside his home. He recently donated three hundred hospital beds to charitable organizations.

"The people where I live are not bad people," Manny says. "They are only poor. If I can help, it is my duty. I know what they're feeling. I remember, as a little boy, I ate one meal a day and sometimes slept in the street. I'm not shy to tell of my life because I want to give inspiration and show how Manny Pacquiao went from nothing to something. It is an honor to me that the people feel about me the way they do. I know that millions of people are praying for me, and that gives me strength. It inspires me to fight hard, stay strong, and remember all of the people of my country trying to achieve better for themselves. I do my best to bring happiness and a feeling of honor to all the people in the Philippines. My fight is not only for me but for my country. Every fight, I dedicate to my country."

Ricky Hatton isn't as iconic a figure as Pacquiao, but his "one of us" persona has made him a hero in Manchester and beyond. There are those who think that his fondness for beer and binge-eating between fights has taken the edge off his intensity as a fighter. But prior to facing Pacquiao, Ricky had won 45 of 46 bouts. His most notable victory was an eleventh-round stoppage of Kostya Tszyu in 2005. His sole defeat came at the hands of Floyd Mayweather Jr in a fight that Team Hatton believes should have an asterisk next to it in the record book because referee Joe Cortez appeared to tilt the playing field in Mayweather's favor.

"It wasn't a humbling experience because I'm humble to begin with," Ricky says of that loss. "But it was devastating."

Hatton, at his best, pressures his opponents until they break. His win-ning personality and the fervor of his fans add to the excitement of his fights.

Last year, Ricky tried his hand at stand-up comedy and told those in attendance, "What an absolute pleasure it is to be entertaining an audience without someone trying to smash my teeth in." But he has acknowledged, "No matter how many pints you have, no matter how many parties you go to; when you get your hand raised at the end of a fight, it's the greatest feeling in the world."

"In boxing, the glory is your own," Hatton says. "But I'm also doing it for Manchester, and I'm doing it for England."

There was the usual posturing during the negotiations that preceded the making of Pacquiao-Hatton.

Hatton (who is promoted by Golden Boy) was willing to accept a 65–35 split in Pacquiao's favor if he were allowed to carve out and keep all of the television money from the United Kingdom. That was unac-ceptable to Bob Arum of Top Rank (Pacquiao's promoter), who bar-gained for and got a 50–50 split on all revenue. Then Manny decided that he wanted better than 50–50 and refused to sign the contract. That elicited an aggravated response from Golden Boy CEO Richard Schaefer who, in a fit of pique, declared, "What a waste of time, money and effort. We had booked the planes, the hotels, printed the press kits for the press tour. It was all ready to go, a big production. Frankly, I'm disgusted at the behavior of Manny Pacquiao. He's a spoiled young kid who doesn't know how to behave."

The following day, Team Pacquiao responded in kind, issuing an "Official Pacquiao Statement" that read in part, "In the new age of Barack Obama where equal opportunity and fair play are now the norm, Ricky Hatton's chief negotiator Richard Schaefer apparently is still living in the past. The Swiss banker-turned CEO of Golden Boy Promotions has blocked a potential mega-fight with pound-for-pound boxing champion Manny Pacquiao by acting on emotion rather than dealing on the merits of the fight and by not giving what is rightly due the four-time, four-division champion."

The statement went on to declare that Pacquiao was "disgusted" by Schaefer's comments and quoted Manny as saying, "I find Schaefer's actions and words too aristocratic. He's the one who is acting childish. He is not professional and civil enough to give merits to the negotiating table." Then, in the ultimate insult, Pacquiao declared, "I say, 'Schaefer is a bad businessman.'"

One day later, the parties settled on a reported 52–48 split in Pacquiao's favor with a $12,000,000 guarantee for each fighter.

The sport of boxing has been sleepwalking through what, in reality, has been a "post-Oscar" era for some time. Pacquiao-Hatton was the start of the post-Oscar pay-per-view era. The marketing of the fight began with a media tour that kicked off in Manchester. Six thousand fans were in attendance. Manny challenged Ricky to a game of darts at a local pub (Ricky won). Then the tour moved to the British Museum of Military History in London.

Hatton sounded a familiar theme throughout the proceedings. "I don't think I can express how much I'm looking forward to this fight," he told the media. "Every youngster dreams of becoming a world champion. But I have to be frank. Never did I dream of being in a position to fight for the pound-for-pound title, which means you're the best champion out of all weight divisions. This fight means everything to me. To become the pound-for-pound champion would be almost beyond belief."

But there was another, less appealing, side to the promotion.

One of the problems with boxing today is that fighters and others who behave badly outside the ring get an inordinate amount of attention. Too often, trash-talking and ugly acts are encouraged as a way of selling tickets and pay-per-view buys.

For the past eight years, Pacquiao has been trained by Freddie Roach. During that time, Manny (who relied on speed and a powerful left hand to become a world-class fighter) has evolved into a complete practitioner of the art of boxing. It's possible that no fighter in history has improved to the degree that Manny has after reaching elite status. Much of the credit for this improvement goes to Roach.

The chemistry between Roach and Pacquiao is special. They have bonded in a unique way.

"It's not like I'm the dictator and tell Manny what to do and he does it," Roach explains. "If I say something and Manny is uncomfortable with it, we discuss it. And it's wrong to say that I made Manny. He was a very good fighter when I got him. Besides; we can work on a game plan and do things in the gym. But when the bell rings, it's Manny who has to win the fight."

Pacquiao has a similar appreciation of the relationship and adds, "Freddie and I are not only a team in boxing. We are friends, like family."

Enter Floyd Mayweather Sr, the self-described "greatest trainer in the world."

In late-2008, Mayweather was brought in by the Hatton camp to replace Ricky's longtime trainer, Billy Graham. Initially, the change carried at least one positive. The tension between Ray Hatton (Ricky's father) and Paul Speak (a business-media adviser and friend) on the one hand and Graham on the other had begun to weigh heavily on Ricky's mind. That irritant was now gone.

But Mayweather is given to public utterances that extol his own talents and demean others. "It's night and day between me and Freddie 'The Joke Coach' Roach," one sample comment began. "Don't ever compare us. Freddie Roach is in the Hall of Fame. He should be in the Hall of Shame. We're going to whip Pacquiao's ass, because I got the best fighter and because I'm the best trainer."

For a while, Roach engaged with Mayweather. "As long as Floyd is in Hatton's corner," Freddie maintained, "I have absolutely no concerns. Floyd training Hatton for this fight is our biggest advantage."

Later, Roach acknowledged, "I got caught up in the bullshit a little bit. For a while, Floyd got under my skin. Then Manny told me, 'Just be a gentleman, stay humble, and I'll take care of it. I'll give you a present in the fight.'"

Neither Pacquiao nor Hatton is into trash-talking. "Saying is one thing," Ricky observes. "Doing is another."

Still, HBO made a conscious decision to highlight the Mayweather-Roach feud by focusing on the trainers in its 24/7 promotional series. Top Rank and Golden Boy took a similar marketing approach.

Would the NBA promote its championship series by encouraging Phil Jackson of the Los Angeles Lakers and Mike Brown of the Cleveland Cavaliers to demean each other? Would Major League Baseball market its games on the basis of trash-talking between Yankee manager Joe Girardi and his Red Sox counterpart, Terry Francona? Intelligently run sports give trophies to their participants. Pacquiao-Hatton was marketed in part as "The Battle of the Trainers" with a gaudy five-foot trophy promised to the winner.

As fight week progressed, the boxing world converged on Las Vegas.

"In Pearce Egan's time," A. J. Liebling wrote of the early nineteenth century, "the migration to a fight would begin days in advance when the foot-toddlers set out on the road for the rumored meeting place. Rumors were all they had to go on because, in England at that time, prizefighting was illegal. A day or so later, the milling coves and the flash coves (fighters and knowing boys) would set out in wagons with plenty of sporting girls and gin to keep them happy. Last, the Corinthians (amateurs of the fancy and patrons of pugilists) would take to the road in their fast traps and catch up with the others in time to get their bets down before the fight."

For Pacquiao–Hatton, the migrants came by plane from the far reaches of the globe.

There was a nice buzz in Las Vegas prior to the fight. A lot of people in the media were there, not just because their jobs required it but because they wanted to be. The bout had been sold out since mid–April with tickets selling at a premium. The major world sanctioning organizations were absent, but no one seemed to care.

Throughout the week, Bob Arum extolled the virtues of his fighter to anyone who would listen.

"Manny Pacquiao isn't 'me, me, me,'" the promoter declared. "He thinks first about other people, and that's unusual for a great athlete in any sport." On numerous occasions, he referred to Pacquiao as "a future president of the Philippines" and went so far as to advise an interviewer for National Public Radio, "When Manny's career in boxing is over, he will lift the yoke of oppression of a corrupt government off the backs of the Filipino people and lift the entire country to greatness."

For good measure, Arum then added, "Manny Pacquiao is a Roman Catholic; Freddie Roach is an agnostic; and I'm Jewish. But we all agree that God is looking over Manny Pacquiao."

"God gives me the strength and looks over me," Pacquiao noted in response. "But I still have to do my best."

The fighters treated each other with respect. Again and again, Manny sounded the refrain, "Ricky Hatton is a good person. I have a lot of respect for him. There is nothing personal for this fight. We are just doing our job."

Hatton responded in kind, saying, "We're both nice men out of the ring; just not so nice inside it. Manny has done it the hard way, and I respect everything that he has achieved in boxing."

That left Floyd Mayweather Sr to be heard from. At the final pre-fight press conference, "the world's greatest trainer" was his normal charming self, referring again to his counterpart as "Freddie 'The Joke Coach' Roach" and adding the appellation "Cockroach." That was enough for some members of the British media to suggest that their loyalty to Ricky was being tested. But Mayweather was undeterred. "I'm having fun with this," he announced.

Meanwhile, more than one member of Team Hatton grumbled not-so-privately that Mayweather's conduct was beneath their dignity. And dignity wasn't the only issue. There was unhappiness in the Hatton camp over Floyd's habitual tardiness, which, some felt, had impacted adversely on Ricky's training. Indeed, "the world's greatest trainer" would arrive in Hatton's dressing room late on fight night. And after Ricky lost, he was slow to return, dressed quickly, and left without consoling his fighter.

By eleven o'clock on Friday morning (the day before the fight), several thousand Brits were waiting outside the Garden Arena at the MGM Grand Hotel and Casino in anticipation of the three o'clock weigh-in. The arena was configured to accommodate six thousand people for the weigh-in. By 2:00 PM, every non-media seat was filled and another thousand fans were unable to gain admittance.

The Ricky Hatton Band was in full swing, with "Walking in a Hatton Wonderland" and "God Save the Queen" sung again and again. The Brits outnumbered Pacquiao's fans by roughly 3-to-1. But Arum tossed that fact aside with the explanation, "Filipinos are hard-working people, so they're not here today because they're working."

Pacquiao weighed in at 138 pounds; Hatton at 140 (the contract weight). By the time they stepped into the ring twenty-nine hours later, Manny had gained ten pounds; Ricky, twelve.

Pacquiao was a 5-to-2 favorite. Both camps were genuinely confident. Most "boxing people" were picking Manny to win. However, there was often a "but."

"But I wouldn't be surprised if it turns out that Ricky is too big and strong for Manny."

After all, Hatton had never entered the ring at less than 138 pounds. Pacquiao began his career at 106 pounds and had fought above 130 pounds on only two occasions. Manny, it was thought, had never faced an opponent who brought as much size, strength, and pressure to bear as Ricky would bring.

Former featherweight champion Barry McGuigan voiced that view, stating, "Pacquiao is unproven at this weight. Apart from one assignment at lightweight against David Diaz and the Oscar De La Hoya bout at welter, he has not fought above 130 pounds. Diaz was the weakest of the champions at 135 pounds and De La Hoya turned out to be little more than a carcass. Hatton will probably come in a stone [14 pounds] over the 140-pound limit, feeling as strong as a bull. Pacquiao will not have dealt with that before."

Hall of Fame trainer Emanuel Steward was in accord, saying, "Manny looked better than he is against Oscar and David Diaz. Oscar was dead at the weight, and Diaz is slower than most heavyweights. I think that Ricky will be too big and tough for him."

Hatton, of course, voiced similar sentiments, declaring:

• "I'm bigger; I'm stronger. Pacquiao may have fought at 147 pounds. But trust me; this is a new weight division for him. I have always stated that no one in the world can beat me at 140 pounds, and I stand by that statement. I'm undefeated at this weight in twelve years. At 140 pounds, I'm too strong and too big for anyone."
• "Pacquiao is a slick, fast, effective boxer. But if you look at the defeat by Erik Morales in 2005 and the close fights he had with Juan Manuel Marquez, he doesn't like sustained pressure. I am a fighter that is constantly in your face, constantly throwing punches. I'm bigger than him. He'll be thinking, 'Jesus, this is going to be tough. This fella doesn't leave you alone.' Believe me; Ricky Hatton will be the toughest fight he has ever had."
• "People are looking at the Oscar performance and suggesting that Pacquiao will finish my career, too. But he won't. Any victory over Oscar is outstanding and I never like to be disrespectful. But Oscar was like a walking corpse that night. It was clear that Oscar wasn't right. Dead man walking. No one will ever convince me that, on that night, I couldn't have done the same job, probably quicker."
• "It's a very very tough fight. But to say I'm confident would be an understatement. I've never felt more certain of victory than I do right now. I know his strengths and his weaknesses, but I also know what I

am capable of doing. Everything has fallen perfectly into place. There's no doubt in my mind who is going to win the fight. I've never been so certain; I've never been more confident. I believe that, as long as Ricky Hatton does what Ricky Hatton does best, I'm going to be too much in all areas for Manny. If people want to re-mortgage and put a few quid on me, they should. There's just no reason why I should lose this fight."

In sum, Hatton and his partisans thought that he could employ basic boxing skills and overpower Pacquiao the way he'd overpowered Kostya Tszyu four years earlier. But Ricky is now on the downhill slide (as Tszyu was then). And Manny is better than Kostya ever was.

"I don't predict before my fights," Pacquiao said when asked how he thought the bout would end. "Ricky Hatton is a good fighter. I know that he is a little bigger than me and a strong fighter, but I am faster. I just want to do my best and give a good fight and bring happiness to the people who see me fight."

Freddie Roach was less reticent, declaring, "I've watched tapes of Hatton's last twenty fights. We know his strengths and his weaknesses. Ricky is a world-class fighter, but he doesn't have the ability to adjust. He fights the same way over and over again. And his balance is poor. When he has you on the ropes and sets his feet, he can throw a good hook to the body. But in the center of the ring, he's not a puncher. Manny has to stay off the ropes. If he does that, his speed and power will be too much for Ricky. He'll walk him into some shots and knock him out. I'm not saying it will be an easy fight, but Manny is a much better fighter than Ricky."

When fight night came, Roach was the first member of Team Pacquiao to enter dressing room #3 at the MGM Grand Garden Arena. He arrived at 5:45 PM, and began organizing the tools of his trade (tape, towels, and various pieces of boxing equipment) on a long table opposite the door. Fifteen minutes later, Pacquiao arrived with twenty people in tow: among them his wife (Jinkee), his mother-in-law and sister-in-law, assistant trainer Buboy Fernandez, conditioning coach Alex Ariza, and team physician Dr. Allan Recto.

Pacquiao sat on a rubdown table. After several minutes of conversation, he took off his sneakers and socks and began putting protective pads on his toes to guard against blisters.

More friends and girlfriends of friends filtered into the room. Thirty-eight people were there. The scene conjured up images of the two-bedroom apartment in Los Angeles that Pacquiao lived in with a dozen friends during training. "It is easier if you have friends around, laughing," Manny says. "Always, there should be laughing."

Now there was just quiet conversation. The first pay-per-view fight of the evening could be seen on a flat-screen television in a corner of the room. The voice of HBO commentator Jim Lampley filled the air. Without the television, the room would have been as quiet as a library. It was hard to believe that thirty-eight people made so little noise.

At 6:25, Roach moved to the center of the room and told the gathering, "In five minutes, anyone who doesn't belong here has to leave."

Five minutes later, a half-dozen women (including Jinkee) and a few others left. Twenty-eight people remained.

Pacquiao put on his socks and laced up his shoes. Larry Merchant came in for the ritual pre-fight HBO interview and mentioned to Roach that Hatton had elected to enter the ring first. As the holder of a 140-pound belt, Ricky had the prerogative of walking last. But he was taking the view that Manny's pound-for-pound title was the real prize at stake. To motivate himself, he wanted to enter the ring as the challenger.

"That's fine with me," Roach responded. "If they want to walk first and wait for Manny and get cold, I have no problem with that."

Merchant finished his interview and left. Once again, Roach moved to the center of the room.

"Please; if you don't belong here, leave."

No one moved.

Two members of the Las Vegas Metropolitan Police Department were summoned and cleared the room of unauthorized personnel.

Lee Beard (Hatton's assistant trainer) came in to watch Pacquiao's hands being wrapped. For the most part, remarkably, Manny performed the chore himself, singing softly as he worked. When need be, cutman Miguel Diaz assisted the fighter as Roach looked on.

"It used to be that I helped out with the taping," Freddie explained. "But when Manny fought Oscar, we thought it would be a good idea for me to watch them tape Oscar's hands to maybe rattle Oscar, so Miguel helped Manny that night. Manny liked the way Miguel did it. He was afraid it might hurt my feelings to have Miguel do it again, but I said 'no problem.' It's not about me. It's about what's best for Manny."

The television, which was turned off when Merchant came in to conduct his interview, hadn't been turned on again. The hum of the air-ventilation system was the loudest noise in the room.

Manny finished taping his left hand, held it up, smiled at his handi-work, and began applying gauze to his right hand.

The television was turned back on. Middleweight prospect Danny Jacobs was midway through an eight-round whitewash of an overmatched Michael Walker.

"Can we change to the basketball game?" Manny inquired. "Chicago Bulls and Boston."

The answer, after tinkering with the television set, was "no." Pacquiao shrugged and continued wrapping his hands. When he was done, he stood up, slapped his fists together, and cried out, "Let's get ready to rumble." Then he shadow-boxed briefly in the center of the room.

At 7:30, a prayer group led by Marlon Beof (a Filipino priest now liv-ing in New York) entered the room. There was a brief prayer.

Referee Kenny Bayless gave Manny his pre-fight instructions.

Pacquiao resumed shadow-boxing and loosening up in what seemed to be the cardiac equivalent of a light aerobics class.

At eight o'clock, Manny put on a pair of white boxing trunks with black trim; then a red-white-and-blue robe.

Roach gloved Pacquiao up.

The room was cleared again. Now only Manny, his cornermen, a commission inspector (and this writer) were present.

At 8:10, serious padwork with Roach began. Unlike most fighters in the dressing room before a fight, Pacquiao worked with his robe on. Periodically, it slipped open and Buboy Fernandez retied it.

The padwork grew more intense. Pacquiao's fists were a combination of blinding speed and power, culminating in a flurry of punches that seemed to explode on the pads.

"Oooo! See ya," Roach said approvingly.

"And if he goes like this," Manny added (imitating Hatton coming in), "I go BOOM!" At which point, he launched a slow-motion counter right hook aimed at Roach's jaw.

Then Manny smiled the smile of an athlete who was primed and ready to play a game. He was completely relaxed, as though he believed he was protected by a higher power. Or maybe he was simply confident in knowing that he's the best fighter in the world.

The hopes and dreams of 100,000,000 people were resting on the shoulders of one soft-spoken diminutive man.

The fight began as expected, with Hatton moving forward and Pacquiao, in his southpaw stance, circling out of harm's way. Thirty seconds in, a sharp counter right hook shook Ricky. That was followed by more hooks and straight lefthands punctuated by a sharp counter hook at the two-minute mark that sent Hatton tumbling face-first to the canvas. He rose at the count of eight, was pummeled around the ring, and decked again for another eight-count with nine seconds left in the round.

That left Hatton's fans with the fragile hope that Pacquiao-Hatton would somehow be like Pacquiao-Marquez I (where Marquez was decked three times in the opening stanza but rallied to salvage a draw). However, Pacquiao is a much better fighter now than he was then. And Marquez makes adjustments well on the fly, whereas Ricky doesn't.

In round two, Hatton came back for more and Pacquiao said "I'll give it to you" with his fists. Speed alone might not kill, but speed plus power does. Ricky fought as well as he could, which kept him on his feet until the 2:52 mark when a straight lefthand landed flush on the jaw and deposited him unconscious on the canvas.

It was a knockout that will appear on highlight reels forever and a career-defining demolition. Hatton has a pretty good chin, and Pacquiao reduced it to English china.

The "punch-stats" compiled by CompuBox reflected the carnage. In round one, Pacquiao landed 35 punches compared to 8 for Hatton. In round two, the margin was 38 to 10. Manny scored with a remarkable 62 percent of his power punches, landing 65 blows in that category.

After the fight, Pacquiao returned to his dressing room and embraced a throng of admirers (Denzel Washington among them).

There was a group prayer.

Manny signed his ring stool, various fight-night credentials, and other memorabilia.

A member of Team Pacquiao handed him a cell phone and announced, "It's David Diaz."

"Hello, my friend," Pacquiao said, beginning the conversation.

"I'm so happy," Diaz told him. "On all the advertisements for the fight, they've been showing me on television, lying face down on the canvas. Now they've got a better knockout to show."

Pacquiao laughed. "Thank you, brother."

The conversation ended.

Manny laughed again and gleefully threw a straight left hand in slow motion into the air. "BOOM! Good-bye."

In his mind, the punch that sent Ricky Hatton into unconsciousness was the equivalent of a five-hundred-foot home run into the bleachers; not an act of violence.

Freddie Roach sat in a chair opposite the rubdown table, surveying the scene. One suspected that he felt a little like Phil Jackson felt after coaching Michael Jordan and the Chicago Bulls to yet another NBA championship.

"Manny makes me look good," the trainer said. "He's such a pleasure to work with. He was good when I got him and I knew there was room for improvement. But I wondered, 'How good can he really be? Will he listen?' Because a lot of guys get to the level Manny was at eight years ago and think they know everything. But Manny works hard. He listens. He keeps getting better and better. I know I have something to do with it. But really, the credit belongs to Manny."

Freddie smiled. "You know; you work on something in the gym again and again, and you hope you see some of it on fight night. And tonight . . ." Roach shook his head in wonder. "Whenever Manny fights now, you see the things you worked on the gym being executed perfectly, right in front of you."

"Floyd told everyone that he had the better fighter," someone offered. "So I guess that makes you the better trainer."

Freddie laughed. "No; I had the better fighter. Besides; trainers are overrated. We can guide our fighters in the right direction, but it's up to them to carry out the game plan. I'm not the best trainer in the world. I just have the best fighter."

In the far corner of the room, several members of Team Pacquiao had rewritten the lyrics to *London Bridge is Falling Down* and were singing:

> Ricky Hatton's falling down
> Falling down
> Falling down

Ricky Hatton's falling down
We love Manny

Pacquiao thrust his left hand into the air again and once again pro-
claimed, "BOOM! Good-bye." Then he began singing to the tune of
"Winter Wonderland" (known in boxing circles as "Walking in a Hatton
Wonderland"):

There's no more Ricky Hatton
No more
Ricky Hatton

A reporter from a Filipino radio station reached toward him with a
tape recorder in hand.

"No tape; please," Manny told him. "Ricky Hatton is a good fighter
and my friend. I only want to show respect to him."

So . . .

What is one to make of Pacquiao-Hatton?

The first thing to be said is that it symbolizes the globalization of
boxing. The heavyweight division today is ruled by Eastern Europeans.
The consensus pound-for-pound rankings are dominated by fighters from
outside the United States. Now the biggest fight of the year thus far has
featured a Filipino versus a Brit.

Forget the rhetoric about Pacquiao having won world titles in six
weight divisions. The way things are in boxing today, any world-class
fighter with connections can win a belt. Better to say that, at various
times, Manny has earned the right to call himself the best flyweight,
super-bantamweight, super-featherweight, and super-lightweight in the
world.

Boxing is a skill. Fighting is the spirit that determines how a fighter
employs his skill. Pacquiao excels at both. He has won his last four fights
in four different weight divisions against opponents who ranged from
good to great. He moved up in weight to go 5-1-1 against Marco
Antonio Barrera, Erik Morales, and Juan Manuel Marquez. None of the
other three fighters has a winning record in that round-robin demolition
tournament.

Other fighters reach a certain level of proficiency, think they know everything, and never get any better. Pacquiao keeps improving. He's getting better as he gets bigger. Another remarkable thing about him is that his body shows so little wear and tear after fourteen years of hard fighting.

Of all the fights that Pacquiao has won in his storied career, only his victory over Oscar De La Hoya looms larger than Pacquiao-Hatton. Many observers of the boxing scene thought that Manny would cut Ricky to pieces. Others considered it likely that he'd beat Hatton down over time. But few experts believed that he would simply overwhelm, dominate, and obliterate his foe.

Pacquiao is now on the verge of crossing over into the American consciousness. His English is good but not fluent. He doesn't always understand the nuances in questions that are put to him. But he speaks English far better than 99.999 percent of Americans speak Visayan (his native language). He has an endorsement deal with Nike. During the week preceding Pacquiao-Hatton, he was interviewed by CNN, National Public Radio, and the *Wall Street Journal*.

On the home front, Manny speaks of undertaking a political career in the not-too-distant future. "I have a heart to help the people in the Philippines," he says. "That is why I will be good in politics."

One assumes that his effectiveness as a candidate (and more so, as an office-holder should he win) will depend in large measure on the people around him. He has a short attention span, particularly as it relates to business matters.

But regardless of what happens in the political arena, Pacquiao is a living reminder of what a great sport boxing can be and how a single fighter can lift the spirits of an entire nation.

In certain times in certain places, boxing has been more than a sport. It has been a rallying point for large segments of society. A handful of great fighters have transcended the sweet science to become symbols for their people.

Two days before he fought Ricky Hatton, Manny Pacquiao told this writer, "My dream is, when I am finished with boxing, my people won't forget me."

That dream is secure.

Wladimir Klitschko entered 2009 as the best heavyweight in the world.
But boxing was without a true heavyweight champion.

A Note on Klitschko-Chagaev

"The notion of a universal heavyweight championship doesn't come across as legitimate any longer," writes Patrick Kehoe. "The heavyweight championship today is a statement of political expediency and marketing-speak. Courts and committees and cable executives and the ubiquity of promotional influence have seen to the extinction of the championship as won via merit and the lineage of ritual combat."

Wladimir Klitschko's June 20th match-up in Gelsenkirchen, Germany, against Ruslan Chagaev was the latest exhibit in support of Kehoe's thesis.

Klitschko-Chagaev began as Klitschko against David Haye.

Haye got the fight in large measure because he sounds like a foul-mouthed version of Naseem Hamed. During the pre-fight build-up, he went out of his way to offend Wladimir, calling him "Bitchko" and demeaning his skills as a fighter.

Among the thoughts that Haye offered were:

- "The heavyweight division has been shit for the last four or five years. It's a joke. It really sucks."
- "Wladimir doesn't engage in battle the way people want to see. I'm different. I don't go out to jab and move and try to steal the fight. I come out from the first round and throw bombs. I smash my opponents to bits.
- I've got a PhD in trash-talking and kicking ass. We'll see whose PhD matters on June 20th."

Klitschko (who has a doctorate in sports science) was particularly offended by a T-shirt that Haye wore during the kick-off press tour. The T-shirt depicted David standing in a boxing ring, holding the severed heads of Wladimir and his brother Vitali in his upraised hands with their decapitated bodies lying on the canvas beneath his feet.

"The T-shirt bothers me," Klitschko acknowledged. "The way he does it with my brother's body; he is doing it in an ugly, not acceptable way. It's not funny. It has nothing to do with sport. He talks a lot, but actions speak louder than words. He is immature as a person and as a fighter. I will not underestimate him, but I know my strong side and his weak side. He has fast hands and a lot of nothing. David Haye is going to eat his words after the fight, and I would like him to eat his T-shirt too."

Klitschko and Haye have bodies that baseball players who hit seventy home runs in a season would admire. But Klitschko is the naturally bigger man. Much bigger. David was a good cruiserweight, but there are questions as to whether he can take (as opposed to talk) a heavyweight punch. Or even has one.

Moreover, Haye had been stopped in five rounds by Carl Thompson and never fought a quality heavyweight. Wladimir figured to be a much tougher opponent than Giacobbe Fragomeni, Ismail Abdoul, or Lasse Johansen (some of Haye's earlier victims).

Then, on June 3rd, it was announced that Haye had suffered a back injury in training and was withdrawing from the fight. Adam Booth (his business representative) described the news as "the most disappointing and devastating that David has ever had to deliver."

In response, Klitschko noted, "If something like that happened to me, he would talk dirty, which I'm not going to do. I will not throw garbage at a person who is down on the floor. I won't kick a man when he is down, but he would to me."

Meanwhile, there were reports that Setanta (the television network slated to carry Klitschko-Haye in the UK) was teetering on the edge of bankruptcy. And given the way Haye's fight contract had been structured, he was to receive most of his purse from Setanta.

Thus, when Floyd Mayweather Jr announced shortly thereafter that a rib injury had forced the postponement of his July 18th fight against Juan Manuel Marquez (which was doing poorly at the box office), Steve Kim of Maxboxing.com was moved to ask, "What's more credible? David Haye's back injury or Floyd Mayweather's ailing rib?"

Adding to boxing's medical report, Ruslan Chagaev (the WBA "world heavyweight champion in recess") had been scheduled to fight Nikolai Valuev (the WBA "world heavyweight champion") in Finland on May 30th.

Chagaev (for those who care) had won the WBA title with an April 14, 2007, majority decision over Valuev. But after Ruslan pulled out of one fight too many (including a rematch against Nikolai, the WBA ruled that Valuev was once again its champion on the basis of a split-decision victory over John Ruiz and declared Ruslan its "champion in recess."

One day before Valuev-Chagaev was to take place, Finnish officials announced that the fight could not proceed because Ruslan had tested positive for hepatitis B.

That wasn't a problem for German officials (who had okayed Klitschko versus Lamon Brewster in 2007, even though Lamon was on medical suspension in the United States and suffering from impaired vision in one eye).

Hence, Klitschko-Chagaev.

Wladimir is a safety-first fighter. That isn't necessarily a bad thing, but it does take some of the drama out of a fight. Klitschko-Chagaev was nine rounds of tedium that could be summed up as "Klitschko jab, Klitschko jab, Klitschko straight righthand."

Chagaev kept trying to work his way inside, but couldn't get past the jab. Part of his problem was that, to get inside, a fighter has to work behind something (like a jab of his own). And Ruslan rarely did. The only blow of consequence he landed during the entire fight was a lefthand after the bell ending round seven.

Give Chagaev points for determination. It takes a special person to get hit in the head again and again, land nothing in return, and not vary from his fight plan. But those were the only points that Ruslan got. He was knocked down once and bleeding from a gash on his left eyelid as well as an ugly cut inside his mouth (remember the hepatitis B) when the ring doctor called a halt to the proceedings after nine rounds.

Prior to the fight, *Ring Magazine* had announced that Klitschko-Chagaev would be for its own vacant heavyweight title. Klitschko also wears the IBF, WBO, and IBO crowns. Perhaps he is now also the WBA "champion in recess."

The best way to make good fights is to put good fighters in tough.

The Lesson of Ortiz-Maidana

On June 27th, HBO televised what was supposed to be Victor Ortiz's coronation as the WBA "interim junior-welterweight champion of the world."

The twenty-two-year-old Ortiz has been groomed for stardom and still might make it there someday. But at a point in his career when the competition should have been stepped up to harden him for a championship run, he was put in soft. That enabled Victor to preserve his shiny record and look great on television. But it didn't prepare him to fight Marcos Maidana (a rugged Argentinean with a solid punch who comes to fight).

At the start of HBO's June 27th *Boxing After Dark* telecast, Max Kellerman surveyed the 140-pound division beginning with Manny Pacquiao and optimistically proclaimed, "Victor Ortiz may have the most star potential of them all."

Then reality set in.

Ortiz dropped Maidana midway through round one, only to have the favor quickly returned. Unlike Marcos, Victor was hurt. But he fought back and did enough to even the stanza. In round two, he knocked Maidana down twice.

The slugfest continued in round three with each man aggressively forcing the action. Kellerman informed the viewing audience that, while he had heard "whispers" about Ortiz's chin, "clearly, Ortiz has a lot of heart."

Actually, in boxing, the chin is often connected to the heart, as became evident three rounds later.

In round four, Ortiz seemed to be tiring. Gut-check time was fast approaching.

Round five was a big one for Maidana. He began landing solid righthands; took everything that Ortiz had to offer; and when backed against the ropes, landed a hard left hook that opened a terrible gash along Victor's right eyebrow.

In some jurisdictions, when that happens to the house fighter, a phantom clash of heads is said to have caused the wound. Referee Raul Caiz Sr properly ruled that the cut was caused by a punch.

By the end of round five, Maidana was pummeling Ortiz at will with right hands.

In round six, Marcos picked up where he'd left off, trapping Victor against the ropes and putting him on the canvas with a left hook to the body. At that point, either the referee or Ortiz's corner could have stopped the action and no one would have complained. Instead, Victor rose and waved the fight off himself.

Caiz went through the charade of taking Ortiz to the corner to be examined by the ring doctor, but it was clear that Victor had no intention of fighting anymore. The time of the stoppage was forty-six seconds of the sixth round.

Afterward, Ortiz informed a national television audience, "I'm not going to go out on my back. I'm not going to lay down for nobody. I'd rather just stop when I'm ahead. That way, I can speak well when I'm older. I'm young, but I don't think I deserve to get beat up like this. I've got a lot of thinking to do."

Give Ortiz credit for candor. But getting hit hard is part of the deal if you want to be a boxer.

So let's look at the lessons to be learned in the wake of Ortiz-Maidana.

At the start of 2009, HBO told boxing fans that the next generation of stars included Victor Ortiz, Alfredo Angulo, James Kirkland, and Robert Guerrero. All four were put in soft to build their reputations.

Kirkland is now in jail. Angulo was exposed (and beaten) by Kermit Cintron. Guerrero begged out after being cut by an accidental headbutt in a fight against 10-to-1 underdog Daud Yordan. Now, Ortiz has been knocked out.

A television network has the power to give fighters exposure. A television network has the power to steer fighters to a particular promoter. A television network cannot (repeat, cannot) create stars.

In boxing, stars create themselves. Very few people knew who Marco Antonio Barrera, Erik Morales, and Arturo Gatti were before HBO put them on *Boxing After Dark* a decade ago. But the public tuned in because they trusted HBO to deliver quality fights. And the fighters who delivered in those fights became stars.

Instead of trying to anoint stars, HBO should create the next generation of stars by continually matching the best young prospects against the best young prospects (not against overmatched foes). If a fighter doesn't want to go in tough, let him fight somewhere else for ten thousand dollars.

Ortiz-Maidana was a great fight. It might not have been great for Ortiz or his manager or his promoter. But it was great entertainment for the viewers who watched it because Ortiz was in tough.

So apply the lessons of Ortiz–Maidana to the future.

HBO won't televise another fight until August 22nd, when Paulie Malignaggi goes to Houston to take on Juan Diaz, the referee, and three judges. Let's hope that, when the network finalizes its fall schedule, it demands competitive fights across the board.

A fight that looks one way on paper sometimes unfolds very differently in the ring.

Juanma's Desperate Hour

Three days before he fought Rogers Mtagwa, Juan Manuel Lopez sat on the sofa in his suite at the Parker Meridien Hotel in New York.

"Juanma" is the WBO super-featherweight champion and the latest in a line of elite Puerto Rican fighters. In an age of proliferating beltholders, he's widely regarded as the best 122-pound fighter in the world.

Equally important from a marketing point of view, he has charisma. There's a joy about him. Juanma has a ready smile and an effervescent bubbling personality. He has IT.

Earlier this year, Lopez signed a three-year contract extension with Top Rank (which has promoted him from his first pro fight). Bob Arum has dreams of Juanma becoming a Puerto Rican version of Manny Pacquiao.

Ricardo Jimenez (who serves as Top Rank's ambassador to the Hispanic media and interacts with all of the promoter's Spanish-speaking fighters) puts the matter in perspective when he says, "Juanma sees the big picture. He understands what he has to do to be great in the ring and also the larger business issues. He's very friendly with the media, very mature, very nice. He has a personality that all of Puerto Rico can fall in love with. He isn't just comfortable in the spotlight. He loves it. When it comes to dealing with the public and the media, he's the most natural one I've ever had."

"I like the media," Lopez says. "I've never had a problem with them. Sometimes, they ask the same questions again and again. But I know they have a job to do just like I do, and I try to help them do their job."

Juanma's father is a security guard. His mother is a secretary. He's twenty-six years old. His wife has three children from a previous relationship. Together, they've had two more; Belissa, age five, and Juanma (not Juan Manuel), age three.

"I'm a family guy," Lopez says. "After a fight, I want to be with my family to celebrate my win; not at a party."

Sitting in his hotel suite at the Parker Meridien on October 7th, Lopez reflected on his journey to date. He understands some English but is more comfortable speaking in Spanish. Jimenez translated for him.

"I was a kid who fought a lot in school," Juanma reminisced. "When I was nine, they sent me to the gym. I liked it right away. Boxing was inside of me. After a week, they said, 'Let's see what you can do.' They put me in the ring to box with a boy who was about my age, and I just threw punches. In fifty-six seconds, I knocked him out. My mother told me then, 'If you are going to be in boxing, you must be serious about it.' So I was serious about it. When I was twelve, I entered a tournament for the first time. I won the tournament and they gave me a trophy. It was the most exciting thing that ever happened to me."

More exciting things have happened since then. "I love boxing," Lopez said. "I love watching boxing. I love being part of boxing. I'm surprised at how fast my career has gotten to where it is now. I thought I'd get here, but I didn't think I'd get here so fast."

Lopez also spoke of the line of kings from Puerto Rico who have ruled the world,

"I admire Jose Torres because he was a good fighter and he was proud of his heritage. Even though he lived most of his life in New York, he never forgot that he was Puerto Rican. When I think about how much Wilfredo Benitez accomplished when he was young—a world champion when he was seventeen, a champion at three different weights by the time he was twenty-two—it humbles me. Wilfredo Gomez; to me, he was the best ever. He always says to me that I can accomplish everything that he accomplished. That makes me so happy. Miguel Cotto invented the word perseverance. I'll have to work very hard to get to where those guys got. But that's my dream."

And Lopez voiced special feelings for Felix Trinidad.

"When I was growing up, Tito was my idol. I met him for the first time when I was fifteen. I was at a boxing show and he took a picture with me. I asked if he would come to my school. He said 'sure' and gave me his card. After the 2004 Olympics [in which Lopez represented Puerto Rico], I met him again. He let me in the gym when he was training to fight Ricardo Mayorga. Now he's my friend. We talk on the phone every day about family, about boxing. It's hard to believe. I never thought that could be possible. I spend a lot of time now going to schools. I see kids looking up to me the way I looked up to Tito. It feels great. I try to be nice to them the way Tito was nice to me."

There were also words that proved eerily prophetic given the battle that would unfold three days hence.

"Boxing isn't enough," Lopez said, sitting on the sofa. "You need heart. Either you have courage and a fighting spirit inside you or you don't. I've been hit hard; I've been hurt. Cuauhtemoc Vargas hit me in the ear in the first round [of a fight in 2007] and my ear exploded. The whole fight, it felt like I had water in my ear. But I won. People say I'm the best in the world at 122 pounds. I think I'm the best. But I know that fighters better than the fighters I have fought so far will come along and I will have to do more to win. And I have to work on some things defensively. There's room for improvement."

All of that was put to the test at Madison Square Garden on October 10th. Lopez entered the ring with 24 knockouts and 26 wins in 26 fights. He was on quite a few pound-for-pound lists and being groomed for a spring 2010 showdown against Yuriorkis Gamboa (who knocked out Whyber Garcia on the same MSG card).

Juanma's opponent, Rogers Mtagwa, was of lesser pedigree. Professional boxing is a world with a small number of haves and a vast majority of have-nots. Mtagwa is one of the have-nots. His record as he stood opposite Lopez was 25 wins, 12 losses, and 2 draws. Too many of his losses had come against less-than-stellar opposition.

Hugh McIlvanney once wrote, "Boxing is basic, but it's not always simple." Mtagwa makes it simple. He comes forward swinging from the heels and doesn't stop. He'll take three punches to land one. His saving grace is that he has an iron chin.

Lopez began the bout with the confidence bordering on arrogance of a world champion who has never tasted defeat. He won the first six rounds and picked up an extra point for a knockdown in round five. But Mtagwa's relentless pressure was forcing him to fight as much as box. And to the degree that Lopez could make choices, he was fighting a stupid fight. Because Mtagwa isn't a big puncher, Juanma was brawling with him.

Thus, Lopez was getting hit with punches that he shouldn't have gotten hit with. Also, referee Eddie Cotton (who failed to call knockdowns on two occasions when Mtagwa's gloves brushed against the canvas) was allowing Rogers to lead with his head, which resulted in a cut above Juanma's left eye in the third round. Then Juanma was visibly stung by a body shot in round four. By round five, he was losing form.

In the second half of the fight, Mtagwa was telling Lopez with his punches, "I'm still here, and now I'm hurting you." By round eleven, Juanma was on shaky legs, holding onto the ropes to stay upright.

"In the eleventh round, he really hurt me," Lopez admitted afterward. "I was never able to recuperate."

The twelfth round was high drama, the longest three minutes of Juanma's life, and proof positive that a good fight is the best "reality television" in the world. For the entire round, Lopez was virtually out on his feet and on the verge of going down. There was pandemonium in the arena. Mtagwa needed a knockout to win and went for it, but he didn't have the power to finish the job.

Lopez survived, barely.

"He was catching me with some good punches," the champion acknowledged afterward. "He was definitely hurting me. A lot of people think that I'm Superman. I'm not. The twelfth round was all heart."

The judges scored it 116–111, 115–111, and 114–113 in Juanma's favor. This observer scored it 115–111.

It was a great great fight, made even more exciting by the phenomenon of a decided underdog having a potential superstar in serious trouble.

Then again, as Eric Raskin has noted, "Few fighters are actually as good as they appear to be when everything is going their way."

Or as James Braddock famously observed, "All fighters are born equal. If one of them looks better, a couple of good chops to the whiskers will bring him back to the field."

The current plan is for Lopez and Gamboa to fight again in separate bouts on January 23, 2010. Then, assuming that each man keeps winning, they'll face each other at some point in the future.

"I don't think Juan Manuel Lopez is better than me," Gamboa declared after Lopez-Mtagwa. "He's not a challenge for me. If we fight, I will show that. I was better than him in the amateurs, and I'm better than him as a professional."

Maybe; maybe not.

Meanwhile, Juanma's balloon didn't burst against Mtagwa. But some of the air leaked out.

As Yuri Foreman was progressing as a fighter, he was developing outside the ring as well.

Yuri Foreman: A Spiritual Journey

On November 14, 2009, on the pay-per-view undercard of the mega-fight between Manny Pacquiao and Miguel Cotto, twenty-nine-year-old Yuri Foreman will challenge Daniel Santos for the World Boxing Association 154-pound crown.

Santos-Foreman shapes up as a competitive fight, but there's a more significant selling point. When the bell rings, Foreman will become the first Israeli citizen ever to fight for a world title. And he's a rabbinical student to boot.

Between 1901 and 1938, there were twenty-six Jewish world champions, most of them from New York and Chicago. Abe Atell was the first. Benny Leonard and Barney Ross followed. But over the past seventy years, there have been few world-class Jewish fighters. As legendary trainer Ray Arcel observed, "Punching people in the head isn't the highest aspiration of the Jewish people."

The last "Jewish" world champion was Mike Rossman, who knocked out Victor Galindez of Argentina in 1978 to capture the WBA light-heavyweight title. But Rossman fought under his mother's maiden name, rather than that of his father-manager Jimmy DiPiano, and there were questions about his authenticity. "It doesn't matter," Rossman said when asked about the situation. "My mother's a Jew. And in the Jewish religion, whatever your mother is, that's what you is."

Foreman's religious identification is on solid ground. He was born in Belarus. When he was eleven, his family moved to Israel.

"At first it was difficult," Yuri recalls. "I was missing my friends. And sometimes in Israel, there was discrimination between the Russians and the Jews. The Russians were also Jewish, but the Israelis would call us Russians and say we didn't deserve to be there, so there would be fights in school between the immigrants and the Israelis."

In Israel, Foreman learned the rudiments of boxing in an outdoor lot. There was no ring; not even a heavy bag. "They wouldn't give us a gym because we were just Russians," he remembers. "We went to City Hall and begged for a place to hang a bag and put up a ring. All they told us was, 'Go box with the Arabs.' So finally I went to the Arab gym. The first time I walked in, I saw the stares. In their eyes, there was a lot of hatred. But I needed to box; and boy, did they all want to box me. But after a while, the wall that was between us melted. We all wanted the same thing. I traveled with them as teammates. It helped that I won almost all the time. And finally, we became friends."

In Israel, Foreman compiled a 75-and-5 amateur record and was a three-time national amateur champion. In 2001, he came to New York. His first job in America entailed sweeping floors and making deliveries for a clothing store in Manhattan's garment district. He also began learning English and is now fluent in three languages (Russian and Hebrew being the other two).

"If boxing was just a job for me," Yuri says, "I'd choose a different job because boxing is very tough. But I love boxing. I like training; I like the competition; I like pushing myself to the limit. To me, boxing is an intellectual sport; almost like chess. You make your move; and if you make a wrong move, you pay for it. You have to use your brain very fast. It's a great sport, and it's an honor for me to be part of it."

When Foreman came to the United States he had little religious training and no interest in the rituals of Judaism. He went to synagogue occasionally with his employer, but that was all.

Five years ago, things began to change. "I was struggling financially," Yuri recalls. "I was feeling the challenges in boxing and with my money situation and my desire to be a good provider for my wife. I realized that I needed to become stronger spiritually so I could become stronger physically."

Then Foreman men Rabbi Dov Ber Binson.

"He's a Chabad rabbi, which is orthodox," Yuri explains. "He started inviting me and my wife to his house for dinner, and things happened from there. I can't observe something that I don't understand, so I took my time with the religion. It didn't make sense to me to eat Kosher and not use electric devices on Shabbos until I understood why. But the more I learned, the more I wanted to know. I started studying Judaism seriously, reading books and taking classes with my rabbi. I questioned everything because questioning makes for better understanding. Then, when I understood the reasons for the laws—the Kosher law, the Sabbath law, the family purity law—I could say, 'Okay; now it makes sense to me. Now I want to follow these laws.' My religion doesn't mean that I do everything right all the time. But it gives me guidance to make my decisions."

In 2006, at Rabbi Binson's invitation, Foreman began studying to become a rabbi. "We meet twice a week," Yuri says. "I'm taking it at my own pace, because my first priority is to be a good provider for my wife and right now that comes from boxing. But the study of Judaism has made me like a tree that grows for years and finally gives fruit. For all of my life, this was inside me. Now it comes out."

Yuri smiles. "My rabbi says that Brooklyn is the closest thing on earth to Jerusalem. I lived in Israel for eight years, but I didn't know about Judaism. I had to go into exile in Brooklyn to learn about Judaism."

In a few more years, Foreman will face a day of reckoning outside the ring. "They'll test me on everything I know," he says. "I hope that, at that time, I will become a rabbi."

But first there's the matter of Daniel Santos.

Santos will go into his battle against Foreman as the betting favorite. He's a world-class fighter with a 32-3-1 record and 23 KOs. He won the WBO welterweight title by knocking out Ahmed Kotiev (who'd defeated him by decision in their first encounter). Last year, he knocked out Joachim Alcine to claim the WBA 154-pound crown. Along the way, he has beaten Antonio Margarito and Jose Rivera.

Foreman is a technically sound fighter with a 27-and-0 record. His Achilles heel is a lack of power; eight knockouts with only one of them coming in his last twelve fights. The English equivalent of "Yuri" is "George." When it comes to punching power, George Foreman and Yuri Foreman are vastly different fighters.

Still, in recent years, Yuri has gone in reasonably tough. His last seven opponents had a composite record of 163 wins against 22 losses with 2 draws. There's a school of thought that he got a gift decision against Anthony Thompson (the toughest of those opponents) when they met at Madison Square Garden two years ago. But Foreman's co-manager, Murray Wilson, puts the matter in perspective when he says, "I was at the Thompson fight. I saw it as well as anybody else. The judges said that Yuri won it. That's it; game over. What's Yuri supposed to do? Jump up and down and complain that he lost?"

More to the point; Santos will be thirty-four years old when he and Foreman meet on November 14th. He will have been out of action for sixteen months and fought only once in the preceding two years. Also, in mid-August, there were whispers that Santos weighed 194 pounds. In other words, the champion is there to be taken. It's up to Foreman to do the job.

What would a Foreman victory mean for boxing? Bob Arum (Yuri's promoter) notes, "Certainly, it would energize a new fan base. Whether that fan base would be large or small, I have no idea. But for me as a Jewish person, to give a young Jewish man from Israel the opportunity to fight for a world championship and then have him win it would be enormously satisfying. I'd consider it one of the most significant achievements of my career."

Foreman has his own thoughts in that regard. "I see myself as smashing stereotypes," he says. "I know that, if I win, it will do a lot for boxing in Israel and make many Jewish people proud."

"But not just Jewish people," Yuri adds. "Last month, the father of one of the boys I boxed with in the Arab gym called and told me, 'We follow your career. We're all rooting for you. We'll be very proud when you become a champion. After you win, we want you to come to our village for a celebration and we'll kill the nicest of the sheep for you.'"

But will the dinner be kosher?

People will be writing about Muhammad Ali and Joe Frazier forever.

Rediscovering Joe Frazier through Dave Wolf's Eyes

Muhammad Ali and Joe Frazier fought three fights that are the pyramids of boxing. Dave Wolf was in the Frazier camp for each of them.

Dave was a gifted writer who later gained recognition as the manager of Ray Mancini and Donny Lalonde. He died in December 2008. Three months later, his daughter and brother gave me a carton filled with file folders containing handwritten notes that detail Dave's years in the Frazier camp.

The notes are fragments; a phrase here, a sentence there. I've reviewed some of them and joined Dave's words together to form an impressionistic portrait.

Everything that follows flowed from Dave's pen. Joe Frazier is often referenced as "JF" because that's how Dave's notes refer to him. For the same reason, Muhammad Ali is frequently referred to as "Clay." As explained in the notes, "JF calls him 'Clay.' Knows his name is 'Ali.' Called him 'Ali' until he heard what Clay was saying about him. Now calls him Clay out of disrespect."

In several instances, I've added an explanatory note to clarify a point. These clarifications are contained in brackets.

I don't agree with everything in Dave's notes. Some of it runs counter to views I've expressed in *Muhammad Ali: His Life and Times* and other works I've written. What I can vouch for is that this article is faithful to Dave's contemporaneous recording of the relationship between Muhammad Ali and Joe Frazier as seen through Joe's eyes.

★   ★   ★

Born in Beaufort, South Carolina, on January 12, 1944 . . . Grew up rural poor. Quit school in ninth grade . . . Married Florence Smith at age sixteen . . . Lived in Brooklyn and Philadelphia . . . Worked in slaughterhouse; took home $125 a week.

Frustrated by poverty . . . Starts boxing in 1962 . . . 1964 Olympic gold medal.

Post-Olympic problems . . . Hand operation . . . No help from Olympic committee . . . Cold Christmas . . . Father dies.

Turns pro on own . . . Modest goals. Some material things. Wanted to be important. Believed he'd become somebody.

Others doubt his potential . . . Not a natural athlete . . . Small compared to past heavyweight champs.

Likes to fight . . . Fighting style like his personality . . . Hit often but doesn't mind. Doesn't feel most punches. High pain threshold. Accepts punishment as part of job.

Formation of Cloverlay to back him . . . Embarrassed at times by lack of education. Problems with public speaking. Called Cloverlay a "cooperation" at first press conference.

Has been a drinker in past. Knows little about drugs.

Inspires loyalty.

Spartan training camp regardless of fight . . . Roadwork at 4:00 AM . . . Brutal training routine. Punishes body.

JF: "I love to work."

Can't understand sparring partners' lack of desire . . . Eats and lives with them. Pushes them hard. Only the tough last.

Gambling with sparring partners as diversion; mostly loses. Doesn't understand odds. Fleeced by crooked dice.

Yank Durham is great manager and friend. Yank succeeds because he wins
JF's complete unquestioning dedication and trust.

JF: "I still remember the look on Florence's face [Joe's wife] when I told
her about no sex before fights. Imagine the look on my face when Yank
told me."

JF liked Clay at first. Understands how others like him.

JF: "I liked his humor and style. Till I got to know him, I admired him a
lot; so it's not hard for me to see why others do."

When Clay first switched to Muslims, JF thought he was sincere. Knew
little about the religion. Shared many racial feelings.

JF: "You feel more comfortable when you're around your own people. I
don't care who you are. That's the life you know. When you're around
them, you can say little bad words. You can call each other niggers and
everything else. You can talk that talk. When you're around a mixed crowd
of people, white and black, you got to be careful."

Always, JF ambition was to beat Clay. From first pro fight, training for him
. . . Watched Clay's fights on TV with Yank. Imagined self in ring. Always
felt he would win.

Upset by Clay's treatment of Patterson . . . JF: "I feel like, why take advantage of a great champ. Once, he was a great champion. And if you're
gonna knock the man out, go ahead and knock him out. You don't suffer
people, especially a good athlete. After seeing him playing around with
Patterson, I felt like I could straighten that out. Why pick on somebody
like that? Try me."

Watched Clay-Mildenberger. Not impressed.

Watched Clay-Williams in theater. Felt sorry for Williams . . . JF: "Why
that fight allowed?"

Yank moved and matched JF perfectly. Protected him from too much pressure.

First Bonavena fight a problem. JF disdainfully overconfident; forced fight but careless. Floored lunging in by sneaky right. Floored again; in danger of losing by three knockdowns. Still aggressive. Split decision. Most writers had JF a clear winner. JF thought he'd lost fight. Most impressive: ability to get off the canvas. Durham furious. JF held hands low and didn't bob and slip. JF realizes things had gotten too complacent; thought he couldn't be hurt.

Doug Jones fight. Left hook in sixth, Jones hanging on ropes. JF might have killed him but held up punch. Jones fell, unconscious for two minutes.

George Chuvalo fight . . . JF: "Joe Louis picked against me. I was a little upset when I heard. But Yank said, 'You got to realize, they brought him in for publicity. The Garden tells him who to pick. They pay him. He needs the work.' I was surprised why a man like him go through these scenes. Seems like a man could stand up for what he believe and not have to choose who somebody else say. I always thought, if I could be like Joe Louis, I'd have it made. Thinking about it was depressing."

JF [on being shaken by George Chuvalo before knocking him out]: "It's a feeling that, if you get up in the morning and raise up out of the bed; you not fully awake and you not giving your blood time enough to circulate through your body; everything is not quite together yet and you fall back on the bed, tired. It's not pain; it's just that everything isn't quite focused. It's a little hazy or something. It's like a TV where the thing is a little out of focus and you think you ought to mess with the focus dial a little bit."

JF [on the party after the Chuvalo fight]: "I got to the party and my mom was there. I came over and hugged her. She was smiling but I could see she looked uneasy.

JF: "How'd you like that?"

Mother: "I was yelling at the referee to stop my son from killing that man."

JF: "Mom, that's the fighting game."

Mother: "The man was bleeding. You could have killed him."

JF: "Mom, you should have been hollering for me, not him."

Mother: "Well, I seen you was all right."

JF: "I felt a little sad that she wasn't happy like I felt. It would have been better if she'd just come to visit without seeing the fight. She'd never seen me act like that before. I felt she must be thinking, 'My son has become a killer.' I got the feeling she wouldn't want to see too many more fights."

First meeting with Clay. In Madison Square Garden basement. Clay sparring for Folley fight. Joe in ring for picture session. Clay condescending; mocks Joe's suspenders.

JF disappointed when Clay was stripped of title for refusing induction. Wanted to win title from him. Had worked three years for shot at Clay. Felt Clay shouldn't lose title except in ring. Didn't want to capitalize on Clay's misfortune.

Respected Clay's draft stand. Believed a man should stand up for his religious beliefs . . . While most press and even many blacks attacked Clay early, Joe often defended Clay in street arguments. Argued with Yank about him.

WBA sanctions eight-man tournament for championship . . . Durham convinces Cloverlay to pass up tournament. Didn't like fixed money; $50,000-$75,000-$125,000 for three fights. Doesn't want so many risky fights. Frazier angered by Yank's decision. Later sees it was correct.

WBA dropped Frazier from #2 to #9. Jimmy Ellis won WBA title.

Joe knocks out Buster Mathis to win New York State championship at Madison Square Garden.

JF: "I knew I'd never feel like the champ till I beat Clay in the ring."

Clay moved to Philadelphia . . . JF met doing roadwork . . . Clay seemed
down and out. Said he had financial problems. Unable to leave U.S. to
fight. Unable to get license to fight in U.S. Buried by legal fees and
alimony problems . . . Muslims wouldn't loan him money. Told Joe his
friends and supporters had abandoned him. Very depressed.

Beginning of strange relationship that existed during next few years . . . JF
felt sorry for Clay. Wanted to help Clay because black brother . . . Once
joined Clay at mosque.

Contact during next few years mostly by phone. Got to know Clay better.

One time, JF teased Clay about car. Felt bad when Clay seemed embarrassed.

Phone conversation: Clay said he wished he'd gone in Army. Said he'd
been misled; lawyers told him he'd get off easy.

JF began to wonder about Clay's relationship with Muslims . . . Clay
seemed trapped . . . Joe convinced Muslims are phony. Learned hypocrisy
of leaders . . . No longer respected Nation of Islam. Impressed they are
anti-drug and for black business. Respects their pride in blackness. But
feels they are hypocrites. Their ministers don't practice what they preach.
Leaders live in luxury; followers are poor. They are violent, even against
each other. They use the black movement and the little man as a front.

Clay asked JF for publicity . . . "Don't leave me out here alone." . . . Said
he didn't care what name JF used. Joe originally used "Ali" and "Clay"
interchangeably. Joe asked what name he wanted: "I don't care. Call me
nigger."

Chance meeting. Joe doing roadwork in Fairmont Park. Clay suggested
mock fight. Joe rejected: "I don't go for crap."

Yank and Clay press Joe to knock Clay. Joe reluctant. Really, nothing
against each other . . . Clay encourages . . . Joe doesn't like it but goes
along. Inner suspicion Clay will turn on him and "use this stuff on me"

. . . But dismisses idea: "He's a brother and a religious man." Assumes Clay will eventually defuse phony feud.

JF calls Clay "un-American" . . . Not true feelings. Believed much Clay said was valid. Joe opposed Vietnam war . . . "It does no good" . . . He opposed killing. People assumed opposite because he was Clay's rival . . . Didn't speak out against war because he knows little and doesn't presume to tell others.

JF agrees to series of staged confrontations with Clay.

PAL 23rd Street Gym in Philadelphia. Joe got angry at "real champ" taunts. Police called.

Mike Douglas taping, next day. Clay friendly in private. Joe asks him before show to "cool it" . . . On set, Clay whispers "hold me" and starts scene. Joe angry.

Cheetah in New York City, next night. Joe invited Clay into dressing room . . . "But cut the shit." . . . Clay beats on and breaks door. Joe angry. Disliked surprise scenes.

Joe tiring of Clay's act . . . "He's like a little kid that can't stop." . . . Dislikes role that has so many blacks down on him. Frustrated that people, especially blacks, appear to be against him and for Clay . . . Complained to Yank: "It's making us look bad" . . . Yank dismissed: "Don't worry; there's no harm." . . . Yank saw big money down the road.

Frazier reputation growing. Perceived as legitimate opponent for Clay.

Regardless of rivalry, Yank not convinced Joe is ready. Bruce Wright [Frazier's attorney] told Joe he could avoid Clay: "You don't have to fight him. He won't get a license if you say you won't fight him. Clay is finished if you say 'no.'"

Joe always said "yes." When promoters or writers called about Clay, Joe said he would fight him. At banquets, told [New York State Athletic

Commission chairman] Dooley and [Pennsylvania State Athletic Commission chairman] Wildman that he wanted them to license Clay.

JF victories over Manuel Ramos, Oscar Bonavena [rematch], and Dave Zyglewicz.

June 1969, Joe training for Quarry fight . . . Yank told Bruce Wright, "Joe's ready for Clay."

Movement to get Clay-Frazier . . . Yank had kept contact and had good relationship with Herbert Muhammad [Ali's manager]. Yank and Herbert agreed to 50–50 split.

Series of false alarms . . . Murray Woroner offer, $1.2 million [for Ali-Frazier fight] in Tampa or Orlando. Vigorous political and veterans opposition . . . Astrodome offer. Roy Hofheinz promises governor will license. Contracts sent to Texas. Hofheinz admits governor wouldn't go along. Deal killed by Texas politics . . . Joe met with Detroit promoters at Yank's house. Clay parties at meeting. Contract signed. Nothing happens.

Joe began to doubt fight would take place. Yank pessimistic. Convinced Clay going to jail. Bruce Wright to Harry Markson [president of Madison Square Garden boxing]: "Get Ellis."

Eddie Futch comes in to help train JF for Ellis fight. Much to Yank's credit, he accepted Futch. Delicate situation. Futch importance grows. Works well with Yank. Futch did the fine-tuning.

JF destroys Jimmy Ellis, KO 5.

Prospects for Ali fight brightened as mood of nation changed . . . Campaigns of Bobby Kennedy and Eugene McCarthy . . . Cambodia, Kent State . . . Feelings grew against war . . . Much draft resistance. Ali stayed while others fled . . . Ali an athlete whose battle to avoid military service transformed him into a kind of folk hero.

Clay license for Atlanta . . . Boxes exhibition . . . Fights Quarry in Atlanta.

Treated like conquering hero . . . Clay licensed in New York . . . Beats
Bonavena. Frazier unimpressed, feared Clay might lose.

Now JF knows Clay fight inevitable if Clay doesn't go to jail first . . .
Wanted Clay bad . . . People bugged him on street, reporters' questions.

Negotiations for fight, simmering for several months, boil. Ante rising fast.
Clearly headed for richest purse in history . . . Garden offered $1.3 mil-
lion; Astrodome offered $1.3 million . . . Yank, Herbert, and Arum pushing
for Houston. Bruce Wright suspicious; felt offer too low. Frazier not aware
of specific negotiations.

Series of meetings in Arum's office. Jesse Jackson roughly rebutted.
Christmas coming when Bruce Wright calls Joe and says it looks like
something about to happen . . . Jerry Perenchio offer; $2.5 million for
each fighter. Fight set for Madison Square Garden.

Nation polarizing . . . Ali becoming hero of left and Frazier hero of right
. . . Clay escalates feud to unsettle Frazier for fight . . . JF: "It got out of
control."

JF hurt by Clay's better ability to communicate to white press . . . JF
becomes symbol of Ali's oppression. Clay trying to make him appear
enemy of black people.

JF becoming aware of unpopularity with blacks. Began to find self perceived as "Uncle Tom." Unfair but inevitable.

JF: "Clay is a phony. He never worked. He never had a job. He don't
know nothing about life for most black people. He talks out both sides of
his mouth. Doesn't act as he preaches. Lies to the public. Gets people riled
up. Exploits race problems and real black pride. No real minister would
act that way."

Clay issues more inflammatory quotes. JF hurt and surprised when he
intensifies insults. Real dislike growing.

JF often teased in street . . . Reaction to being called ugly.

JF: "Black people are ashamed of me. They don't know what I'm really like."

JF thought Clay liked him . . . JF: "He never did. He wants to be bigger than everyone else, so he tries to make them small. Even when we signed to fight, he still looked down on me as nothing. I'm his black brother, but he used me."

Night before the fight. Joe tense, didn't sleep . . . Believes he'll win, but will feel no shame if he loses.

In dressing room before fight, Futch is calm center of storm.

Joe beats Clay in the most famous fight of all time. Knockdown, unanimous decision, little press disagreement. JF says afterward, "He's the greatest I ever fought."

Traditionally, fighters who achieve great victory allowed to enjoy acclaim that goes with it. Loser treats winner with respect of fellow athlete, even if momentary controversy or rivalry very intense.

JF victory tarnished. . . . Ali attacks Frazier after fight: "I didn't lose the fight. The white people said I lost it." . . . Spends next two years trying to diminish JF victory. Occasionally admitted he lost. But most often, in public, claimed he had won; that fight was "stolen" for "political reasons."

Period of title not as pleasant for JF as might have been. Clay attacks make victory appear suspect. JF not fully appreciated as a fighter or a man.

JF: "Clay was responsible for my time as champion not being as happy as it could have been."

What it's like to be champ: People awed. Everyone recognizes you and feels it's an honor to be in your presence. JF visits Nixon at White House.

Invited to speak before South Carolina legislature. Requests to appear on major TV shows. Marvels at how far he has come.

JF setting stage for losing title. Too involved with being champ. Demands on time.

Relationship with Yank changed. Not together as often. Joe more assertive.

JF much too involved with music group, Joe Frazier and the Knockouts. Argued with Yank over music. Yank caved . . . Bad reviews for group. European tour bombs.

Yank privately hurt by Joe. But Yank had changed also. Much more abrasive and self-important. Decided secretly that Joe should avoid tough fights. Didn't tell Joe, who thought no contender would fight him.

For 22 months, no tough fights . . . Two overmatched opponents, Terry Daniels and Ron Stander . . . JF didn't work as hard. Overweight for both fights. Put less pressure on opponents, not doubling up. Wins came too easily.

Eddie Futch saw changes in Joe. Tried to tell him. Can't when still winning. JF feeling invincible.

JF: "I lay my hands on and they fall."

JF: "Nobody can knock me out."

Joe decides he wants to fight George Foreman . . . Loses in two rounds.

Dealing with defeat . . . "The former heavyweight champion of the world."

Back to the drawing board . . . JF gives up most outside activity. Draws closer to Yank. Happy in training . . . Decision over Joe Bugner in London.

August 1973; Yank dies.

Eddie Futch takes over

Negotiations for Clay II . . . Fight made.

JF feelings about Clay had mellowed . . . Thought attacks were over . . .
Clay escalates feud, stirs racial issue again.

Joe cries in back of car . . . Still not accepted or understood by many
blacks . . . Many painful incidents . . . Hassled by people in street.

JF: "We'll never get along. I got the best of him in ring, but he caused a
lot of my own people to turn on me."

Bombardment continues.

Joe bothered by lack of formal schooling. Can't read.

JF: "Clay goes out of his way to mock my education. Makes this image of
me that I'm dumb and ugly. I don't think this guy have any kind of feeling for anybody. Maybe his wife and his kids. But general people, I don't
think so."

Problems in training . . . Joe misses Yank . . . Inconsistent and unimpressive
in gym. Up too high, taking too many rights . . . Complaining about sore
shoulder and other aches, lingering cold.

Studio brawl when Clay calls Joe "ignorant."

Joe increasingly paranoid, restless . . . Self-doubts without Yank . . . Futch
admits JF uptight too soon; fears JF losing confidence in him.

On fight night, dressing room too chaotic . . . Confusion on exit time. JF
warms up twice.

First fight without Yank . . . Clay wins unanimous decision.

Clay beats Foreman to regain championship.

JF: "I admire him regaining the title. He KO'd the man who KO'd me."

Ali-Frazier III in Manila.

Pre-fight, Ali labels Joe a gorilla.

JF: "Every once in a while, the ugliness that's behind that cocky smile sees the sunshine . . . Clay is a phony and a hypocrite who uses people, mostly his own people . . . He must be bigger than anyone else or he tries to make them smaller."

Wanted to actually kill Clay in ring, hated him so much.

[Ali-Frazier III was contested on the outskirts of Manila at 10:45 AM on October 1, 1975.]

Evening of September 29 . . . Joe on kingsized bed, watching TV, running fingers over guitar strings . . . "One day, I'm gonna learn how to play this thing."

Ali on TV, predicting, "The first combination, he will fall."

JF: He's still trying to make himself believe. But it's too late, way too late. I got the noose around that cat's neck."

TV coverage of Ali workout . . . JF hand tightens around handle of guitar when Ali jokes, "Joe's so ugly, when he was a baby and cried, the tears turned around and ran back up his face into his eyes."

Commentator in ring with Ali says, "He calls you 'Clay' because he can't spell 'Muhammad.'" . . . JF face clouds and he shakes his head silently . . . "Shut it off."

September 30 . . . JF up at 3:30 AM. Walks one mile . . . Back in room, pulls off boots, strips to underwear, pours alcohol on chest, lets it run down . . . Discusses letters he's getting from Christians.

JF: "They say don't worry about the fight. God will take care of everything . . . That's cool. When the bell ring, I'll just sit on the stool and say, 'Okay, God; take over.' . . . Maybe I better not take no chances. I'll do a little fighting too."

Takes a nap. Sleeps till 10:30 AM . . . Stays in room playing blackjack most of afternoon . . . Face grim.

Lies on bed, watches TV . . . *The Flying Nun* and *Porky Pig* . . . Chewing gum, cracking it.

At 5:30, JF eats fried fish, peas, and rice

Florence comes into room and sits by bed . . . Florence sacrifices. JF doesn't always appreciate her . . . JF and Florence have long quiet talk . . . Florence leaves.

JF: "Florence been sacrificing for years to make things happen for me. When we got married, we was so poor, she needed her sister's ring. Now she's got her own Cadillac."

8:10 PM: JF shuts off light, goes to sleep.

October 1, 1975 . . . Joe leaves room at 7:15 AM . . . Wearing green shirt, beige slacks, brown suspenders . . . Siren wailing . . . Arrives at arena . . . Sits on red couch.

7:45 AM. Ali-Frazier III in three hours . . . JF lays back with head on red pillow, closes eyes, and sleeps.

★   ★   ★

AUTHOR'S NOTE: Muhammad Ali has always defied expectations. In the 1960s, he was one of the most loved and hated men in America. Then he became a symbol of good will and courage, embraced by the world.

Now a new wave of revisionism is influencing how people think about Ali. Several high-profile books and documentaries have emphasized

Muhammad's shortcomings and the less attractive aspects of his make-up (such as the cruelties he visited upon Joe Frazier). Meanwhile, at the other end of the spectrum, those with a financial interest in Ali's name and likeness have blurred his past (often obscuring his revolutionary acts and utterances) for economic gain.

I won't defend Ali's treatment of Joe Frazier. It was wrong. I will say, as I've said many times before, that Muhammad Ali in the 1960s stood as a beacon of hope for oppressed people all over the world. Every time he looked in the mirror and uttered the phrase, "I'm so pretty," he was saying "black is beautiful" before it became fashionable. When he refused induction into the United States Army, he stood up to armies around the globe in support of the proposition that, unless you have a very good reason for killing people, war is wrong.

Nelson Mandela later declared, "Ali's refusal to go to Vietnam and the reasons he gave made him an international hero. The news could not be shut out even by prison walls. He became a real legend to us in prison."

As for African Americans, Reggie Jackson put the matter in perspective when he said, "Do you have any idea what Ali meant to black people? He was the leader of a nation; the leader of black America. As a young black, at times I was ashamed of my color; I was ashamed of my hair. And Ali made me proud. I'm just as happy being black now as somebody else is being white, and Ali was part of that growing process. Ali helped raise black people in this country out of mental slavery. The entire experience of being black changed for millions of people because of Ali."

Joe Frazier was an unnecessary casualty of that era.

The last big fight of 2009 was also the most important.

Boxing Gives Thanks for Manny Pacquiao

Thanksgiving and Christmas came early for boxing this year. The November 14, 2009, mega-match between Manny Pacquiao and Miguel Cotto was the biggest and most important fight of 2009. Think of it as a holiday festival with Pacquiao in the role of Santa Claus. Or maybe Manny is better characterized as a non-stop Energizer Easter Bunny, whose fists exploded like Fourth of July fireworks and turned Cotto's face into a gruesome Halloween mask.

Andrew M. Kaye writes, "Like royalty, the reign of a particular fighter can instantly evoke an era, reminding us of some of the values held by his generation, people, or nation."

Pacquiao is the perfect symbol of the hopes and aspirations of the Filipino people.

The Philippines are mired in a culture of poverty and oppression. "Pacquiao," *Time Magazine* observes, "has a myth of origin equal to that of any Greek or Roman hero." He grew up amidst squalor that most Americans can't begin to comprehend. At age twelve, he ran away from home to escape his abusive father. Thereafter, he survived by selling water and donuts on the streets and worked occasionally as a gardener's assistant. Then he fell into boxing, living for two years in a tiny room adjacent to the workout area in a Manila gym. He fought for pennies under all manner of circumstances; then professionally for as little as two dollars a fight.

Now, *Time Magazine* proclaims, "In the Philippines, Pacquiao is a demigod."

Pacquiao is dedicated to improving the spirits of his people. "There is bad news all the time in my country," he says, explaining why Filipinos love him. "There is not enough food. We have typhoons. There is corruption in the government and too much crime. So many people are suffering and have no hope. Then I bring them good news and they are happy."

Filipino journalist Granville Ampong speaks to Pacquiao's mass appeal when he writes, "Pacquiao has been a saving grace for the government. The Philippines is in a state of political chaos and economic meltdown. There are many controversies around the current administration. The masses could have overthrown the government; but each time Manny fights, he calms the situation. When he enters the ring, a truce is declared between guerrillas and the national army and the crime rate all over the Philippines drops to zero."

"To live in the Philippines is to live in a world of uncertainty and hardship," notes Nick Giongco (one of that country's foremost boxing writers). "Filipinos are dreamers. They like fantasy. And what is more of a fantasy than Manny Pacquiao?"

During the past year, Pacquiao has also become a standard-bearer for boxing. In recent decades, the powers that be have balkanized the sport, depriving the public of legitimate world champions. As a result, boxing has become more dependent than ever on "name" fighters.

Pacquiao fights with the look of a video-game action hero. He's a remarkable blend of speed, power, endurance, determination, and (in recent years) ring smarts. He first came to the attention of boxing fans in the United States when he challenged Lehlohonolo Ledwaba for the IBF 122-pound crown in 2001. At the time, he was an unknown twenty-two-year-old, who'd fought only in the Philippines, Thailand, and Japan.

Entering the ring on two week's notice, Pacquiao lit up the screen and won every minute of every round against Ledwaba en route to a sixth-round stoppage. Since then, he has been on an extraordinary run.

Over the past year, each Pacquiao victory has been more remarkable than the one before. The snowball keeps getting bigger. At a promotional event in Manchester, England, to promote Pacquiao's May 2, 2009, fight against hometown hero Ricky Hatton, Manny's fans were so exuberant that Pacquiao was moved to comment, "I think Manchester is now Mannychester."

Pacquiao's November 14th encounter with Cotto shaped up as Manny's toughest test to date. Miguel had amassed a 34-and-1 record with 27 knockouts. His sole loss was an eleventh-round stoppage at the hands of Antonio Margarito. Subsequent events led to the suspicion that Margarito's handwraps had contained gauze sprinkled with plaster of Paris.

Cotto is respected but not adored in his native Puerto Rico. "I know that some people are happy with my accomplishments in boxing," he said a week before the Pacquiao fight. "Others do not believe in me. I have to do my work whether the people believe in me or not. I am here for me, my family, and the people that want to follow Miguel Cotto."

As for his place in Puerto Rican boxing history, Cotto declared, "I am going to be wherever the fans put me. I am never going to claim something that the people won't give me. Wherever they are going to put Miguel Cotto, I am going to be happy."

Prior to fighting Pacquiao, Cotto was no stranger to going in tough. The list of opponents he'd vanquished included Shane Mosley, Joshua Clottey, Zab Judah, Paulie Malignaggi, Carlos Quintana, and Randall Bailey. His loss to Margarito had been followed by two less-than-scintillating victories. But the assumption in boxing circles was that Miguel would have dominated Oscar De la Hoya and Ricky Hatton (Pacquiao's most recent opponents) as thoroughly as Manny had.

Then there was the issue of weight. Pacquiao-Cotto would be fought at a catchweight of 145 pounds. On March 15, 2008, Pacquiao defended his super-featherweight crown at 129 pounds. Four weeks later, Cotto defended his WBA welterweight belt weighing 146. In other words, twenty months ago, there was a differential of three weight classes between the two men. Being the best fighter in the world pound-for-pound (an honor accorded to Pacquiao) doesn't mean that a fighter can beat any opponent at any weight.

Breaking down the fight, most prognosticators began with the premise that Pacquiao was faster while Cotto was bigger and stronger. They further agreed that Miguel would be Manny's toughest test to date. Pacquiao had beaten two great symbols (De la Hoya and Hatton) in his last two fights. Now he'd be facing a great fighter. Cotto had proved that he could deal with speed when he defeated Shane Mosley and Zab Judah. And Judah, like Pacquiao, was a southpaw.

"Everyone is so intrigued over Pacquiao and thinks that he wins big," trainer Emanuel Steward posited. "I just don't see it that way. Miguel is going to have to improve his defense; in particular, his defense against punches right up the middle. If he boxes and keeps his defense a little bit tighter and if he starts banging those hard left hooks to the body on the smaller guy, this could be a tough fight for Manny because Manny is not really a welterweight. I see it as almost a toss-up."

Cotto radiated confidence. "His weaknesses are obvious to me," Miguel said during a teleconference call. "He is coming from a lower weight division. If he thinks he is going to have the same power as Miguel Cotto, his thinking is very wrong. He's a fast fighter. You know what? That's why we prepare ourselves. We know he has speed and we are prepared to beat it. I am prepared for anything he can show me."

Miguel, the media was told, was having his "best training camp ever." Meanwhile, Team Pacquiao was reportedly in chaos.

Freddie Roach (Pacquiao's trainer) would have preferred that Manny prepare for the fight at the Wild Card Gym in Los Angeles. But United States law dictated that Pacquiao's tax bill would rise considerably if he spent more than three weeks training in America.

Initially, Roach wanted the early stages of training to take place in Mexico. "Toluca is the best option," he maintained. "It's private, quiet, not a vacation-type of area. The gym is owned by the government. It's a very safe place. A federal marshal works there. He'd be with us the whole time, so security wouldn't be a problem."

But as of September 1st, the training site still hadn't been agreed upon and Roach was having trouble contacting his charge. "My gut feeling," he said, "is that we'll end up in the Philippines. The thing is, there are a lot of distractions in the Philippines. One weekend, this governor will want to fly him here. The next weekend, another governor will want to fly him there. It's a hassle."

Eventually, Baguio (in the Philippines) was chosen as the camp site. Then that region of the country was hit by typhoons and there were reports that civil war had broken out within Team Pacquiao.

Roach, it was said, had been conspiratorially lodged in a separate hotel away from Pacquiao. Manny, according to some newspapers, was spending as much time helping typhoon victims as he was training for Cotto. Strength-and-conditioning coach Alex Ariza and Pacquiao adviser Michael Koncz were engaged in a much-publicized feud that culminated in a physical confrontation.

Meanwhile, Roach was fearful that the long flight from the Philippines to Los Angeles (where Pacquiao would conclude training) would result in several days lost due to jet lag.

Pacquiao tried to keep things in perspective. During a teleconference call, he was asked about the problems inherent in training in an area that had been devastated by typhoons.

"It is very difficult for me," Manny acknowledged. "But I have to focus on my fight because nobody can help me in the ring. I am not only fighting for me. I am also fighting for my country. It is my responsibility to focus on training."

Then more typhoons threatened and the training camp was moved to Manila.

How did it all work out?

"Much better than I thought it would," Roach reported. "It was very emotional in Baguio. We saw a lot of death and destruction. But when Manny walks into the gym, he leaves the distractions behind. We had to run inside with the treadmill because the rain was so heavy, but it didn't affect our preparation. We worked right through it. We had good sparring partners. We didn't miss a day. The first month was the best first month of training I've had with Manny. He was in great shape. I'd go back to Baguio with Manny in a minute. We had a great four weeks there."

And Manila?

"The five days in Manila sucked," Roach said. "Everyone wanted a piece of Manny. Filipino politicians, governors, mayors, councilmen; all dragging him every which way. The American Embassy, entertainers, you name it. Too many distractions; too many people in the gym. Manny's mind was all over the place. His focus wasn't there."

Then Pacquiao journeyed to Los Angeles for the final days of training, and what passes for normalcy within Team Pacquiao reigned.

"Manny trains hard for every fight," Freddie said afterward. "If he was fighting me, he'd train hard and be in perfect shape. He sees that as his responsibility to his country and himself, and he's right."

On paper, Pacquiao and Cotto were fighting for Miguel's WBO welterweight crown. In theory, that offered Manny the opportunity to win a world championship in the seventh weight division of his career. But given the multiplicity of belts in boxing today, that was of secondary importance. The real prize was Pacquiao's pound-for-pound title.

There was a buzz in the media center at the MGM Grand Hotel and Casino during fight week. Pacquiao-Cotto wasn't a manufactured event. It was a legitimate super-fight, and the promotion had caught fire.

Time Magazine ran a five-page feature article on Pacquiao in its United States edition and placed him on the cover of its Asian counterpart. The

New York Times ran daily stories on the fight. Pulling out all the stops, Top Rank (which was promoting the bout) spent $150,000 to rent a twenty-one-foot-high cylindrical LED video screen that was suspended above the ring and was evocative of a rock concert. Google and Twitter reported record numbers for Pacquiao traffic. The fight was completely sold out.

"Not one ticket left," Top Rank CEO Bob Arum chortled. "We got a list of one hundred names of people that want tickets, and we don't have any. It's not my problem. Everybody had an opportunity to buy tickets. The peopled that snoozed lose'd."

Arum was in his glory. His run as Pacquiao's promoter began with Manny's first fight against Juan Manuel Marquez in 2004 and has been highlighted by two bouts against Marquez, Pacquiao's second fight against Marco Antonio Barrera, three fights against Erik Morales, and one fight each against Oscar De La Hoya and Ricky Hatton.

Arum is also Cotto's promoter. "One reason this promotion has gone so well," he noted, "is that I have no co-promoter to argue with and give me tsuris." But for the first time in his ring career, Miguel was the "B-side" in a promotion. Fight week was The Manny Pacquiao Show.

"Fights like De La Hoya-Trinidad and De La Hoya-Mayweather were big," Arum proclaimed. "But they were boxing stories, and boxing people live in a very insular world that's all about HBO, Showtime, and the boxing websites. This fight has created interest in non-traditional ways. There's *Time Magazine,* the *New York Times,* the *Wall Street Journal.* People who know nothing about boxing have heard about Manny Pacquiao and are becoming interested in him."

"Manny has gotten bigger since he fought De La Hoya and Hatton," Arum continued. "Neither of those fights had this kind of feeling. The interest in this fight is global. Oscar was charming and good-looking and a very good fighter, but Manny is something more. Globally, Manny is now bigger than Oscar ever was. And Manny is going to get bigger and bigger because the world has changed. The stars no longer have to come from America."

At the center of it all, Pacquiao seemed to glide effortlessly through the storm of attention.

Despite an unspeakably hard childhood, Manny looks younger than his thirty-one years. Women describe him as "adorable." There's a gentle childlike quality about him, much like a young tiger cub. He's partial to casual clothes, has a ready smile, and laughs easily. Left to his own devices, he text messages constantly on two cellphones that he carries with him. Reflecting on the fame that has overtaken him, he says, "It's a big change in my life. That's for sure."

Fame like Pacquiao's can eat a person alive (think Elvis Presley and Michael Jackson). To survive, either a person sets rigid boundaries in the manner of Michael Jordan or gives himself to the public like Muhammad Ali.

Pacquiao immerses himself in his celebrity status the way a fish takes to water. He might wonder sometimes, "What's going on here? What's this all about?" But he loves being Manny and is enjoying the ride. He understood early on the value of speaking English and has learned it well. He acts and speaks without media advisors telling him what to do and say. He loves the big stage. He makes movies. He sings.

"There's no spotlight that's too bright for Manny," says Freddie Roach. "He likes being famous and he handles it well. He's got class and a great way about him. He brightens every room he enters."

Meanwhile, Roach has been on a remarkable ride of his own. Like Pacquiao, he's one of boxing's feel-good stories.

As a young man, Freddie had a promising ring career that began with 26 victories in 27 fights. Then the opposition got tougher and he got older. By the end, he was an opponent, losing four bouts in a row to fighters with a composite record of 81-2-2. He closed the active-fighter portion of his life with a 39-and-13 career mark. Then Parkinson's syndrome struck.

Roach is now one of the best-liked and most respected trainers in boxing. He'll be fifty years old in March. Despite his physical condition, he's constantly in the ring with Pacquiao and other fighters, working the pads and otherwise engaged. His workload would exhaust a younger healthy well-conditioned man.

Freddie has a self-deprecating sense of humor. At the start of a satellite TV interview two days before Pacquiao-Cotto, a sound technician asked him to count to ten for a microphone check.

Roach dutifully complied: "One, two, three, four, five, six, seven, eight, nine, ten." Then he added, "Didn't think I could do that, did you?"

"I get more anxious as a trainer than I ever did as a fighter," Freddie acknowledges. "When I'm lying in bed at night before a fight, I go through things over and over again in my mind. I do it for hours. Finally, when I'm satisfied that I've covered all the bases, I fall asleep."

Pacquiao is Roach's monument. Freddie never achieved greatness as a fighter. But as a trainer, he has reached glorious heights. Skyhorse Books (a division of Simon & Schuster) has contracted for his autobiography to be written with journalist Peter Nelson. *Time Magazine* calls him "the most popular foreigner in the Philippines."

"Training a fighter like Manny is what a guy like me lives for," Roach says. "As far as the attention is concerned; I'm like Manny. I enjoy it. It's nice to be recognized for what you do, and it's not that hard to smile and be nice to people. If I can make someone happy by taking a picture with them or signing my name, I do it."

Three days before the fight, Roach supervised Pacquiao's final intensive workout at the IBA gym in Las Vegas. The early odds had favored Manny at slightly better than 2-to-1. Now they were 3-to-1 and would settle on fight night at 5-to-2.

Manny never trash-talks. In the days leading up to the bout, he spoke respectfully of his opponent, telling the media, "Cotto is a bigger guy and a hard puncher and strong. He has a good left hook and a good uppercut. He is a good fighter and a champion. For this fight, it is a challenge."

Early in the promotion, Roach had predicted that Pacquiao-Cotto would be "the toughest fight of Manny's life."

"This guy beat Shane Mosley, a speed guy," Freddie explained. "He knows how to nullify speed. Cotto is better than Oscar De La Hoya, better than Ricky Hatton. He's the biggest, strongest guy we've ever fought. To beat Manny, you have to slow him down. Cotto knows how to do that with body shots. And low blows. I'm a little concerned about the fact that, when Cotto gets hurt, he goes to low blows. I try to teach fighters, 'If the other guy hits you low, hit him back low.' But Manny won't do it."

However, as the fight approached, Roach seemed increasingly less troubled. Among the thoughts he offered were:

• "I'm not worried about Cotto's size. Size and brute strength might win a weight-lifting contest, but they don't win fights. Boxing ability wins fights, and Manny is a better boxer than Cotto. Hatton was bigger and stronger than Manny until the fight started. So was Oscar."
• "We're not reinventing the wheel. We're adjusting to the styles of our opponents. We study them and we find their habits and adjust to them. I don't look for mistakes. Every fighter makes mistakes, and you don't

know when they'll come. I look for habits. I've seen all the tapes on Cotto. The idea is to not get hit with the hook. Cotto cocks his left hand before he throws it, so it shouldn't be that hard for Manny to take it away from him. And Cotto makes certain adjustments when he fights a southpaw, which is something we'll deal with."

• "Working the mitts with Manny at this weight; he's punching so much harder than he ever has. He's used to the extra weight now and has learned how to use it to his advantage, especially on the inside. I've never seen Manny better than he is now. He's punching harder than I've ever seen him. He's as fast as I've ever seen him. Cotto has never fought a guy with speed like Manny. That's where he's going to have trouble; with Manny's speed. I don't think he can handle it."

• "I'm very confident in my guy. Manny is one hundred percent ready for this fight and he knows exactly how to win this fight. It's like a choreographed dance. Manny knows what Cotto will do, and he knows how he'll respond to it. We have a Plan A and a Plan B. I don't think we'll need a C."

• I don't think Cotto has enough. He's hittable; and people that Manny can hit, he knocks out. I feel like Manny, with the power he's punching with right now at this weight; he's going to knock Cotto out. I think I have the greatest fighter in the world today, and I think we'll prove that again with Cotto."

In the IBA gym, Roach worked with his fighter for close to an hour. During a break, he observed, "Sometimes, when I'm working the pads with Manny, I ask myself, 'What would I do if I was fighting this guy?' Let's be realistic. What could I do if I was fighting Manny?"

Then the conversation turned to the issue of weight. There's a school of thought that the division Pacquiao is fighting in now is more appropriate for him than the lower weight classes that he competed in for years. He was undernourished as a child, eating mostly rice until the age of sixteen. Then he suffered through another decade of having to make weight. Now (the theory goes), for the first time, Manny is eating what he should be eating.

"I'm not a nutritionist, so I can't answer that," Roach said. "I think that Manny's best fighting weight is probably 140, but the biggest fights are at 147. What I do know is that, when Manny had to make weight at 126 or 130, he was unhappy all the time. Now he can eat the week of a fight. He can eat on the morning of the weigh-in. The whole time leading up to the fight, he's in a much better frame of mind."

Then there were the intangibles.

"It's what you can't see that's inside a fighter that makes the difference," Freddie offered. "Manny has all the right things inside. One of the questions I have about Cotto is, 'What did the loss to Margarito take out of him?' I was 26-and-1 when I got knocked out for the first time, and I never believed in myself quite the same way again. Cotto can tell himself that the reason he got beat up by Margarito was the gloves. But whether he believes that in his heart is something else. I don't think Cotto is the same fighter he was before Margarito. His first fight back [against Michael Jennings], he wasn't that good. And I wasn't impressed with Cotto against [Joshua] Clottey either. Cotto is slower now than he used to be. I don't think he has the confidence he once had. Manny is better now than ever and he feels like he's fighting with a hundred million Filipinos behind him. Nothing is certain in boxing, but I'm as certain as I can be that Manny will beat Cotto."

The fighters weighed in at the MGM Grand Garden Arena at 3:00 PM on Friday. Fans started lining up at 5:45 AM. At one o'clock, fire marshals closed off access to the arena because the six thousand seats available to the public were filled to capacity.

Cotto tipped the scales at the contract weight of 145 pounds; Pacquiao at 144. Spirits were high. There was partisan cheering. The only thing missing was the Ricky Hatton Band.

One discordant note accompanied the proceedings. Earlier this year, Cotto split with his uncle, who had trained him throughout his career. Evangelista Cotto's replacement, Joe Santiago (formerly a Cotto camp assistant), was training Miguel for only the second time.

Initially, Santiago and Roach were respectful of one another. "I have a lot of respect for what Freddie Roach has done," Joe said early in the promotion. "But he won't be able to fight for Pacquiao. It's the fighters that are going to do the fighting."

Then people started questioning whether Santiago was qualified to train a fighter at the elite level. Joe got huffy and made a few intemperate remarks about Freddie that led Roach to respond, "He's never fought in his life and he has no idea what it's like being in the ring. He's got a towel on his shoulder and gives water and all of a sudden he's a coach. Cotto trains himself."

One issue prior to the fight was whether Cotto would have trouble getting down to 145 pounds. At the weigh-in, as the scale registered Miguel's weight, Santiago turned to Roach and said, "145, asshole."

"He's supposed to weigh 145," Roach countered. "And if you call me 'asshole' again, I'll punch you in the face."

The harsh words escalated from there until cooler heads prevailed.

On fight night, Roach was the first member of Team Pacquiao to arrive at the arena. He entered dressing room #3 at 5:30 PM and emptied his bag of the tools he'd need in the hours ahead.

Pacquiao was due at 6:00 PM. Word came by cell phone that his van was stuck in traffic.

"I'm not worried," Roach said. "The earliest we'll walk is eight o'clock. HBO likes the fighters here two hours early, but I can get Manny ready in an hour. And whatever happens, they're not starting the fight without him."

Pacquiao arrived at 6:40 PM, accompanied by an entourage far larger than Roach or the Nevada State Athletic Commission would have liked. He went into the toilet area to give a pre-fight urine sample to a commission inspector. Then he returned to the main room, took off his shoes and socks, and began putting band-aids on his toes to protect against blisters. When that chore was done, he stood up, intoned, "Ladies and gentleman; from the Philippines . . ." and threw several punches in Roach's direction.

At seven o'clock, NSAC inspector Jack Lazzarotto began the process of clearing unauthorized personnel from the room, winnowing the number from thirty to twenty.

Over the next twenty-five minutes, Pacquiao wrapped his own hands, singing softly to himself as he worked.

Several of Manny's friends who had balked at the earlier removal order were escorted to the door.

Pacquiao did some stretching exercises and shadow boxed for fifteen seconds. He had the look of a boy who was warming up for a youth soccer game.

At 7:45, referee Kenny Bayless entered and gave Manny his pre-fight instructions. After Bayless left, there were more stretching exercises and a brief prayer.

The number of people in the room had risen again due to the presence of several entourage members who had hidden in the shower area during the earlier sweeps. This time, with help from the Las Vegas Metropolitan Police Department, the room was cleared for real.

At 8:10, assistant trainer Buboy Fernandez gloved Pacquiao up. There was an almost casual feeling in the air. Manny had the calm demeanor of a man who felt fully protected against the storm to come.

At 8:20, Pacquiao began hitting the pads with Roach; his first real exercise of the night. World-class fighters have a snap to their punches. The crack of leather against leather sounds like an explosion. There was intensity in Manny's eyes.

Roach gave running instructions in a soft voice.

Crack! Pop!

Blazing speed.

HBO production coordinator Tami Cotel entered the room. "Ten minutes, guys," she said.

The padwork ended at 8:30. "You're ready to go," Roach told his fighter.

On a large television monitor at the far end of the room, Miguel Cotto could be seen in real time throwing left hooks toward the body of his trainer.

"That's what he does," Roach reminded Pacquiao. "He cocks the left when he goes up top and opens himself up when he reaches with the hook to the body. Either way; you nail him with a counter-right."

Manny sat on a chair. He looked happy and serene.

No one spoke.

Then it was time.

Pacquiao stood up and turned toward Peter Nelson, who'd been granted access to the dressing room because of his work with Roach on the trainer's autobiography.

"Do you have a good story?" Manny asked.

Nelson looked startled that his book would be of concern to Pacquiao at this moment.

"Yes," he answered after a moment's pause.

Each time a fighter steps in the ring, he has to prove himself all over again. Against Cotto, Pacquiao did just that.

The first round belonged to Miguel. He neutralized Manny's speed with his jab and fought a smart measured three minutes. Pacquiao turned the tables in the second stanza, getting off first and giving every indication of relishing a firefight.

The pendulum swung several times in round three, most of which was controlled by Cotto. He landed several hard shots and seemed the stronger of the two men. Manny took the punches well and scored a knockdown with a sharp right hook of his own. But because Miguel didn't seem hurt and was superior for the rest of the round, two of the three judges appropriately scored it 10–9 in Manny's favor instead of 10–8 (which a knockdown usually warrants).

Round four belonged to Pacquiao. He decked Cotto again; this time with a hard left-uppercut that hurt Miguel.

Round five was close. All three judges gave it to Pacquiao. But many observers (including this writer) thought that it belonged to Cotto.

At this point, as predicted, Pacquiao was the faster of the two men, but Cotto looked to be physically stronger. Certainly, Miguel was competitive.

"I was a little concerned," Roach admitted afterward. "Cotto looked pretty good. And for a while, Manny was fighting Cotto's fight. He was laying on the ropes, and Miguel caught him with some punches that got his attention."

Then, in round six, Pacquiao turned a great fight into a great performance. The "smaller" man started digging to the body and scoring up top, staggering Cotto twice. By the end of the round, Miguel was badly cut on the left eyelid and Manny was dominating the action.

From that point on, Pacquiao beat Cotto up. The second half of the bout saw Miguel in full retreat, backpedaling and circling away in an effort to get to the end of the fight with as little additional damage and pain as possible. He looked like a man who was trying to escape from a spinning airplane propeller. Manny relentlessly pursued him and, when Cotto landed, simply walked through the punches.

"When Cotto started backing up, I knew it was over," Roach said afterward. "His corner should have stopped the fight three rounds before it ended. All that happened after Miguel started running was that he took a beating."

Cotto himself later acknowledged, "I didn't know from where the punches come. I couldn't protect myself. After round seven, I tell Joe [Santiago] to stop the fight, but I think better and I prefer to fight."

Roach was right. Santiago should have stopped it. As the fight progressed, Cotto's face became more and more disfigured. He was bleeding from the nose and mouth. His lips were horribly swollen.

One could make a strong case that round nine was 10–8 in Pacquiao's favor even though there was no knockdown. Rounds ten and eleven were more of the same. Meanwhile, Manny wasn't playing it safe. Great fighters have the ability to finish strong and close the show. He was going for the kill.

Fifty-five seconds into round twelve, Bayless did what Cotto's corner should have done earlier. He mercifully stopped the slaughter.

The entourage was waiting when Pacquiao returned to his dressing room after the fight. After embracing several friends, he began to sing:

> You raise me up so I can stand on mountains;
> You raise me up to walk on stormy seas;
> I am strong when I am on your shoulders;
> You raise me up to more than I can be.

Then he grimaced. Manny had been in a fight. There were bruises under both eyes and, of greater medical significance, he'd suffered torn cartilage in his right ear. The ear hurt and was starting to swell. Unattended, it would lead to the condition known in boxing as a "cauliflower ear."

Dr. Jeffrey Roth (a plastic surgeon) took Pacquiao to an adjacent room and drained his ear. When they returned, white gauze was wrapped around Manny's head. The merriment resumed. Roach stood quietly to the side.

"Manny is such a great guy to work with," Freddie said. "He's unbelievable, one of a kind. I'm working with the greatest fighter of my time and one of the greatest fighters ever. Sometimes I can't believe how lucky I am."

How good is Pacquiao?

It's axiomatic in boxing that either a fighter is getting better or he's getting worse. Remarkably, at age thirty-one, Pacquiao is getting better; much better. He's on a roll where each new fight (first De La Hoya, then Hatton, now Cotto) becomes his signature outing.

Part of that is Roach's influence. Freddie has worked with some of the best fighters of our time and three of the most famous (De La Hoya, Tyson, and Pacquiao).

"Oscar was a slow learner," Roach says. "Oscar needed repetition. He had to do something over and over again to get it right. Tyson, at the point in his career that I was with him, wasn't interested in learning. Manny is very teachable and an incredibly fast learner. He's carrying his punch and his power with him along with his speed as he moves up in weight. He's getting better all the time."

Against Cotto, Pacquiao made a world-class fighter look ordinary and turned him into a foil. "His performance," Gordon Marino wrote in the *Wall Street Journal,* "was absolutely jaw-dropping; a fistic work of art." His ability to take punches and walk through punishment is astounding. And speed is only part of the problem that Manny poses for opponents. He punches with power too.

"We thought Pacquiao was great," Larry Merchant said after the fight. "He's better than we thought."

Pacquiao frequently talks about entering the political arena. In 2007, he ran for Congress and was defeated decisively by incumbent Darlene Antonino-Custodio. But his popularity has grown since then and another campaign in 2010 appears to be in the cards. Manny's motives are pure, but some of his biggest admirers fear that politics could be his unmaking; that depending on his associations, he could be tainted by the political process, especially if he wins.

"Manny might find out that politics isn't as much fun as boxing," Roach says. "And it might be rougher. I've been wrong before, but I think Manny can do more for his country as a boxer than he can as a politician."

What we know for sure is that Pacquiao is doing a lot for boxing.

"What did Manny Pacquiao achieve?" Jerry Izenberg (the dean of American sportswriters) asked after Pacquiao-Cotto. "He brought boxing back into newspapers, back onto television, and back into an unbroken chain of conversations across America, from its office water coolers to its neighborhood saloons. Yankee Stadium and the new Dallas Cowboys Stadium are now talking about outdoor championship fights with guess who as the magnet that will pack them in. The face of all of boxing is indelibly stamped with that of Manny Pacquiao today. This wasn't just a great fight. It was a coronation."

For years, the people who run boxing worried, "What will happen when Tyson retires?" Then it was, "What will happen when Oscar retires?" Now Manny Pacquiao is ushering in a new potentially-golden era.

Pacquiao–Cotto showed that boxing is still capable of thrilling entire nations and giving the world magical nights. It wasn't the last big fight of the current decade. It was the first big fight of the future.

For too long, boxing has been rooted in the past. Ten years ago, the conventional wisdom was that all things good and profitable in the sweet science flowed from the United States. The Internet was an afterthought insofar as marketing was concerned. Now boxing has gone global and digital. And Pacquiao is reaching critical mass. His fights keep getting bigger.

Boxing has taken Manny Pacquiao on a journey that's almost beyond belief. In return, he has put his mark on the sport forever.

Round 2
Curiosities

It's remarkable how many fight fans have never been to a pro fight.

A Fight Fan's First Fight

From time to time, I'm asked why I like boxing. The best answer I can give is, go to a fight and see for yourself. Television covers the sport well, but there's no substitute for live action. Better yet; go to a club fight so you can get close to the ring, feel the action, and see the emotions etched on the fighters' faces.

Lance Kolb is a longtime fight fan. One of his great-grandfathers was Giovanni Giuseppe Terranova, who was born in Italy and fought in the United States under the name "Red Cap Wilson" from 1912 through 1927.

Lance's own early life wasn't a bed of roses. His first crib was a dresser drawer. Thereafter, in his words, "I was tossed back and forth between my parents and foster homes until my mother died from a combination of hepatitis B and drugs. Then I was adopted by a fabulous family and my life turned around."

Kolb, now forty-three, remembers sitting next to his grandfather on the sofa on Saturday and Sunday afternoons, watching fights on television. Sugar Ray Leonard, Marvin Hagler, and Ray Mancini turned him on to boxing. He graduated from Bridgewater State College and spent sixteen years in the military, rising from private to captain.

"There were things I did when I was in the Army that were hard to do and I didn't want to do," he says. "But they were necessary and had to be done." He has never boxed but was trained extensively in hand-to-hand combat.

"They don't really correlate," Lance says. "One is life and death, and the other is entertainment."

Kolb is now responsible for managing the building infrastructure of a large cooperative residence in Manhattan. When there's a big pay-per-view fight, he gets together with a half-dozen friends to watch the action on television.

"I love the one-on-one aspect of boxing," he says. "It's pure. Two guys, no one else, and you have to out-skill and out-will the other guy."

Like many fans, Kolb is ambivalent about the current state of boxing. "I loved watching Roy Jones when he was Roy," Lance recalls. "I thought it was amazing the way Bernard Hopkins put it all together to destroy Felix Trinidad. And it was very satisfying for me when Lennox Lewis took Mike Tyson apart. Right now, I like Kelly Pavlik and Miguel Cotto, but there's no heavyweight for me to root for. Wladimir Klitschko fighting Ray Austin in Germany? Who cares?"

"And the bigger problem," he continues, "is, if you want to see great boxing on television today, you're forced to pay through the nose. The only alternative is to watch films of old fights. No sport can survive without fans; and you can't get fans if it's close to impossible to watch."

Significantly, until last month, Kolb had never been to a fight.

Why not?

"When I was young," he explains, "I never had the money. Now the tickets for a big fight cost a fortune if you want to sit anywhere near the ring. And the way things are, you don't even know when and where the club fights are or how to buy a ticket for them."

As a writer, I benefit from viewing things through new eyes. Thus, on February 25th, I invited Kolb to join me at B. B. King's Blues Club and Grill in New York for the latest installment of Lou DiBella's "Broadway Boxing" series.

"I'm psyched for this," Lance said as we arrived.

B. B. King's accommodates 550 people (sitting and standing) for boxing. It's an intimate atmosphere that accentuates the camaraderie within the fight community. Before the first bell, there was a steady stream of handshakes from insiders like the venerable Lou Duva, ring announcer Joe Antonacci, and New York State Athletic Commission inspectors Felix Figueroa, George Ward, and Mike Paz.

"Seeing a fight in person is very different from watching it on television," Steve Farhood told Lance. "I've never brought anyone to the fights for the first time who didn't love it."

"You hear the punches," former junior-welterweight champion Paulie Malignaggi added.

Then the fights began.

DiBella's goals for the evening were fairly straightforward. He'd make or lose a few dollars. More significantly, he hoped to get some publicity for the fighters on the card who he had under contract and advance their careers a bit.

The first bout of the evening saw local heavyweight Bedarin Toma making his pro debut against Joseph Rabotte of South Carolina. Last October, Rabotte journeyed to New York as the opponent in Tor Hamer's pro debut. He'd arrived with a 2-and-3 record (all three losses coming by way of knockout) and left with four "KOs by."

Against Toma, Rabotte circled constantly to his left, jabbed occasionally, and avoided contact whenever possible. Toma had no idea how to cut the ring off, and the bout was boring. Rabotte won a majority decision, although most ringside observers thought the nod should have gone to Toma.

"It's different without the commentators," Lance said.

"Do you miss them?"

"I'm not sure."

Next up; four rounds, junior-lightweights; Luis Del Valle (4–0, 3 KOs) from Newburgh, New York, against Tommy Atencio (3–0, 2 KOs) from Denver. It's unusual to see two fighters this good go in this tough early in their careers. Del Valle was better and won all four rounds, but Atencio made him work for everything he got.

"It's interesting," Lance noted. "The rounds seem longer when you're watching them in person. And there's more tension."

The rest of the card shaped up as four prospects from New York against four punching bags from around the country.

Fight number three wasn't much. Sadam Ali (a member of the 2008 United States Olympic team with one knockout victory in one pro fight) was up against Ralph Prescott (0–1) from Seattle. A left hook upstairs ended matters in the second round.

That was followed by light-heavyweight Will Rosinsky (5-and-0, 5 KOs) versus James McAvey (2–3, 1 KO). Rosinsky, age twenty-four, is a four-time New York Golden Gloves champion and a graduate of Queens College. He sells tickets. DiBella would love to sign him; but right now, Rosinsky is playing hard to get.

The difference in skill between Rosinsky and McAvey was quickly apparent, with the prospect landing lead right hands and thudding body shots.

"I heard that one," Lance said with a wince.

It was over at 2:43 of round one.

"Rosinsky impressed me," Lance noted. "I'd like to see more of him."

The semi-final bout matched Tor Hamer (3–0, 3 KOs) of Harlem against late-substitute Clarence Tillman (1-1-1, 1 KO) from Henderson, Nevada.

Hamer is a "small" heavyweight (225 pounds). He began boxing in 2004 and compiled a 34-and-1 amateur record, winning the 2008 super-heavyweight division in the National Golden Gloves. Lest one get carried away by that achievement; the last National Golden Gloves super-heavyweight champion to win any version of the heavyweight crown as a pro was Greg Page.

Hamer is trained by Bobby Miles and Shaun Raysor (his amateur coach). After two quick knockdowns that put Tillman on queer street, referee Ken Ezzo appropriately stopped the fight at 1:44 of round one.

Afterward, Lance and I went to Hamer's dressing room for a quick visit. "Next heavyweight champion of the world," Raysor proclaimed. "I told you I had a heavyweight," Miles chortled.

Hamer turned twenty-six years old on January 20th (the day that Barack Obama was inaugurated). How had he felt, watching the ceremonies on television?

"I thought back to a day when I was thirteen years old," Tor answered "I remember it very clearly. I was in the car with my father. We were driving across the Triborough Bridge. I told my father that someday I wanted to be president of the United States, and he said, 'It will never happen. You're black and you don't work hard enough in school to get good grades.'"

"He was half-right," Tor added. "I never got the grades."

We returned to ringside as the bell was sounding for round one of the main event. Light-heavyweight Shaun George (17-2-2 with 8 knockouts) of Brooklyn against Jaffa Ballogou (46–7, 40 KOs).

George is pushing thirty and nearing make-or-break time in his career. In his last fight (on May 16, 2008), he stopped a faded Chris Byrd in nine rounds. Ballogou is from Togo and now lives in New York. He began fighting as a junior-middleweight and is forty years old. In other words, Ballogou has seen better days (and his better days weren't all that good). George turned him into a human piñata. The fight ended at 1:26 of round one.

"I wasn't thrilled with tonight," DiBella told us afterward. "The key guys looked good and I'm happy they won. But I would have liked to have had more of a main event for the fans."

As for Lance—

"Do you know what I liked most?" he said. "The atmosphere. I would have liked to see a little better quality fight, but the atmosphere was great. The crowd was into it. I love the way the room was set up. And I loved the boxing people; the camaraderie and glad-handing and the way so many of them came over during the night to say hello."

"Tommy Atencio made it special for me," Lance continued. "Some of the opponents were just here for a paycheck, but Atencio came to fight. The fans got their money's worth on that one. After more than thirty years of watching boxing on television, this experience was long overdue for me. I'd come back again in a minute."

I've often said that the difference between watching a fight on television and seeing a fight in person is like the difference between looking at a photograph of a painting in a book and standing in front of the same painting in the Metropolitan Museum of Art.

A similar sentiment was waiting for me when I checked my email the following morning.

"At 4:20 AM, after re-living the moments in my head a thousand times," Lance wrote, "I realized that the difference between watching boxing live and watching it on television is very simple. It's like watching a Broadway play verses a movie. Live boxing, like theatre is more real, more raw, and a much grander experience."

Sometimes fairy tales come true. And sometimes they don't.

Great Moments in Sports

In the past, I've recounted the memories of fighters who spoke fondly of their greatest moment in a sport other than boxing. The recollections of some notable non-combatants follow:

SETH ABRAHAM: I went to the University of Toledo on a baseball scholarship and was a member of Sigma Alpha Mu. If you were on a varsity team, you couldn't play fraternity ball in that sport. But in my sophomore year [1965–1966], I had back-to-back monster games in football and basketball against Alpha Epsilon Pi, which was our most hated rival.

The football game was first. It was a big event; very physical two-hand touch, six men on a side, referred to on campus as "The Blood Bowl." Both fraternities were predominantly Jewish, and people came to watch the Jews bash each other's brains in. In the second half, I intercepted a pass and ran it back for a touchdown and returned a punt for another touchdown. We won; and that night while most of my fraternity brothers were celebrating by getting drunk, I had a memorable assignation with a young woman I was dating at the time. Then she dumped me and started seeing an Alpha Epsilon Pi guy.

Fast-forward to Winter Homecoming and the Jews are at it again, only this time it's basketball. Sigma Alpha Mu plays Alpha Epsilon Pi on center court in the university field house. I was the fifth best player on our starting team. Normally, my role was passing; but in warm-ups that day, I was hitting everything. Our coach was a basketball player named Bob Aston, who was first-team all-conference but wasn't allowed to play basketball in the fraternity league because of his varsity status.

When the warm-ups were over, Bob said to me, "I saw what you were doing. Let's see what you have in the game." He designed the first offensive play for me. I got the ball; shot it; nothing but net. Next possession; my teammates get the ball to me again; I shoot it; swish. Now I'm constantly getting the ball and scoring. We won in a rout. And when the game was over, the woman who had dumped me for the Alpha Epsilon

Pi guy came over and said, "Obviously, I made a bad choice." That was more than forty years ago and the memory of it still warms my heart.

JIM LAMPLEY: The year is 1960. I'm eleven years old, playing in the twelve-and-under Little League in Hendersonville, North Carolina. Virtually all of the teams are named for local churches or tiny outlying communities. I'm the starting pitcher for the Presbyterian team, which is the league doormat. We can't score at all and lose all sixteen of our games that year. I look good in the batter's box; I have great form; and I can't hit a thing.

First great moment; we're playing Etowah. Their pitcher is Buddy Lydecker, who's twelve years old and looks like he's seventeen. Two years earlier, Buddy was the pitcher for my first Little League at bat and hit me in the stomach with a fastball. It's hard to get hit in the stomach with a fastball, but I'd managed to do it by turning into an inside pitch. Etowah is the best team in the league. They'll go through the entire season undefeated. There are two outs in the sixth inning, which was the regulation length for league games. Buddy is one out away from pitching a no-hitter, and I'm at the plate. I drop a bunt down the third-base line and beat it out for my first hit of the year. Sweet revenge.

Second great moment; it's now the last game of the season. This one is against the Methodists. Because of the natural rivalry between Presbyterians and Methodists, it's our biggest game of the year. Waddy Stokes is on the mound for Methodist. His real name is Roddy; but when his sister was young, she couldn't pronounce Roddy. Hence Waddy. Once again, we're losing with two outs in the sixth inning. Once again, I'm at bat. And once again, we're facing the embarrassment of being no-hit. Waddy had a curveball, which I never would have been able to put my bat on, but he made the mistake of throwing me a fastball. I bunted it down the third-base line and made it to first. Those were my only two hits that year. Thank God for tiny victories.

DAN GOOSSEN: My brothers and I used to play roller hockey on the street in front of our house with the rest of the family and a few friends. Our garage looked like a locker room with all the sticks, skates, shin-guards, and two big goals. The games got pretty rough. We took it seriously. Once the puck dropped, we weren't brothers anymore.

One day, a carload of guys drove by, saw us playing, and challenged us to a game. We met them later that day at Van Nuys High School, where there was a big field. You could tell by the way they warmed up that they were good. They even had uniforms.

We knew that our only chance to win was to play like the Hanson Brothers in that movie, *Slap Shot*, so that's what we did. Three minutes into the game, my brother Joe won a face-off and got the puck to my nephew, Jimmy Buffo, who skated in and scored. The guys on the other team were upset because my brother Tom had checked one of them into a chain-link fence to clear the way for Jimmy. And they didn't like the way we were celebrating the goal. So there was a big brawl that ended with a few of their guys lying on the ground. That was the end of the game, which meant that we won 1–0. I broke my hand during the brawl, but I knocked one of their guys down so that was satisfying too.

GARY SHAW: I started bowling when I was seven years old. By the time I got to high school, I was pretty good; maybe a 190 average. I bowled a lot in Jersey City and was on a team that was sponsored by Pepsi Cola. One time, we were in a tournament in North Bergen. I knew I was in a groove early. It felt like I couldn't do anything wrong. Just lay the ball down, and it would go in the pocket.

Six frames, six strikes. I started getting a bit nervous.

Seventh frame; another strike.

Eighth frame; everybody in the place started gathering around our lane to watch me. Strike.

Ninth frame. Strike

Now the crowd looked like the gallery watching Tiger Woods at Augusta. I could hardly hold the ball. Strike.

Two away from a perfect game.

Strike.

It was like an out of body experience. One more strike and I'd have a perfect game. I'm superstitious, so I was trying to remember everything I'd done that day. How I'd picked the ball up each time; whether or not I'd wiped it with a rag.

Then I choked. I released the ball and there was a loud thud as the ball hit the floor; nothing like the smooth delivery I'd had before. It wasn't pretty. I left five pins standing, and never came close to rolling a perfect game again.

AL BERNSTEIN: It was in Babe Ruth baseball when I was seventeen years old. I was the starting catcher on the Archer Manor all-star team, which was a league on the southwest side of Chicago. We were playing in the state all-star tournament and had won our first game. I was the number-three hitter in the line-up and I was in a slump. This was our second tournament game. The score was tied 4-to-4. I was scheduled to lead off in the bottom of the eleventh inning, and the coach wanted to pinch hit for me. Nothing like that had ever happened to me before. Then one of my teammates talked him out of it, and I went up to the plate.

As a rule, I was a line-drive hitter; a lot of singles and doubles, not much power. And here, I was aware of the fact that I hadn't been hitting well and wasn't the guy the coach wanted at bat. All I wanted to do was make contact.

First pitch; the pitcher hung a curve. I swung. And somehow, I got under the ball just enough. It was a perfect home run stroke. I'd never hit a ball that far before. It went over the left-fielder's head, over the fence, out onto the expressway.

I've had more important moments as an athlete. But that was the one that gave me the most joy. How many guys have actually hit a walk-off home run in an all-star tournament game? And as I was rounding third base, the coach just stared at the ground. He wouldn't look at me.

LOU DiBELLA: When I was in law school [at Harvard], two teams dominated intramural basketball. One of them was a group of guys who'd been jocks in college and were a self-contained clique. Their team was called the Armadillos.

I was on a rag-tag team called The Lurking Funk. Our best player was a guy named Bob Dozier, who'd been good in high school but had ballooned up to 300 pounds. The rest of the guys on our team had never really been basketball players. I was tall and had a big ass, so I was useful as a rebounder; that's about all.

We squeaked into the playoffs and wound up playing the Armadillos in the first round. Dozier had his worst game of the year. Everything he threw up missed by a mile. But somehow, I had the greatest game of my life. The chances of me hitting six or seven shots in a row were negligible; particularly if someone was guarding me. But that day, every shot I took went in.

For the first time, I understood what it felt like to be in a zone. Then another guy on our team, George Seeberger, who was half the size of a midget, got into a rhythm. It was like a kids movie; the jocks against the nerds. The lead see-sawed back and forth the entire second half. Finally, with twenty seconds left in the game, we got the ball, down by one point. One more shot; if we make it, we win and heaven and earth turn upside down.

I'd love to tell you I hit the final shot, but I didn't. Dozier got the ball. He'd been frustrated all afternoon, put up one last shot, and missed that one too. We lost by a point. I was heartbroken, but I felt good about what we'd done. We gave those guys hell and it was the greatest game of basketball I ever played.

JERRY IZENBERG: When I was ten years old, my father bought me a baseball glove. It was a Chanukah gift, which mixed the religion of the old country with the new religion in my life, which was baseball. He took me to a sporting goods store in Newark called Davega's to pick out the glove. Then we got home and went outside to play catch, even though it was December with huge snowflakes whipping around in the wind.

I remember throwing the ball back and forth. The snowflakes got bigger and the wind blew harder. My father reached back and threw the ball high into the air. I had to squint up through the snowflakes to see it. Then the ball started falling; I reached up; it landed smack in my glove. And in that moment, I felt as close to my father as I would ever feel in my life.

2009, like its predecessors, brought its share of miscellaneous insights and humor.

Fistic Nuggets

Barney Frank has been in Congress since 1981 and is chairman of the House of Representatives Financial Services Committee. That makes him one of the most powerful people in government. His career is also notable because, in 1987, he was only the second member of Congress to openly acknowledge being gay.

What does Barney Frank have to do with boxing?

Not much. But earlier this year, in a profile for *The New Yorker,* he was quoted as reminiscing, "My first day of high school, I was sent to the vice principal for discipline because I got in trouble for talking too much. When I got to her office, Chuck Wepner was already there. He'd gotten into a fight with the toughest kid in the school."

Actually, Wepner was probably the toughest kid in the school. In later years, he compiled a professional record of 35 wins, 14 losses, and 2 draws against opponents like George Foreman, Sonny Liston, and Ernie Terrell. But the most notable encounter of "The Bayonne Bleeder's" career was a fifteenth-round knockout loss at the hands of Muhammad Ali. Chuck's courage that night inspired an unemployed actor named Sylvester Stallone to write a screenplay entitled *Rocky.*

As for Barney Frank and their time together at Bayonne High School, Wepner recalls, "I was two years ahead of Barney. I would have graduated in 1956, but I was two credits short and went into the Marines. I got my GED later on. Barney and I didn't have much to do with each other. He was active in the different political forums they ran, but politics wasn't my thing. I came from a pretty rough background. My mother and father split up when I was a year old. We lived in a converted coal shed until I was thirteen. Then we moved to the projects, so I had other things on my mind."

And the fight in school that Frank remembers?

"It was with a guy named Cuno Canella. I didn't push guys around, but I didn't like guys pushing me around either. We got into it in the school cafeteria. I was beating him up pretty good when they stopped it. I lost sometimes in the pros, but I was undefeated in the cafeteria."

And last; what does Wepner think of Barney Frank today?

"I'm very proud that I knew Barney. He seems like a nice guy. He's a good politician. And it took courage to come out of the closet when he did. I give him credit for that. You know; I've been a Democrat my whole life. I like Barack Obama. He's a good man with a tough job, and I'm glad that Barney is there to help him."

★   ★   ★

Reg Gutteridge, who died on January 24, 2009, was a boxing journalist of the highest order and the voice of boxing for ITV.

As a twenty-year-old soldier with the King's Royal Rifle Corps, Gutteridge lost a leg in World War II. That gave rise to numerous anecdotes, one of which was recounted last week by Jerry Izenberg.

In 1962, Gutteridge journeyed to Chicago for the first fight between Sonny Liston and Floyd Patterson. Liston was in the habit of trying to intimidate virtually everyone he met. Thus, when Jack Nilon (Sonny's manager) arranged for his fighter to have dinner with Reg, the fighter gave Gutteridge his most baleful stare.

"Let's see who's tougher," Reg suggested. Then he picked up a steak knife and jammed it deep into his leg (which unbeknownst to Sonny) was made of wood.

Liston cringed and said reverentially, "You bad, man. You bad."

★   ★   ★

Top Rank and Golden Boy are the two most powerful promotional companies in boxing today. Recently, their CEOs reminisced about the first professional fight they ever saw.

BOB ARUM: It was the first fight I promoted; Muhammad Ali against George Chuvalo [on March 29, 1966]. Jim Brown put me together with Herbert Muhammad [Ali's manager]. We formed a promotional company called Main Bout, and the first fight we did was a nightmare. It started as Ali against Ernie Terrell in Chicago. Then we got kicked out of Illinois because Ali had said he had no quarrel with them Vietcong, and I ran around the country without any luck looking for a state where we could have the fight. Finally, I took it to Montreal and then it was Toronto and then Terrell pulled out and we wound up with Ali-Chuvalo. On fight night, I went to the arena [Maple Leaf Gardens] and all I cared about was the fight should happen. I didn't walk in and look at the ring and say "wow." I knew nothing about the preliminary fights because, at the time, I knew nothing about boxing. All I knew was, I wanted the bell for round one of Ali-Chuvalo to ring because I'd been promoting the fight on my Diners Club card and had something like $29,000 in charges to pay off.

RICHARD SCHAEFER: After I moved to the United States, I became friendly with Gabriel Brener, who was from a prominent family that lived in Mexico City. Gabriel was living in Los Angeles and asked if I would like to go to a live boxing event with him. He was friends with the Azcaraga family, which owned Televisa and Azteca Stadium in Mexico City. So we went to see Julio Cesar Chavez against Greg Haugen [on February 20, 1993]. We arrived in Mexico City and drove to the stadium. As we were driving, I could see the magnitude of the event on the streets. There was this wave of humanity, all going in the same direction. I remember walking into the stadium and looking up at all these faces [the announced attendance was 132,247]. It was absolutely amazing. We walked through the crowd to the middle of the field and sat in the third row. Then I saw this guy in the ring, dressed in a tuxedo with his hair standing up in the air, waving Mexican and American flags, shouting, "Viva Mexico." That was my first look at Don King. I have to hand it to him. Don created an extraordinary event. I was very impressed by what he did. So there was Don King; there was the crowd; and then the fight [won by Chavez on a fifth-round knockout]. I was thinking, this is the way it must have been in the old days of Rome with the gladiators. It was a remarkable experience. And as we were leaving, Gabriel said to me, "Be careful; they throw stuff. It's a tradition at fights in Mexico." So there I was, leaving the field, a Swiss banker, with piss in cups being thrown at me.

★   ★   ★

One of the best things to happen in heavyweight boxing this year was David Haye pulling out of a proposed September 12th fight against Vitali Klitschko in favor of a November 7th date against Nikolai Valuev. At that point, Haye didn't have the credentials to be taken seriously as a challenger to the Klitschko brothers, who share the de facto heavyweight championship of the world. Now David has done what he should have been doing all along. By beating Valuev, he began the process of establishing his credentials as a challenger for the heavyweight throne.

Meanwhile, Haye's trash-talking might get him attention, but it turns a lot of people off. "My mum hates it," he acknowledges. "She's not amused by it one bit. I get reprimanded all the time. She says it makes people think she didn't raise me right."

Good for David's mum.

★   ★   ★

For those who are keeping score, the silliest thing to come out of the WBC's 47th annual convention held this year in South Korea was . . . (drumroll, please):

WBC welterweight champion Andre Berto requested approval to make a voluntary title defense against WBA champion Shane Mosley. Berto's request was approved on the condition that Mosley publicly apologize to the WBC for giving up the sanctioning body's crown earlier this year in order to challenge Antonio Margarito for the WBA title. But approval was granted only after Berto addressed the convention and proclaimed, "I'm a very proud champion of the WBC. Sometimes I can't sleep at night and I push my girl out of the bed and lay the belt next to me."

The honorable mention for idiocy goes to the ruling that heavyweight Chris Arreola be removed from the WBC rankings and precluded from fighting for the organization's title for six months because he used foul language (aimed mostly at himself) after his September 26th loss to Vitali Klitschko.

★   ★   ★

Ricky Hatton has long been known for binge-eating and heavy drinking between fights. His fondness for beer gives new meaning to the phrase "six-pack abs." Then he goes to training camp and works his way into shape.

"But the last few pounds are murder," Ricky says of making weight. "And temptation is always there."

That temptation was never more difficult to resist than the Sunday before Hatton fought Luis Collazo in Boston three years ago.

"The promoters arranged for us to go to a baseball game at Fenway Park," Ricky recalls. "We had great seats behind home plate, but I was miserable. I couldn't understand the game. And the vendors going through the crowd with hot dogs, pizza, and beer drove me absolutely nuts."

★   ★   ★

Earlier this year, I recounted the memories of some boxing luminaries who spoke fondly of their greatest moment in a sport other than boxing. Light-heavyweight champion Chad Dawson's recollections follow:

"When I was a sophomore [at Hyde Leadership High School in New Hamden, Connecticut], I played small forward on the school basketball team. My brother Ricky was the star. He played guard and averaged 22 points a game. I was a bench-warmer. One game, the coach let me start over my brother because he'd gotten in academic trouble. I played the first quarter and scored seven points. Then my brother went in for me. That's the way it was. I didn't mind. I knew I had to wait my turn to play. At the end of the season, we were in the Class S [small school] State Tournament championship game. With two seconds left, we scored a basket and won by one point. Everybody in the arena was on their feet, screaming. I didn't play in the game. But just sitting on the bench, being part of a championship team with my brother, was special to me. I've always loved basketball. In boxing, you do it by yourself. The victory is your own and that feels good. But it's also nice to share a win with a team. If I could be pound-for-pound in boxing or MVP in the NBA Finals on the winning team, I think I'd choose basketball. But I never found out how good I could be because I dropped out of high school after tenth grade."

★ ★ ★

A tip of the hat to two men who deserve it.

Whenever there's a big fight at the MGM Grand in Las Vegas, Nathan Lee and La Mont Starks can be found sitting at a desk outside the media center.

Nathan was born in Arkansas in 1939. When he was nine, his family moved to California. In the 1960s and early '70s, he was a station manager for Hughes Air West. Then the station closed and he relocated to Las Vegas, where he was a supervisor at McCarran Airport. He retired in 1996 and, a year later, took a part-time job at the MGM Grand.

La Mont Starks ("remember the first four letters of my last name," he says) was born in Los Angeles in 1942. His professional resume includes a stint as the varsity basketball coach at Verbum Dei High School. He also taught political science and economics. He left teaching in 1977, went into sales, and moved to Las Vegas in 1989. After retiring in 2004, he went to work on a part-time basis for the MGM Grand.

Nathan and La Mont work big fights and other special events. During fight week, they're on duty outside the media center from 8:45 AM to 6:15 PM on Tuesday through Thursday and 8:45 AM to 8:15 PM on Friday and Saturday. They eat at the desk and leave only for restroom breaks.

"Our job," Nathan explains, "is to make sure that anyone who enters the media center has the proper credential. Most of the people we deal with are nice. We never have difficulty with the people who belong. They adhere to the rules. If they need a credential, they go where they're supposed to go and get the credential."

That sounds simple enough. But what about people who don't belong?

"Most of the people who aren't allowed into the media center accept it," La Mont says. "Very few of them tell us they're going in whether we like it or not. If they try to play hardball, we talk with them on a logical basis. We tell them, 'Look; we have rules and regulations, and we expect you to follow them. You came to Las Vegas to have a good time; not to wind up in trouble. If this turns into a problem, it won't be the two of us that deal with it.' That always defuses the situation."

Nathan and La Mont are incredibly nice. They have a kind word for everyone. There are times when circumstances require them to be firm, but they're never confrontational.

"And we like each other," Nathan notes.

"Yes, we do," La Mont says, seconding the notion. "The job would be less fun without each other."

"Those two guys are special," says Golden Boy CEO Richard Schaefer (who has been in the media center for his share of big fights). "You come in at nine o'clock in the morning, and they're there, smiling. You leave at six o'clock in the evening, and they're there smiling. Everyone likes them."

And another first fight . . .

Jessica Goes to the Fights

Jessica won my heart completely, totally, and without reservation when she was three years old.

I was forty-two at the time. My brother, Jim, had come east from Oregon, where he lived with his wife and daughters (Cathy and Jessica). They were visiting my parents, who lived in the suburbs of New York. Cathy was seven and too sophisticated for the game that Jessica and I were playing.

At Jessica's urging, I was carrying her around the house on my shoulders. We went into the living room, where the family was gathered, and I asked, "Does anyone know where Jessica is?"

That was met by a chorus of, "Oh, no. We have no idea where Jessica is."

Then, from above my head, a little voice instructed, "Look in the kitchen."

So I announced, "I think I'll look in the kitchen and see if Jessica is there."

That was followed by a trip to the kitchen.

"No. Jessica isn't here in the kitchen."

"Look in the bathroom," the voice from on high ordered.

Which was followed by "Look in the bedroom . . . Look in the closet . . . Look in the basement . . ." Although by this time, Jessica was sufficiently excited that she was flailing her arms around and whacking me on the head with each command.

Finally, I wearied of getting hit in the head. And the bundle of joy on my shoulders was getting a bit heavy. So I stopped in front of a mirror, stared at the image, and said, "Wait a minute! Wait a minute!"

At which point, Jessica put her hands over her eyes on the theory that, if she couldn't see me, then I couldn't see her either.

Jessica is now twenty-two. The little girl who once advised me that "four plus four equals two" graduated from the University of Washington in June. During the first trimester of her senior year, in addition to carrying a full course-load, she worked fifty hours a week for the Obama campaign in Seattle.

On election day, Jessica's picture was on Barack Obama's national website. She was wearing an Obama sweatshirt, holding a clipboard, ordering people around (which she likes to do). That night, after the polls closed and the results were in, she telephoned and joyously told me, "This is the best night of my life."

Jessica also practices what she preaches. Later this month, she'll enter the Peace Corps for a twenty-seven-month tour of duty in Cambodia.

Jessica has met her share of boxing personalities. In November 1992, Riddick Bowe was training in Sun River, Oregon, preparatory to challenging Evander Holyfield for the heavyweight championship. Eddie Futch (who was Bowe's trainer) invited my brother and his daughters to camp for a day. Jessica wasn't overly excited about meeting Riddick. She was five years old at the time. But she often talked about how much she liked "Mr. Futch."

Then, in 1993, Jessica met Muhammad Ali. The Smithsonian Institution was honoring "five great American athletes" at a weekend extravaganza that included a White House reception, an elaborate dinner, and a televised entertainment special. Muhammad was among the five. I had four invitations, which I shared with my brother, Cathy, and Jessica.

It was quite a weekend. Friday evening, Jim, Cathy, Jessica, and I had dinner with Muhammad and Lonnie Ali. Muhammad performed a series of magic tricks that left the girls transfixed. Lonnie gave each of them a shopping bag filled with presents. On Saturday, she took the girls sightseeing in a limousine provided by the event organizers.

ESPN was tracking Ali that weekend. Jessica and Cathy are the proud possessors of ESPN footage showing them sitting on Muhammad's knee. They're singing "the Barney song" together.

After the weekend, I asked the girls what they'd liked most about the trip. Seeing Bill Clinton? Meeting Muhammad Ali?

They'd enjoyed all that and also thought that Arnold Palmer (another of the honorees) was cool. But none of those things topped their list.

Cathy was impressed by the fact that there was a television in the hotel bathroom. Jessica liked the TV in the back of the limousine.

Fast-forward to September 2006. Jessica was in New York, and I took her to Gallagher's Steak House for the kick-off press conference for Evander Holyfield vs. Fres Oquendo. Afterward, I suggested that she earn the lunch she'd just eaten by writing about the day's events. She did so in an article for Secondsout.com that quoted Lou DiBella (Oquendo's promoter) as saying, "Boxing is a horrendous miserable vile business full of miserable thieving motherfuckers. But with this miserable pathetic crop of heavyweights, anyone can become heavyweight champion."

All of which brings us to July 11, 2009, at the Prudential Center in Newark. Jessica had seen many fights on television, but she'd never been to a fight. We decided to remedy that situation while she was visiting in New York.

During the past year, Main Events has carved out a niche for itself at the Prudential Center. The surrounding environs have a large Polish-American population, and Tomasz Adamek (born in Poland but now living in Jersey City) is the company's flagship fighter.

Main Events had hoped that July 11th would witness Adamek defending his IBF cruiserweight title against Bernard Hopkins. That would have been a big fight. But Golden Boy (which promotes Hopkins) refused to put more than $500,000 on the table for Adamek's services. Thus, Hopkins-Adamek became Adamek vs. Bobby Gunn.

On paper, that wasn't much of a fight. Gunn began fighting professionally in Arizona at age fifteen and is now thirty-five years old. The most notable thing about his 18-3-1 record was an eleven-year absence from the ring between 1993 and 2004. More ominously, he'd never lasted past the first round against a world-class fighter.

Don't blame Adamek for the level of competition. After Hopkins-Adamek fell through, Tomasz was willing to fight Glen Johnson or Matt Godfrey. But those fights were turned down by HBO and Showtime. Hence the absence of dollars to pay for a quality opponent.

At the final pre-fight press conference, Gunn optimistically told the media. "This is a modern-day Cinderella story. No one expects great things of me. A lot of the media has ripped me. Beware of a dangerous man."

That earned a riposte from Andrew Gmitruk (Adamek's trainer), who advised, "It's really nice to hear fairy tales, but those stories are for children. We are going to teach reality on Saturday."

When Saturday arrived, Jessica and I took the PATH train to Newark. After picking up our media credentials, we walked inside the arena and the first person we saw was Don Elbaum.

For those not in the know; Elbaum is a quintessential boxing guy. The sweet science is in his soul. As far as he's concerned, nothing transcends boxing because boxing is everything.

Elbaum came over to say hello (which, I explained to Jessica, is like walking into the Sistine Chapel and being greeted by the Pope). Don was at the fights because he's an advisor to an Israeli cruiserweight named Ran Nakash, who would be in the third bout of the evening.

"Nakash is amazing," Elbaum told us. "He's taught martial arts to every paramilitary organization in Israel. He's tough as nails; a great great fighter. I don't think anyone under two hundred pounds can beat him."

[Note to readers: Elbaum is the man who once proclaimed, "I got a kid who might be the next heavyweight champion of the world. The only problem is, he weighs 145 pounds and can't punch."]

Either one "gets" Don Elbaum or one doesn't. Jessica liked him immediately. They bonded in about thirty seconds, after which he took her to Nakash's dressing room, so she could watch Ran's hands being wrapped.

They returned to the press section just before the start of the first fight. "Remember," Elbaum said in parting, "there's nothing like boxing. I've been to the Super Bowl, the World Series, the Kentucky Derby, and none of them come close. A good fight is the greatest entertainment on earth."

The first bout of the evening saw Delen Parsley, a junior-middleweight from Brooklyn, making his pro debut against Tyrone Miles, who'd won his only previous pro bout. Parsley broke him down with body shots and stopped him in round four.

That was followed by a quick trip to the press room for penne and Caesar salad. "The first rule of boxing writing," I explained to Jessica, "is, if there's free food, grab it."

Then, having missed the second bout, we returned to ringside, where Parsley joined us. He's a likeable young man and was in a good mood, having just won his first pro fight.

"They don't expect a fighter as tall as me to go to the body like I do," Delen told us. "But I was digging to the body and saw him cringe, so I kept doing it. I'm building my career and this is a good start. Now I can say I've made my pro debut right."

Did he have any insights into the sweet science to share with Jessica?

"No fighter is one hundred percent sane," Delen counseled. "I'm not saying I'm crazy, but you have to be a little off to do this."

Then Ran Nakash entered the ring to face William Bailey. Nakash was more flawed than a 12-and-0 fighter should be. But Bailey (who had 10 victories in 28 fights) wasn't there to test him. He'd come from Virginia to pick up a paycheck. One more loss on his record wouldn't matter. The Virginian quit in round four.

Meanwhile, Jessica liked the music that was booming over the public address system. To me, it sounded like noise, but she explained that it was "top-ten iTunes download." And she loved the fights. "It's not boring," she said. "That's for sure. I'm really into it."

Then we got bored; both of us. Welterweights Henry Crawford and Kaseem Wilson, two cautious counter-punchers, engaged in a stultifyingly boring non-fight. How bad was it? After a while, the crowd wasn't paying enough attention to boo. Crawford won a unanimous decision.

That was followed by the most interesting match-up of the evening. Piotr Wilczewski (22–0, 7 KOs, the first of three Polish fighters on the card) vs. Curtis Stevens (20–2, 14 KOs, from the Brownsville section of Brooklyn). Super-middleweights.

It was a good action fight. Stevens knocked Wilczewski down with a left hook in round one and smacked him around the ring until the bell brought a temporary halt to the proceedings. Piotr recovered sufficiently to land the more numerous (if not harder) blows in round two. Then, in round three, Wilczewski was decked by another left hook, rose, and was being battered against the ropes when referee Earl Morton intervened to save him from the inevitable.

The crowd jeered and Wilczewski protested, but it was the right call. Stevens then celebrated a little more boisterously than Piotr's fans thought appropriate. The jeers turned more hostile and it was suggested that Curtis leave the ring expeditiously to avoid further provocation.

Polish pride was restored somewhat in fight number six, when cruiserweight Mateusz Masternak (13–0, 8 KOs) stopped Naser Mohamed Aly (4–3, 2 KOs) in five rounds. Like Wilczewski, Masternak had a padded record. But he wasn't fighting Curtis Stevens.

Now it was time for the main event. Tomasz Adamek (37–1, 25 KOs, the best cruiserweight in the world) against a club fighter.

"First time I saw this place," Adamek has said of the Prudential Center, "I thought it is beautiful. There is nothing like this in Poland. Many Polish people live near Prudential Center. I feel very at home here. It is very exciting to look up and see all the Polish people."

Now Adamek was surrounded by a sea of red and white, the colors of the Polish flag being the dominant sartorial theme among the 5,590 fans in attendance.

As for Gunn; he looked like a guy who had no chance; he fought like a guy who had no chance; and he had no chance.

Adamek, a habitually slow starter, easily dominated round one. From that point on, he beat Gunn up. Give Bobby credit for courage and heart. Each round that he survived was a small victory. But being game is different from being good.

In round four, the beating turned ugly. Gunn takes a pretty good punch, but he was taking too many of them without landing anything in return. Before the bell for round five, the ring doctor stopped it.

"I feel sorry for him," Jessica said of Gunn. "But it is boxing."

After the fights, Harold Lederman, who was at the Prudential Center with his wife, Eileen, and eldest daughter, Julie, drove us home. That's some pair of bookends for an evening of boxing: Don Elbaum and Harold Lederman.

Eighteen hours later, Jessica flew back to Oregon. In a matter of days, she'll leave for Cambodia to embark upon the next chapter in her life. I'll miss her and I'll be concerned about her welfare in a faraway land. But she assures me that she's "adventurous, not reckless."

She has become a wonderful young woman. I wish her godspeed on the journey ahead.

People often write about the adoration that the Filipino people feel for
Manny Pacquiao. This article personalized that adoration.

Tina Meets Manny

When the bell rings, Manny Pacquiao's eyes turn to burning coals.
His ring skills have made him what Steve Kim calls "the Filipino version
of Michael Jordan, Babe Ruth, and the Beatles."

Pacquiao carried the Filipino flag at the opening ceremony for the
2008 Beijing Olympics. He's the only Filipino boxer to appear on a
postage stamp. Earlier this year, *Time Magazine* listed him among its "100
most influential people" in the world.

Manny takes himself less seriously. "I'm just a regular person who
believes life is simple," he says. "I want to share the good things that God
has given me."

Pacquiao makes his fellow Filipinos happy the way that Muhammad
Ali in his prime made people happy. In the ring, he's their representative.
Face to face, there's adoration.

Tina Cruz was born in the Philippines. She grew up in Santiago
Isabela province. Her parents were rice farmers. In 1983, she came to the
United States in pursuit of a better life.

Five days a week, Tina gets up at four o'clock in the morning and
goes to the design company where she works in cleaning maintenance.
One of her daughters lives in the United States and is married to an Irish-
American. Her other daughter lives in the Philippines.

"Before Manny Pacquiao, I didn't watch boxing," Tina says. "I hate
violence. I don't like people hitting each other. But Manny Pacquiao is
the pride of all the Filipino people. I have to watch him. He is very special
to us. He is our voice to the world."

On September 10th, with the permission of Top Rank (Pacquiao's
promoter), I brought Tina to Yankee Stadium to meet Manny. The occasion was the kick-off press conference for his November 14th mega-fight
against Miguel Cotto.

We took the subway to Yankee Stadium. "I'm very excited," Tina said
as the moment of reckoning neared.

As per instructions, we waited at Gate #2 for Top Rank publicist Lee Samuels. Lee arrived. Tina and I were ushered into a stadium restaurant that was closed to the outside world. Pacquiao was sitting in a chair, text-messaging.

Tina's face lit up with joy and awe. The image she'd seen on television screens for years was right in front of her.

They were introduced. Then the image, a real flesh-and-blood person, was talking with her.

"I have to give people time to take a picture and sign autographs," Pacquiao has said. "I have to be generous to people. It is in my heart. Without that, I would not be Manny Pacquiao. I believe that being famous means one of your responsibilities is to give."

Tina and Manny spoke in Visayan (the dialect in the province where he was born); about his children and hers, life in the Philippines, and her joy in meeting him.

The press conference followed. A dais had been set up between first base and the stands. Tina was ushered to a seat of honor in the Yankees dugout. Fourteen hours earlier, Derek Jeter had come out of the same dugout to tie Lou Gehrig's seventy-year-old record for most base hits by a Yankee.

"Just to be here in Yankee Stadium like this would be exciting," Tina said. "This is like a dream."

The November 14th match-up will be dangerous for both men. Cotto sounded a word of warning from the dais, when he referenced Pacquiao's last two opponents. "I'm not Oscar De La Hoya," he declared. "I'm not Ricky Hatton. I'm Miguel Cotto."

"Cotto is bigger and stronger," Pacquiao acknowledged when it was his turn to speak. "But I will do my best." Then he added several words in Visayan.

The Filipinos in the stands roared.

"What did he say?" I asked Tina.

"I will fight to the last drop of my blood."

After the press conference, Tina posed for a photo with Pacquiao and he gave her autographs for several family members. Then Lee Samuels suggested that they pose again; this time with the WBC "diamond championship" belt around her waist.

Hopefully, the WBC won't send her a bill for a sanctioning fee.

It's unlikely that Manny Pacquiao will remember Tina. She's one of tens of thousands of people who have crossed his path. But on September 10th in Yankee Stadium, he put joy in her heart; and it will be there for the rest of her life.

That night, Tina called to thank me.

"I keep thinking about today," she said. "And it keeps getting better. Manny Pacquiao is the king. He's the most famous person in my country. I'm nobody to him, and he was so nice. He really talked to me."

Round 3
Issues and Answers

HBO is the most powerful force in boxing and thus warrants special scrutiny.

Memorandum for Ross Greenburg: HBO 2009

Hi. It's me again.

Yeah; I figured that would make you happy.

Anyway; HBO seems to be struggling with its boxing programming. Your ratings for boxing last year looked like polls tracking the national approval rating for George Bush's handling of the economy. So I thought I'd pass along a few thoughts.

Prior to 2008, the lowest prime-time *HBO World Championship Boxing* rating ever for a live telecast was 2.8. You did 2.5 for Mosley-Mayorga and Hatton-Malignaggi, 2.3 for Taylor-Lacy, and 2.0 for Pavlik-Lockett. The numbers for *Boxing After Dark* in 2008 were even worse, bottoming out at 1.1 for your October 4th telecast. If there were times when it seemed as though all-time-low records were set on a monthly basis, it's because they were.

I doubt that Bill Nelson (HBO's chief executive officer) likes spending $10,000,000 in license fees, marketing, and production costs for a 4.0 rating (Oscar De La Hoya vs. Steve Forbes). Some of the people who produce HBO's specials say that they can deliver an 8.0 rating for the same $10,000,000.

It would be a shame if HBO pulled the plug on boxing. The sweet science has taken too many hits lately. In October, ESPN2 cancelled *Wednesday Night Fights*. A month later, Telefutura cancelled *Solo Boxeo*. Both cancellations were the result of budget tightening. But their implications were miniscule compared to the shockwaves that would radiate if HBO did the same.

Will Rogers was fond of saying, "When you're in a hole, the first step toward getting out is to stop digging."

But before you do that, you have to understand that you're in a hole.

You're in a hole. HBO's boxing franchise is melting away because you've taken your subscribers for granted and tested their loyalty in ways that are hard to endure. So stop digging and give some thought to the following.

(1) Televise competitive fights

Each year, you tell the media, "We intend to dig our feet in a little more on mismatches and not give in to promoters, managers, and fighters who don't want to take a risk (2007)" . . . "This year, if a fighter wants to be on HBO, we'll expect him to go in tough (2008)."

Then, year after year, you televise mismatches.

Too often in recent years, the formula for *Boxing After Dark* has been putting a potential star in a non-competitive fight. For *World Championship Boxing,* it's putting a star you're building for pay-per-view in a non-competitive fight. One denizen of the boxing world said recently that your slogan should be changed to "HBO: Building beltholders one mismatch at a time."

CBS and Fox don't determine which teams play each other in the National Football League. ESPN doesn't make up the schedule for Major League Baseball. But in many instances, HBO determines who fights whom. You're starting off reasonably well in 2009. Kudos for that. But overall, your matchmaking has been poor and there are fears that you'll revert to form.

College football is popular; right? Did you notice the way ABC and ESPN programmed their prime-time Saturday night games this past autumn? They chose the MOST COMPETITIVE games available among the elite teams; not Oklahoma against Chattanooga.

HBO's subscribers want boxing. They just don't want the mismatches that you keep force-feeding them.

Am I exaggerating? Let's run some numbers.

Last year, *World Championship Boxing* (your flagship offering) televised fights with odds like 12-to-1, 15-to-1, and 18-to-1.

In the final quarter of 2008, HBO televised nine fights on *World Championship Boxing* and *Boxing After Dark*. Eight of those fights were mismatches going in. And the public knew they were mismatches, as evidenced by the one-sided odds. The favorite won all nine of those fights.

Okay; now we get to the really embarrassing part. In nine fights, do you know how many ROUNDS the underdog won?

Take a guess . . . No; guess again . . . Lower . . .

In nine fights on *HBO World Championship Boxing* and *Boxing After Dark* in the final quarter of 2008, the underdog won a total of FIVE ROUNDS.

Five rounds out of sixty-four rounds in nine fights. That's not boxing. That's paying to watch guys get beaten up.

HBO is capable of making competitive fights, even under difficult circumstances. One of the best fights you made in 2007 was Kelly Pavlik against Edison Miranda as part of a double-header. It wasn't easy. Jermain Taylor (promoted by Lou DiBella) fought Cory Spinks (a Don King fighter) in the main event. Pavlik was promoted by Bob Arum; Miranda by Warriors Boxing. But you wanted Pavlik-Miranda; you refused to take an alternative; and you got what you wanted. Not only was Pavlik-Miranda an exciting fight; it lay the groundwork for Kelly's rise to the undisputed middleweight championship of the world. And because of the way the deal was structured, no one had to engage in the all-too-common grotesque practice of giving a promoter options on someone else's fighter to get a date on HBO.

It's not rocket science. Buy competitive fights.

(2) Stop enabling the flow of fights that should be on World Championship Boxing to pay-per-view

You keep speaking out against the exodus of meaningful fights to pay-per-view. "I can't tell you that pay-per-view helps the sport because it doesn't," you said in 2007. "It hurts the sport because it narrows our audience, but it's a fact of life. The promoters and fighters insist on pay-per-view because that's where their greatest profits lie."

In 2008, you told the world, "The sport would benefit from more *HBO World Championship Boxing* fights and fewer pay-per-view events. But we can't turn back the clock and shut the cash register off. If we don't do the pay-per-view shows, someone else will."

Okay; now it's time for a quote from me: "The reality is that, by its conduct, HBO has enabled the flight to pay-per-view. If it wanted to, the network could take steps to reverse the trend. It would be very easy for

HBO to say to promoters, 'Pay-per-view undermines the commitment we've made to deliver the best content possible to our loyal paying subscribers, so we're going to cut back on pay-per-view.' Network executives could also tell promoters, 'We're not going to promo your pay-per-view fight on our regular boxing telecasts. There will be no promotional *Countdown* show. We won't guarantee a given number of buys in the form of an advance against pay-per-view revenue. And by the way; we can't guarantee that we won't counterprogram you.' Then sit back and watch how quickly mid-level pay-per-view shows return to *HBO World Championship Boxing*."

Is there anything in that quote you don't understand?

Bob Arum has figured it out. Last year, Arum declared, "If I was running HBO, I'd get out of the pay-per-view business. Maybe I'd do two huge per-per-view shows a year. Other than that, I wouldn't touch it. I wouldn't produce; I wouldn't distribute; I wouldn't have Jim Lampley at ringside for pay-per-view fights. Right now, it's idiotic."

Let's be honest. When a fight is on HBO-PPV, instead of spending money in the form of a license fee, HBO is taking in additional money. You keep saying, "It isn't as much as you think it is." But on most pay-per-view fights, HBO gets 10 percent of the first three or four million dollars in PPV revenue (after the multi-system cable operators and clearance fees are paid). Then the number drops to 7 1/2 percent.

Also; when a fight is on pay-per-view, more than fifty cents of every dollar in pay-per-view revenue goes to the cable or satellite companies that provide the signal to consumers and the clearing houses through which pay-per-view telecasts are sold to cable and satellite system operators. Time Warner Cable is the second-largest cable operator in the United States with more than 13,000,000 basic video subscribers. Roughly 90 percent of the homes in the United States that are addressable by cable for pay-per-view telecasts are "cleared" by a company called In-Demand. In Demand is owned by Comcast, Cox Communications, and Time Warner. HBO is part of the Time Warner empire.

You have to decide whether HBO Sports is primarily in the subscription television business or the pay-per-view business. It would be better for boxing (and HBO would have more subscribers) if you chose the former.

(3) When HBO-PPV televises a fight card,
give your customers quality undercard fights

HBO-PPV shows take place under the HBO banner. Lousy undercard fights make the network look bad, squander the good will you've earned in the past, and diminish the HBO brand.

I know you adhere to the view that fans buy pay-per-view fights for the main event; that the undercard isn't a factor. Have you considered the possibility that the undercard isn't a factor because fans have come to expect horrific undercard fights on HBO-PPV?

The National Football League doesn't say, "People are going to watch the Super Bowl anyway, so let's give them a crappy halftime show." This year, Bruce Springsteen and the E Street Band will be onstage at halftime. Past performers include U2, Stevie Wonder, Diana Ross, Michael Jackson, Paul McCartney, and the Rolling Stones.

Think about that. The NFL gives football fans Mick Jagger for free. HBO-PPV charges $54.95 and gives boxing fans slop. You put HBO's brand on the slop. And then you wonder why people don't watch boxing on HBO.

HBO's pay-per-view undercards keep getting worse. A lot of people in the industry thought it would be impossible to cobble together a less interesting undercard than the one you presented on your November 8, 2008, telecast of Joe Calzaghe vs. Roy Jones Jr. The naysayers were wrong.

The December 6, 2008, fight between Oscar De La Hoya and Manny Pacquiao was boxing's event of the year; a chance for HBO Sports to put its best foot forward. And you paired it with what might have been the worst undercard in the history of pay-per-view.

De La Hoya-Pacquiao engendered 1,250,000 buys. That means millions of people got together and paid $70,000,000 to watch an HBO telecast. It was an opportunity to make new fans. And what did you give them as an undercard? Danny Jacobs against Victor Lares; Juan Manuel Lopez versus Sergio Medina; and Victor Ortiz against Jeffrey Resto.

Do you know how bad that undercard was?

Nod your head, "yes" or shake your head "no."

If shook your head "no," you weren't paying attention to the fights.

Everyone with a modicum of knowledge about boxing knew going in that each of the three televised undercard fights was a mismatch. Not one of the fights lasted through the second round. The three designated victims landed a combined total of SIXTEEN punches. They were out-landed 99-to-16 and knocked down seven times.

That left Jim Lampley, Larry Merchant, and Emanuel Steward scram-bling to fill air time for two hours. Like you couldn't have figured out in advance, "Hey; we have three mismatches. Let's give some thought to a Plan B."

Not only did you blow an opportunity to win new fans; you lost some old ones.

Dan Rafael of ESPN.com wrote afterward, "We now have an under-card against which all other crappy undercards will be compared. The De La Hoya-Pacquiao undercard totally stunk and is the worst one I have ever seen."

Bob Raissman of the *New York Daily News* was similarly disenchanted. Raissman labeled the undercard "garbage." Then he retracted that char-acterization on the theory that it was unfair to garbage and opined, "If the HBO brand actually stands for quality, the company should try to present a night of competitive fights."

What goes through your mind when you read something like that?

I figure the most likely possibilities are: (1) You say to yourself, "Fuck Rafael and Raissman; how many Emmys have they won?" (2); You write a note to make sure that they're not invited to the next HBO party; or (3) You think about what they wrote, realize that a dozen other writers have written the same thing, and tell your staff, "We're doing something wrong. Let's fix the problem."

Hint: The correct answer is #3.

So let me make a suggestion. At your next staff meeting, if you haven't already done so, ask for a show of hands in response to the ques-tion, "How many of you think that the De La Hoya-Pacquiao pay-per-view undercard was acceptable?"

HBO puts all sorts of clauses in its contracts with promoters. How about a clause requiring them to present a quality undercard when boxing fans are charged $54.95 to watch a night of boxing on HBO-PPV? In fact, I'll go you one further. Think outside the box the next time you have a mega-fight. Structure a deal with the promoter that puts $1,000,000 toward a genuine top-flight co-feature. All you'd need to generate is another 40,000 buys to cover the cost. You'd have a card of historic pro-portions. And boxing fans might fall in love with HBO all over again.

(4) Stop giving preferential treatment to Golden Boy and Al Haymon

There's a joke that's making its way through boxing circles: "Richard Schaefer and Al Haymon aren't as smart as people think they are. They've done a lousy job of running boxing at HBO."

During Seth Abraham's tenure as president of Time Warner Sports, HBO was guided by what were known internally as "the five pillars of HBO Boxing." For example, one "pillar" was that Abraham felt it was important that the "fight of the year" have been televised on HBO.

Out of eleven fights considered by the Boxing Writers Association of America for the 2008 "fight of the year" award, only two (Cotto-Margarito and Pacquiao-Marquez II, both of which were on pay-per-view with Top Rank as the lead promoter) were affiliated with HBO. Meanwhile, there's a widespread belief that, under your administration, the "two pillars of HBO Boxing" are Golden Boy and Al Haymon.

I know you like Richard Schaefer. I do too. He's smart. He's a gentleman (which separates him from a lot of people in boxing). I have no quarrel with his trying to get as many dates as possible for Golden Boy on HBO. That's his job as Golden Boy's CEO.

But it's hard to shake the belief that HBO is tilting the playing field in Golden Boy's favor to the detriment of other promoters. One of your underlings explained it to me as follows: "Arum, King, DiBella; all those guys are headaches. Richard is low maintenance. He knows exactly how to stroke Ross. And as long as Ross gives Golden Boy what it wants, Richard makes it easy for Ross to do business with him."

Unfortunately, one consequence of your being stroked is that fighters are abandoning the promoters who built them and signing with Golden Boy in order to get dates on HBO.

"Part of being a promoter," Top Rank president Todd DuBoef says, "is to be an entrepreneur. That means taking risks and developing your product. Great promoters are developers and builders, not stealers and poachers."

Golden Boy now features Golden Oldies that someone else developed (e.g. Oscar De La Hoya, Bernard Hopkins, Ricky Hatton, Shane Mosley, Juan Manuel Marquez, Juan Diaz, and David Haye). They've used HBO's checkbook to sign them. It's a little like Pat Boone in the 1950s selling a million copies of the cover version of *Ain't That A Shame* and *Tutti Frutti* after Fats Domino and Little Richard first recorded the songs.

Late last year, HBO Sports presented a marketing plan to several pro-moters that would have brought their fighters to New York for a promo-tional shoot designed to support boxing on HBO. The plan was rejected. Why? Because the fighters were to be posed as students in a classroom under the instruction of Oscar De La Hoya.

What message do you think you sent with that?

As for Al Haymon; what is it with you and Al? You seem to bend over backwards for him like Chubby Checker going under a limbo bar.

Al is smart. He can be charming. But the line of mismatches, boring fights, and excessive license fees that you've approved for his fighters is as long as the Great Wall of China.

Did HBO really need Paul Williams vs. Verno Phillips paired with Chris Arreola against Travis Walker? Williams and Arreola (Haymon's fighters) were both favored at better than 10-to-1. The show, televised on November 29, 2008, did a 1.4 rating, so obviously your subscribers didn't care about the fights.

Nor was that an isolated instance. Andre Berto (represented by Haymon) against Michel Trabant, Miguel Rodriguez, and Steve Forbes might have been interesting if Berto had fought all three guys on the same night. Unfortunately, you televised each fight separately last year.

And speaking of another Al Haymon fighter; one of the things I don't understand is why HBO is paying a $3,200,000 license fee for the March 14, 2009, rematch between Chad Dawson and Antonio Tarver.

I know Tarver is one of Al's fighters. But did you see the first Dawson-Tarver fight?

Not many people did. It had a 1.5 rating. You don't strike me as the sort of guy who sits at home on Saturday night watching fights on Showtime, so my guess is that you didn't see it live. Did you watch a tape before you bought the rematch for HBO? Be honest; because if you say you watched it, someone might quiz you on what you saw. If you did watch it, did you watch the whole thing or fast-forward through the bor-ing rounds? You could have fast-forwarded a lot and not missed much. Do you really want to see that fight again?

Could Dawson-Tarver II turn out to be great viewing? Anything's possible. But the chances of showing HBO's subscribers a good fight are better if you start with a fight that looks good on paper. You could have spent your money more wisely.

Most likely, the Dawson-Tarver II telecast will be pretty boring. For creative production values, you'll start with the five-year-old tape of Antonio asking, "Got any excuses tonight, Roy?" Somewhere along the line, Max Kellerman will tell us that Chad Dawson reminds him of some alltime great (hopefully not Bob Foster). And ratings will tank.

By the way; as of this writing, promoter Gary Shaw has a multi-million-dollar license fee from HBO for Dawson-Tarver II but no site. What does that tell you about the fight? How many tickets do you think Gary will sell? I'll bet the under on ticket sales. I'll also bet the under on the Nielsen rating.

(5) Bring license fees into line with economic reality

HBO can deliver quality boxing to its subscribers for less money than you've spent in the past.

Do you recall "HBO: 2008" (the article that I posted on May 28th of last year)?

I thought so. I'm told you held a staff meeting that day and informed the dozen-or-so people in attendance that you were going to find out who the "moles" were and "destroy" them.

"It was a meltdown," one person who was there said afterward. "Ross's eyes were bulging so far out of his head that he looked like Max."

But I digress.

In "HBO: 2008," I referenced HBO's dealings with Ricky Hatton and wrote, "There's something very wrong with the economic model at HBO Sports when the network pays a $2,850,000 license fee for Hatton-Urango and Versus pays roughly five percent of that amount for a double-header pairing Hatton-Lazcano with Malignaggi-N'dou. HBO Sports won't solve its problems with regard to boxing until it learns to allocate its financial resources more intelligently."

So what happened? HBO is continuing to pay oversized license fees and bid against itself with its primary competition being HBO-PPV.

On December 11, 2008, Versus televised two exciting competitive fights: Steve Cunningham against Tomasz Adamek and Joseph Agbeko vs. William Gonzalez. Those fights cost a small fraction of what HBO pays for lesser offerings.

Look at the schedule for *ESPN2 Friday Night Fights* for the first few months of 2009. Some of their bouts shape up as being more exciting and more competitive than fights you gave HBO's subscribers in 2008. And ESPN2 pays as little as $20,000 for some of its shows.

Here's another comparison with ESPN2. On June 21, 2008, *Boxing After Dark* featured Andre Berto in a mismatch against Miguel Angel Rodriguez paired with Chris Arreola vs. Chazz Witherspoon. HBO paid a $900,000 license fee for the show and got a 1.7 rating. By way of comparison, one year earlier, ESPN2 paid $60,000 for a more competitive match-up between Berto and Cosme Rivera plus Witherspoon against Talmadge Griffis. And don't tell me that Chris Arreola was worth the extra $840,000.

HBO has enormous power when it comes to negotiating license fees for fights. And you keep giving in to people who have little or no clout. It's not the end of the world if you lose a particular fight or fighter. HBO Sports survived the loss of Mike Tyson to Showtime. You can survive the loss of Oscar De La Hoya or anyone else. But boxing at HBO won't survive bad fight after bad fight accompanied by ratings that keep going south.

So let me make a suggestion. Construct a chart of all the fights you've televised on *World Championship Boxing* and *Boxing After Dark* during the past three years. Enter the license fee, production and marketing costs, and the rating for each fight. I'd do it for you, but I don't have the production and marketing costs and I'm missing a few license fees.

Once the chart is complete, the first thing you'll realize is that there's often very little correlation between the amount of money you spend on a fight and the rating you get.

Did a lightbulb just go on in your head? That's right. There should be a rational relationship between those numbers. Ratings reflect which fights your subscribers want to see.

Next, cross-index the chart by promoter and fighter. You might also throw Al Haymon into the mix. In other words, are Golden Boy fights giving you more viewers-per-dollar than fights promoted by Top Rank? When an Al Haymon fighter is on HBO, do you get more or less bang for your buck? Which individual fighters bring you the best ratings in terms of dollars spent?

It's a good idea, isn't it?

(6) Forget the heavyweights until a worthwhile fight comes along

One of Seth Abraham's "five pillars" was that HBO should strive to have the heavyweight champion of the world under contract. I know how much you admire Seth. But for the time being, I'd skip that pillar.

The best heavyweights in the world right now are Wladimir and Vitali Klitschko. There is no "champion." HBO has telecast Wladimir's last five fights. The rating for the live telecast of four of those five fights failed to break 2.0 (Klitschko-Austin 1.5; Klitschko-Brewster 1.7; Klitschko-Thompson 1.4; Klitschko-Rahman 1.8).

Wladimir Klitschko vs. Hasim Rahman was HBO's final boxing telecast in 2008. That left quite a taste in everyone's mouth. Wladimir was a 9-to-1 favorite. Lest anyone think that Hasim was committed to winning, he weighed in at 253 pounds. During the bout, Jim Lampley said of Rahman, "He's never been in the fight, not even for a second." Klitschko outlanded Hasim 178 to 30 (40-to-1 over the last two rounds) before the mismatch was stopped.

Stop trying to hammer a square peg into a round hole. Right now, heavyweight boxing isn't very entertaining. And stop shilling for Chris Arreola (managed by Al Haymon) and David Haye (promoted by Golden Boy) as top-flight opponents for the Klitschkos. Haye is a cruiserweight who was knocked out by Carl Thompson. His lone victory as a heavyweight was against a faded Monte Barrett (who was knocked out in two rounds by Cliff Couser). Arreola is an entertaining overweight club fighter, who might someday develop his potential but has never fought (let alone beaten) a world-class fighter.

Arreola against Haye would be a very good HBO fight. Most likely, either Arreola exposes Haye's chin early or he gets outboxed and knocked out himself. Neither guy has earned a fight against Vitali or Wladimir Klitschko or proven yet that he belongs in the ring with either one of them.

(7) Do more to support American fighters.

In recent years, the world sanctioning bodies have outsourced the making of world champions (once American-made) to foreign countries. Now HBO Sports seems to have developed a fascination with things imported.

In 2008, there were 34 fights on *HBO World Championship Boxing* and *Boxing After Dark*. That's 68 slots for fighters. Less than half of those 68 slots were filled by American fighters.

If the price is right, it makes sense to put Ricky Hatton and Joe Calzaghe on HBO. There hasn't been a more compelling British invasion since the Beatles and Rolling Stones. But did we really need to see guys like Robert Steiglitz and Michel Trabant (each of whom fought on HBO in 2008)?

How bad is Michel Trabant? On July 19, 2008, (his first fight after being knocked out by Andre Berto), he lost a unanimous eight-round decision to Roman Seliverstov (a fighter with a 7-and-7 record who had lost seven of his previous nine bouts). Trabant now has one win, two losses, a draw, and one no-contest (he tested positive for steroids) in his last five fights.

If you want to create an environment in the United States in which boxing (and HBO's ratings) can flourish, you should do more to support American fighters. That doesn't mean televising mediocre American fighters and lousy fights. But when the opponent is fungible (as guys like Trabant and Steiglitz are for viewing purposes), there's no reason to not televise an American fighter.

(8) Revamp your announcing teams

Talk with anyone who was a football fan in the 1970s and 1980s. Ask them what's the first thing they think of when they think of *Monday Night Football*. Chances are they'll answer "Howard Cosell."

HBO's "on-air talent" serves as its representative to the boxing community and is essential to branding in the collective mind of subscribers. You've got a problem with your announcing teams on *World Championship Boxing* and *Boxing After Dark*. And you're one of the few people at HBO who doesn't seem to know it.

Deal with it.

(9) Be ever-vigilant to ensure that HBO's journalistic integrity remains intact

HBO is part of Time Warner, whose component parts have a long record of journalistic integrity. HBO has carved a special niche for itself in sports television with regard to the same.

In the past, viewers knew that they could turn to HBO for the unvarnished truth. Whether it was boxing, *Sports of the 20th Century, Costas Now, Inside the NFL, Real Sports,* or any of your other offerings, the line between credibility and hype was clear.

Now that line is blurring.

The four-part *24/7* series promoting the pay-per-view telecast of Oscar De La Hoya vs. Manny Pacquiao is an example of what I'm talking about. The bill for *De La Hoya-Pacquiao: 24/7* was $1,500,000. Golden Boy and Top Rank (the fight's promoters) paid the whole thing. If pay-per-view buys had topped 1,500,000, HBO would have chipped in.

That put HBO in an awkward situation. You don't ask the subjects of *Real Sports* segments to pay production costs. That would put you in a compromising position, wouldn't it?

There were a lot of little problems with *De La Hoya-Pacquiao: 24/7.* I wasn't impressed when Liev Schreiber solemnly intoned, "Freddie Roach has important business to tend to. He needs a haircut." No disrespect to Roach or his stylist; but there are things I'd rather watch than Freddie getting his hair washed and cut.

There were also times when *24/7* gave us false "reality." Steve Kim reported that sound effects were added to the scene showing Manny Pacquiao listening to the heartbeat of his soon-to-be-born daughter because the sonogram didn't work. Bob Arum observed, "They wanted Oscar and Manny to fly to Las Vegas in a helicopter and land on the roof of Treasure Island; like that's a realistic look at what a fighter does before a fight."

But most significantly, *De La Hoya-Pacquiao: 24/7,* while pretending to be sports journalism, was primarily an effort to engender pay-per-view buys and, secondarily, an exercise in image-building for Oscar coupled with a product placement tool for Ring sportswear. The issue of De La Hoya trying to lure Pacquiao away from Top Rank and signing him with Golden Boy by giving him a briefcase filled with $300,000 in cash and the ugly recriminations that followed were never discussed. Why not?

And while we're on the subject of sports journalism; why not do a segment about Al Haymon on *Real Sports?* Here's a guy who comes out of the music business. Articulate, smooth, polished, smart. All of a sudden, he's getting more dates and big paydays on HBO for his fighters than any other manager in the business. That would be great television.

(10) Re-examine your boxing program from top to bottom

"The leadership at HBO Sports today is reactive, not proactive. That's one of the biggest differences between now and the Seth Abraham era."

That's a quote from someone in the industry, who would rather not be identified because he does business with HBO.

HBO Sports has to become proactive again. The best way to start would be to bring someone in from the outside to conduct a full diagnostic study of what needs to be improved with HBO's boxing program, how to implement the necessary changes, and (particularly important in today's economy) where you can save money.

The study can't be conducted from within because those on the inside will simply defend their past decisions.

I'd be glad to conduct the study.

Nah; I didn't think you'd go for that.

Okay; let me throw two more names into the mix.

Seth Abraham built HBO Sports into a colossus and made its boxing program the best in the business. Seth has a small consulting firm with a roster of elite clients. He could do the job.

And if you don't want to go to Seth for advice, how about Jay Larkin? Jay ran Showtime's boxing program for years. He pioneered the network's "great fights, no rights" policy and did your job, Kery Davis's job, Mark Taffet's job, Luis Barragan's job, and Rick Bernstein's job all rolled into one.

(11) A few more thoughts

Let me repeat something that an industry veteran said to me recently: "Ross personalizes everything, and it's not about Ross. It's about HBO and boxing."

I mention that because you've told people that I'm trying to get you fired. That's far-fetched, since I gather your employment contract runs until the end of 2111. Also, I doubt that Bill Nelson and HBO co-presidents Eric Kessler, Harold Akselrad, and Richard Plepler make decisions based on articles that appear on Secondsout.com.

Besides; if my goal was to make life miserable for you, I'd simply give Dan Goossen your home telephone number and suggest he call you five nights a week about putting James Toney on HBO.

I want HBO Sports to be successful. It would be good for boxing, and there are a lot of people I like at HBO.

Where we part ways is in our understanding of what the media is supposed to do. In a free society, its function is to inform. Sometimes that involves praise; sometimes it involves criticism.

In recent years, I've written several articles that were critical of the path you've followed insofar as it relates to boxing at HBO. In researching those articles, I spoke with reliable sources. I respected requests for confidentiality from people who assumed that, if they spoke on the record, they'd be subjected to retaliation. The articles shed light on important issues. In other words, I did my job as a journalist.

You reacted in a manner befitting Lord Voldemort. Quite a few HBO employees were told that, if they were seen talking with me, they were at risk of being fired. Then rational minds prevailed and that edict was reversed. But you did conduct an office computer search in an effort to determine who my sources were.

You might not be aware of it, but morale among some of your troops is low. Search and seizure missions don't help.

Corporate executives have a legitimate interest in keeping confidential information secure. You have every right to tell employees that they shouldn't discuss confidential HBO information with me. But a corporation doesn't have a legitimate interest in regulating the personal lives of its employees unless the personal life embarrasses the corporation (e.g. HBO CEO Chris Albrecht beating up a woman in the parking lot at the MGM Grand). You don't have the right to tell your employees that they're forbidden to socialize with me or punish them if they do.

And the irony is that the most significant quote in any of my articles about HBO didn't come from a confidential source. It was taken from the pages of USA Today at a time when you were planning to replace Larry Merchant with Max Kellerman.

"Larry is still throwing a 95-mph fastball and hitting the corners," the speaker said. "We'd never give him a reduced role."

You remember that quote, don't you? Larry's role has since been reduced (as was contemplated at the time). The speaker was you.

What you should have done after I wrote "Larry Merchant and HBO" was apologize to Larry and Max for putting them in the situation you'd put them in. Then, if you were concerned about "leaks," you could have called a staff meeting and said something along the lines of, "Obviously, I'm doing something wrong because a lot of you feel more comfortable talking with Tom Hauser about problems at HBO that you do talking with me. So let's start fresh. My door is open. If any of you have concerns about the way things are being done, I'm here to listen. We're a team. Let's get the job done right."

Instead, you acted like Mike Tyson on a bad day. As one of your underlings said at the time, "All that's missing is the Maori tattoo."

I'm not always right. I'm one of the guys who thought that Oscar De La Hoya would be too big for Manny Pacquiao. But ask yourself whether the issues I've raised with regard to boxing at HBO are completely without merit; or on reflection, do some of the problems I've referenced actually exist? If you disagree with 90 percent of what I'm writing, implement the 10 percent that you agree with. Then reconsider the rest.

I'm not your biggest critic and I'm far from the most important. The critics who matter are HBO's subscribers, who've stopped watching fights on HBO and are driving ratings to record lows. The problem isn't what I'm writing. The problem is what I'm writing about.

John Duddy is like a magnet. Wherever he goes, people are drawn to him. Some of those people are good. Others raise questions by their conduct.

The Truth about John Duddy

A fighter sacrifices. He tortures his body; he hardens his mind. And all the while, he's surrounded by people, some of whom give him their heart and soul while others view him as prey. Depending on those associations, the business of boxing can be profitable for a fighter or worse than any physical beating that he suffers.

John Duddy is learning that hard lesson now.

Duddy is the most prominent Irish boxer in the world today. He's articulate, handsome, charismatic, and 25-and-0 with 17 knockouts. The WBC lists him as the #3-ranked junior-middleweight in the world. The WBO and IBF place him second and sixth respectively at 160 pounds.

Most of Duddy's fights have been in New York. He has been the headline attraction at Madison Square Garden three times and in the featured undercard bout in the big arena on two occasions. "That means a great deal to me," he says. "There are a lot of fighters out there who are as good as me, but no one has better fans. For a guy from Derry to headline at Madison Square Garden is something special. New York has been very good to me. It's my home for boxing. But at the end of the day, Ireland will always be my home."

Throughout his professional career, Duddy has been guided by two brothers; Eddie and Tony McLoughlin. They used ten different promoters for his first fifteen fights. On the night before St. Patrick's Day 2006, John knocked out Shelby Pudwill in the first round at Madison Square Garden. "Duddy-mania" was in full bloom, and "Clan Duddy" was thought of as one of boxing's "feel good" stories.

Then a bad seed was planted. On April 24, 2006, John signed an exclusive promotional contract with Irish Ropes (a company founded and controlled by Eddie McLoughlin). One day later, he entered into a three-year managerial contract with Tony McLoughlin pursuant to which Tony was to receive 20 percent of John's purses off the top.

It was not in John's best interests to sign those contracts. At that point in his career, many promoters would have given him a substantial signing bonus (which Irish Ropes didn't). Moreover, on many of Duddy's future fights, Irish Ropes wouldn't even perform the nuts-and-bolts promotional work. Rather, they provided John's services to another promoter and took a share of what would otherwise have been a larger purse for John.

And most significantly, Eddie and Tony McLoughlin are brothers with a close personal relationship.

Promoters and managers are in an adversarial position when it comes to negotiating a fighter's purse. The manager's job is to get as much money as he can for his fighter. The promoter tries to give the fighter as little money as possible because, that way, he keeps more for himself.

Dan Birmingham (who knows quite a bit about the business of boxing) has observed, "You have to keep promoters on the end of your jab and watch them on everything."

Tony McLoughlin was less likely to scrutinize, threaten, cajole, and battle with his brother on John's behalf than a fully independent manager would have been.

After the promotional and managerial contracts were signed, Duddy continued his winning ways and his "star power" kept growing. The one concern his team had (and it was a big one) was that he wasn't improving as a fighter as much as they would have liked.

Thus, in June 2007, Harry Keitt (who'd trained John from his fourth through his twentieth pro fights) was replaced by Don Turner. Four fights after that, Turner was replaced by Pat Burns.

Burns made a suggestion that opened a whole new range of possibilities. Duddy had fought as a middleweight for most of his pro career. But very little "drying out" had been necessary to make weight, and the top middleweights are naturally bigger than John. Why not go down to 154 pounds? That way, Duddy would be facing lighter punchers and his own blows would have greater effect.

John concurred. Soon after, opportunity knocked.

On March 27, 2008, Verno Phillips had beaten the odds and won a split-decision over Cory Spinks to capture the IBF 154-pound crown. That left Artie Pelullo (Phillips's promoter) with a champion and a problem. The problem was that Verno, despite his belt, wasn't marketable. And most of the opponents who could sell tickets would be overwhelmingly favored to beat him.

As far as Pelullo was concerned, Duddy was the perfect opponent for his fighter. Phillips-Duddy was a fight for good money that Verno could win.

From John's point of view, the match-up was just as good. Verno was a legitimate world champion who'd won his title honestly in the ring, not by alphabet-soup fiat. But he was a vulnerable champion approaching his thirty-ninth birthday, who'd been beaten on ten occasions and scored only one knockout in the preceding four years. The icing on the cake was that Phillips was willing to defend his title against Duddy in Ireland.

"It's hard to put into words how badly I wanted that fight," John recalls. "I told Eddie, 'Whatever it takes, make the deal.' Eddie said to me, 'Well, it's not enough money and Pelullo wants options.' I said, 'I don't care; make the deal.'"

The deal never got done. Eddie McLoughlin and Irish Ropes matchmaker Jim Borzell say that's because Pelullo refused to give them a dollar number and wanted options on John's future fights. Pelullo says that he offered Irish Ropes a guarantee of $150,000 against 50 percent of the net receipts to make Phillips-Duddy and asked for nothing more than a shared option with Irish Ropes on John's next two fights should Duddy beat Phillips.

Whatever the reason, Eddie McLoughlin didn't seem anxious to make Phillips-Duddy. Pelullo offered to come to New York on two hours notice, anytime day or night, to close the deal. McLoughlin declined to have that meeting. Then Borzell started making calls to members of the media, putting a damper on the notion that the fight might happen.

Phillips-Duddy died. Thereafter, the McLoughlins told John that they'd arranged for him to fight Sam Hill at Roseland Ballroom on November 21, 2008, for a purse of $20,000 and Ronald Hearns at Madison Square Garden on January 17, 2009, for a purse of $75,000.

"That made no sense to me," John remembers. "I was getting less for both of those fights together than I would have gotten for Phillips. Also, I later learned that, when Eddie and Tony made the Hearns fight, they'd agreed to everything that they said was wrong with the Phillips fight, including options. And neither fight was for a world title. It showed me how little control I had over my own destiny with Eddie and Tony, and I began to question other things."

In October 2008, Duddy telephoned Craig Hamilton and asked for advice. Hamilton had carved out a reputation in boxing circles as a key player in guiding Michael Grant to a $3,500,000 payday against Lennox Lewis and seven-figure purses for fights against Lou Savarese and Andrew Golota.

On November 5th, Duddy met with Hamilton and Gary Friedman (who John retained as his attorney). Thereafter, Hamilton and Friedman made some inquiries into the finances surrounding Duddy's fights. Some of the numbers they found were troubling.

Duddy's contract with Irish Ropes specified certain minimum purses that John was to receive during the term of the contract (a $20,000 minimum for fights in the first year; $50,000 for fights in the second year; and $75,000 for fights in the third). Those contractual requirements had sometimes been ignored. For example, for fighting Charles Howe in year three of the contract, Duddy should have received at least $75,000 but was paid only $20,000.

Details regarding Duddy's three fights in Ireland (against Alessio Furlan, Prince Arron, and Howard Eastman) in 2007 were sketchy. John told Hamilton that he'd been paid $60,000 (less Tony McLoughlin's 20 percent managerial fee and certain training expenses) for the Eastman fight. That struck Craig as lower than it should have been, given the risks that Eastman posed and the revenue that Duddy had generated in the past against lesser opponents.

Further with regard to the Eastman fight, New York promoter Bob Duffy (who'd worked with the McLoughlins before) recounted, "Brian Peters promoted John's first two fights in Ireland with Irish Ropes looking on. Then Irish Ropes got licensed to promote over there, and I put together a business plan that showed they could make a $250,000 to $300,000 profit if they promoted Duddy-Eastman themselves in Belfast. I asked Eddie for $12,000 to help run the show. Then Eddie told me that he didn't need me and sold promotional rights for the fight to Brian Peters. I have no idea what Irish Ropes got for providing John's services. But if you think you can make $250,000 to $300,000 for promoting a fight, you'll sell those services for a lot more than $60,000."

Hamilton and Friedman also looked at the finances surrounding Duddy's three most recent fights at Madison Square Garden.

On September 29, 2006, John fought Yory Boy Campas in The Theatre at The Garden. New York State Athletic Commission records show a total attendance of 3,352. Irish Ropes reported that only 2,593 of that was "paid," which means that there were 759 comps. The number of comps seems high. The "gross receipts of ticket sales" reported by Irish Ropes was $264,800. In addition, it reported $25,000 from the sale of television rights. Duddy's purse was $20,000.

Six months later, on St. Patrick's Day Eve 2007, John fought at The Theatre again; this time against Anthony Bonsante. NYSAC records show a total attendance of 4,955. Irish Ropes reported that 4,471 of that was "paid." The "gross receipts of ticket sales" reported by Irish Ropes to the commission was $558,505. In other words, the gross receipts from the sale of tickets for Duddy-Bonsante exceeded the total for Duddy-Campas by $293,705. Yet Duddy received only $20,000 more (a $40,000 purse from which training expenses and Tony McLoughlin's 20 percent managerial fee were deducted). Hamilton calculated that, most likely, Irish Ropes turned a profit of at least $200,000 on Duddy-Bonsante.

Then, on February 23, 2008, John fought Walid Smichet on the undercard of Wladimir Klitschko vs. Sultan Ibragimov in the main arena at Madison Square Garden. Leon Margules of Warriors Boxing (who contracted with Irish Ropes for Duddy's services) says that Irish Ropes received $60,000 plus $200,000 worth of tickets that were reported to the New York State Athletic Commission as having been sold for $190,000 (the other $10,000 in tickets was returned to the promotion). In addition, Irish Ropes was given ten $60 comp tickets and seventy-five $100 comp tickets. Irish Ropes paid $20,000 for Smichet's services out its revenue stream.

Under Duddy's promotional contract with Irish Ropes, if a fight went to purse bid, John was to receive 80 percent of the purse with Irish Ropes getting the other 20 percent. That would have been a fair guideline for the division of revenue from Duddy-Smichet (where K2 Promotions and Warriors Boxing did most of the promotional work). An 80–20 split would have given Duddy approximately $200,000. Instead, he was paid $60,000 minus the usual deductions.

Duddy told Hamilton and Friedman that he'd never been shown a record of the income received by Irish Ropes with regard to any of the cards that he'd fought on. Apparently, other information had also been withheld from him. Promoter Lou DiBella told Hamilton that, before Jermain Taylor fought Kelly Pavlik, DiBella Entertainment had offered Irish Ropes $1,700,000 to provide Duddy's services for a fight against

Taylor. That offer, according to DiBella, was turned down. Duddy said that neither Eddie or Tony McLoughlin had mentioned it to him.

"I guess if you're selling $190,000 worth of tickets on the side," Hamilton observed, "you might not be anxious for your fighter to fight for a world championship under circumstances where the fighter knows how much money is on the table and insists on getting more than you want to give him. So instead, you make deals like the Smichet fight, where John trains, John fights, John gets his eyelids ripped open, Irish Ropes takes in $250,000, and John gets $60,000; but of course, John has to pay $12,000 of that $60,000 to Tony."

The thing that put matters in perspective best for Hamilton was something that Duddy said as they were going over the numbers together. "If I'd gotten my fair share of that money," John noted, "Grainne [his fiancee] and I would be married now."

On November 6, 2008, at Gary Friedman's request, Hamilton and Friedman met with Eddie and Tony McLoughlin and Jim Borzell at the offices of Irish Ropes. The McLoughlins said that, far from exploiting John, they had both incurred losses as a consequence of various extras that they'd given him during the course of their association. Friedman responded that he considered the promotional and managerial contracts void because of various breaches but that, as part of a settlement, John would reimburse the McLoughlins out of future purses for any out-of-pocket losses that they'd suffered. Eddie and Tony said that they'd think about the situation and get back to Friedman with a number.

Two matters (the Sam Hill and Ronald Hearns fights) required immediate attention.

As previously noted, the McLoughlins had arranged for Duddy to fight Sam Hill at Roseland Ballroom on November 21st for a purse of $20,000. The promoter of that fight was Cedric Kushner's Gotham Boxing. It was a small-money bout that made little sense, given the fact that a loss (or even a cut) could jeopardize much bigger pay-days in the near future.

With Eddie McLoughlin's permission, Hamilton spoke with Kushner on November 9th and learned that, in lieu of cash, Gotham Boxing had agreed to give Irish Ropes $35,000 worth of tickets for Duddy-Hill plus a 20 percent commission on all ticket sales over $50,000. Kushner offered to modify the deal so that Duddy would receive $30,000 plus $25,000 in tickets. The promoter would also pay airfare, hotel, and a per diem food allowance for John and Pat Burns.

Duddy wanted to go through with the fight. "I've always lived up to my contracts," he said. "And I need the goal of having a fight in front of me. Right now, I'm in limbo. I don't know if I'm coming or going. The only thing that keeps me straight is that I know I have a fight."

Hamilton advised Kushner accordingly.

The second fight on the table was the proposed January 17th match-up against Ronald Hearns in The Theatre at Madison Square Garden. That fight was to be promoted by Lou DiBella and televised by HBO on *Boxing After Dark*.

The McLoughlins had told Duddy that he'd be paid $75,000 for the Hearns fight. Hamilton learned that Irish Ropes had a deal with DiBella that would give them 100 percent of the Irish television money plus a percentage of all other fight revenue after the deduction of expenses. DiBella estimated that Irish Ropes would receive $300,000 for delivering John's services.

Duddy had never signed a contract for the Hearns fight. Hamilton felt that the McLoughlins had undervalued their fighter in negotiations with DiBella. He also thought that, using Lou's numbers, $75,000 was an absurdly low purse.

"If Irish Ropes takes in $300,000," Hamilton asked rhetorically, "why does John get $75,000 minus Tony McLoughlin's twenty percent? And I see that, if Ronald Hearns beats Duddy, Irish Ropes gets a piece of Hearns. I understand why that might be in Eddie McLoughlin's interest, but how is that in John's interest?"

Then things got ugly. The McLoughlins didn't respond to Gary Friedman's settlement offer. Instead, on November 10th, Tony McLoughlin told the media that John wouldn't be fighting Sam Hill for "unforeseen" reasons and advised fans who'd bought tickets to go to the point of purchase for a full refund. That same day, Kushner called Hamilton and told him that, given Tony's statement, the entire fight card was off.

"It's frustrating for me," Duddy said on hearing the news. "I've been out of the ring for so long. I'd had a good six-week training camp. I was ready to go. And then, without any warning at all, without ever telling me, Tony cancelled the fight."

Hamilton went further, saying, "Tony McLaughlin did here what has been a pattern of behavior throughout his relationship with John. He treated John like a child instead of the intelligent person that he is and went ahead and did something without consulting the fighter. There was no discussion; just cancel the fight. Tony McLoughlin just cost John fifty thousand dollars."

Duddy-Hearns fell apart soon after. Meanwhile, Eddie McLoughlin decided to go public with the dispute and told the media, "I think John was reading his own press clippings. I know that he has people speaking in his ear, telling him that he should be bigger and fighting for more money and that kind of thing. What kills me is all the big things that we had in store for him next year. If he had looked good against Hearns on HBO, it would have probably led to a title shot. But it's not about the money. I'm disappointed that John hasn't even called me to talk about what's bothering him. Because I can tell you that, if he had called, we would have met and worked this out. I'm disappointed that he didn't face me like a man and tell me he was unhappy."

Jim Borzell took things to another level. First, he denigrated Duddy's talent as a fighter ("Considering that John never fought anyone in the top twenty and how high he was rated, I think I did a pretty good job of matchmaking"). Then he questioned Duddy's judgment ("We're all scratching our heads, wondering why he's doing this. This is the worst possible time to pull this nonsense. It's counter-productive to his career. Now he's going to be caught up in litigation, and HBO and Showtime aren't going to want to touch him"). Finally, he attacked John's character ("As far as we were concerned, we were constructing a press personality as much as a fighter. John has an arrogance and nastiness about him that the press and the public never saw.")

In response to those comments, Craig Hamilton declared, "John has more integrity in his little finger than the McLoughlins and Jim Borzell have in their entire bodies put together."

Pat Burns observed, "I've known John for about a year. He's a fine a young man and a person of integrity. Eddie McLoughlin has a lot of charm. He's a guy who, when you start talking to him, the first impression is good. But first impressions can be deceiving. Whether or not Eddie and Tony and Jim Borzell did right by John is in the numbers. And right now, the numbers I'm hearing don't sound good."

Hamilton and Burns have a vested interest in standing by Duddy. They're his current boxing adviser and trainer. Thus, the thoughts of

John's previous two trainers (each of whom was unceremoniously dismissed) are significant.

"John is a good person," says Don Turner. "Outside the ring, there was nothing he ever did other than what I asked of him. As a person, he's one of the better guys that I've trained, and I've trained some great guys."

Harry Keitt has a similar view. "I like John," Keitt says. "I wish everyone in boxing had John's character." Then Keitt adds, "I believe the same thing John does about the money. I'd ask, 'Eddie, where is all the money going?' He'd say expenses this and expenses that. But he would never sit down with me and show me the documented numbers. As John's trainer, the only pay I got was as a percentage of John's purses. So if John got less than he should have gotten, then I got less too. The fans were there to see John; not the McLoughlins. What Eddie and Tony had going with John was the same sort of thing that Don King and Carl King had with fighters. And we all know how that worked out."

The past two months have seen a thicket of legal proceedings involving Duddy and the McLoughlins.

Cedric Kushner and Duddy both filed complaints with the New York State Athletic Commission against Irish Ropes and Tony McLoughlin. After a preliminary fact-finding hearing, the commission issued complaints of its own charging that Irish Ropes and Tony McLoughlin violated state law and engaged in acts "detrimental to boxing." The commission further alleged that Tony McLoughlin "breached the fiduciary duties" he owed to Duddy.

A hearing on the commission complaints is scheduled for February 26, 2009. In each instance, the NYSAC is asking the hearing officer to revoke or suspend the respondent's license and impose "the maximum monetary penalties permitted by law." In the case of Tony McLoughlin, the NYSAC is also asking that the boxer-manager contract be voided.

In addition, Duddy has filed a lawsuit in the United States District Court for the Southern District of New York against Irish Ropes, Eddie McLoughlin, and Tony McLoughlin. The lawsuit alleges that:

(1) Irish Ropes breached its promotional obligations by failing to pay Duddy his contractual minimums for fights such as his June 28, 2008, bout against Charles Howe.

(2) Irish Ropes violated the financial disclosure provisions of the Muhammad Ali Boxing Reform Act, which states, "A promoter shall not be entitled to receive any compensation directly or indirectly in connection

with a boxing match until it provides to the boxer it promotes the amounts of any compensation or consideration that the promoter has contracted to receive from such match." (This is significant because the failure of Irish Ropes to give the required financial information to Duddy left John unable to properly evaluate his worth with regard to each fight going forward.)

(3) Tony McLoughlin breached the fiduciary duty that he owed to Duddy. Here, the complaint states, "Among the obligations that Tony McLoughlin assumed when he became Duddy's manager was the obligation to negotiate against his brother Eddie on Duddy's behalf and, if necessary, to fire his brother in the event Eddie proved unable to live up to the letter of his contractual obligations. Defendant Tony McLoughlin breached his fiduciary obligations to Duddy in numerous respects, including (a) allowing and helping his brother Eddie to distribute hundreds of thousands of dollars of bout tickets without accounting to Duddy; (b) cooperating with his brother Eddie to arrange to pay Duddy bout purses significantly below the minimums stipulated in the promotional agreement; and (c) unilaterally canceling the Sam Hill bout without consulting Duddy."

(4) Tony McLoughlin's relationship with Eddie was such that it violated the "firewall" provision of the Ali Act, which states, "It shall be unlawful for a manager to have a direct or indirect financial interest in the promotion of a boxer or to be employed by or receive compensation or other benefits from a promoter." Among the items that the complaint references in this regard are "cash sales of bout tickets in bars and other establishments outside of the normal box-office channel to Duddy's fans in the Irish-American community." The complaint alleges, "These cash ticket sales were a principal source of revenue for the McLoughlins and Irish Ropes."

Duddy's complaint in the federal lawsuit seeks monetary damages from all three defendants and a judgment that the promotional agreement has been materially breached by Irish Ropes and is thus void and unenforceable. For the time being, the voidance of the boxer-manager contract between Duddy and Tony McLoughlin has been left to the New York State Athletic Commission (as per the requirements of a clause in that contract).

Irish Ropes and Eddie McLoughlin are currently represented by Walter Kane, although Kane has yet to file a notice of appearance as their attorney in the federal proceeding. Tony McLoughlin is represented by Edward Hayes.

In discussing the case, Kane sounds very much like a man who would rather be representing the other side. Walter is a union guy who has stood up for boxers in the past and was one of the co-founders of JAB (the Joint Association of Boxers).

"How do you feel," Kane is asked, "about one brother managing a fighter while the other brother promotes him?"

"I believe it can be troublesome in some situations," Walter answers.

"Is this one of those situations?"

"I can't speculate."

Much of the McLoughlins' defense against Duddy's complaint centers on "extras" that they say they gave John beyond the terms of his contract. More specifically, they point to the fact that they provided him with the use of an apartment and car and gave him cash from time to time.

The apartment was on the ground floor of a two-story row house in Queens (one of New York's five boroughs). Tony was the owner and used the basement as his office. Another tenant lived on the second floor.

The car was a 1998 Dodge that Tony bought second-hand from a garage. Duddy paid for the insurance and upkeep. It was given to John well before the promotional and managerial contracts were signed.

Duddy says that there were times when Tony gave him $250 a week, but adds that the payments were hit and miss ("Originally, he told me they'd be every week, but they weren't").

Hamilton puts the "extras" in perspective when he says, "Even if the not-so-weekly payments and the value of the car and apartment rental are recoverable, which they probably aren't, their total value is less than what Eddie and Tony made on the Smichet fight alone. John owes them zero. And I have a feeling that what we've learned so far about the McLoughlins and their financial dealings with John is only the tip of the iceberg."

As word of Duddy's rift with the McLoughlins spread, Hamilton was contacted by Top Rank, Golden Boy, DiBella Entertainment, Main Events, Star Boxing, Gary Shaw Promotions, and (as Craig puts it) "just about every other promoter with a pulse."

Meanwhile, the McLoughlins seemed to be pursuing a strategy of putting John on ice and keeping him from entering the ring. In that regard, they were inadvertently aided by the New York State Athletic

Commission, which has moved slowly and failed so far to exercise the full range of remedies at its command

For a while, the slow commission pace played havoc with several potential fight cards in New York. Promoters Lou DiBella, Cedric Kushner, and Bob Duffy had put holds on venues in Manhattan for shows to be held in proximity to St. Patrick's Day. Each of them was waiting to see if Duddy would be available to fight on their card.

Irish Ropes put a hold on The Theatre at Madison Square Garden for March 14th, but was denied the right to hold a fight on that date by the NYSAC. Thereafter, David Mossberg (an attorney for the commission) revealed that Irish Ropes's promotional license had expired and its request for a renewal had been denied because of "a deficiency in the application."

On January 13, 2009, Gary Friedman filed a motion on Duddy's behalf in federal court. The motion asked Judge Barbara Jones to grant an injunction prohibiting Irish Ropes from taking any action to interfere with Duddy's participation in any professional boxing match during the pendency of the litigation. To protect Irish Ropes's rights, Friedman offered to put a percentage of John's compensation in escrow pending final resolution of the court action.

Faced with a firm court date, Eddie McLoughlin agreed on January 16th that Duddy could fight anywhere anytime as long as a portion of the profits from his future fights was put in escrow.

"That's fine with us," Hamilton says. "There's no way that John will lose the court case. As far as I'm concerned, the escrow account is a savings account for John. The important thing is that now he can fight. As for Tony, once the New York State Athletic Commission gets through with him, we'll finish off what's left in federal court."

Then, on a pensive note, Hamilton adds. "You know; when I heard that Tony was managing John and Eddie was promoting him, I figured John was getting screwed. That's usually the way those things work. This is a classic case of a promoter and manager working together for their own benefit to the detriment of the fighter. The McLoughlins can promote and manage for the next twenty years. John has only a few years left. Verno Phillips lost his title, so that opportunity is gone for John. Who knows what will come next. The biggest problem with the business of boxing is that bad behavior is rewarded. I'd like to think that, this time, things will be different and everything will work out well for John."

Duddy hopes for a similar resolution. He has learned a hard lesson; to wit, nothing prepares a fighter for the business of boxing except the business of boxing. And he has maintained his dignity through it all.

"Other people have told me about some of the attacks that have been made on me," John says. "It's unnecessary and very petty. There should be a common purpose between a boxer and his manager, and it seems as though that wasn't the case between Tony and myself. The common purpose appears to have been more between Eddie and Tony. This has taught me that, as a fighter, even if you have people you think you can trust, you have to get involved in the financial end of things. Even if you rely on someone else to make certain decisions, you have to see the whole picture and know what they're doing. I'm disappointed with what happened, but I'm lucky to have found out now rather than later. What's done is done. I just want to move on."

"I've tried to put the time I've been out of the ring to good use," Duddy continues. "Not being able to fight has been difficult for me. I'm going to be thirty this year. These are my prime years as a boxer, and I know I can't fight forever. But I've stayed in shape and I've enjoyed being home. Grainne and I don't have a house anymore. We have a home. We just had our first Christmas in our own home. It's ten doors down from her mother and father, so Sunday dinner is easy to handle. Lately, Grainne has had me painting and wallpapering, which means I've been busy in and out of the gym. But it's not the same as fighting. Whoever I fight next, I feel sorry for him. I'm ready to explode."

As a contrast to "Fistic Nuggets," these "Notes" were on the serious side.

Fistic Notes

The epic third battle between Muhammad Ali and Joe Frazier is regarded by many as the greatest fight of all time.

Despite its title, *Thrilla in Manila* (produced and directed by John Dower) is about more than that one fight. It's a look at the greatest rivalry in boxing history through Frazier's eyes. There are glimpses of the Ali who won people's hearts, but not many. The documentary shows a different side of Muhammad and the cruelties that he visited upon Joe, who was (and still is) a good and decent man.

There are several nagging factual errors in *Thrilla in Manila*. And it's frustrating that Dower (who went to great lengths in researching his film) accepted as true the apocryphal story of Ali addressing a Ku Klux Klan rally. But *Thrilla in Manila* puts the final bout in the Ali-Frazier trilogy in the context of the blood feud between the combatants and accords their struggle its rightful place in the world at large.

The climactic fight is presented with all the drama of a feature film and captures the ebb and flow and 110-degree heat that made it seem as though Muhammad and Joe were fighting in hell.

"Normal fighters would not have continued," Jerry Izenberg says on-screen. "This fight could have been stopped six times." Other thoughts come from Frazier confidante Dave Wolf ("Joe was ready to lay his life on the line, and he did"); Ali cornerman Ferdie Pacheco ("The fight became more important than life and death"); and Frazier himself ("We was dead; both of us").

After fourteen rounds, Eddie Futch (Joe's trainer) called a halt to the carnage. Frazier had gone into the battle partially blind in his left eye due to an injury suffered early in his career and his right eye had been closed by Ali's blows. At the very moment that Futch stopped the fight, Muhammad was imploring his own corner to cut his gloves off. No one knows whether either man could have survived a fifteenth round.

The best parts of *Thrilla in Manila* include the scenes of Frazier in the spartan living quarters above the gym that he owned until last year and contemporary interviews with Joe. That footage makes one feel for him. Dower's images of Frazier watching a tape of his third battle against Ali are even more powerful and will linger viewers' minds.

"God marks it down," Frazier said way back when. "God's gonna slap the hell out of him one of these days."

★   ★   ★

Mike Tyson has always been a compelling presence. Many observers of the boxing scene think that, early in his career, he was a great fighter. Others (such as Dave Anderson, who called Tyson "a thug who got lucky") take a contrary view. What's beyond debate is that Tyson, like Muhammad Ali and Joe Louis before him, entered the national psyche. Everyone knew who he was and everyone had an opinion about him.

This year's most ambitious stab at defining Tyson comes from filmmaker James Toback, who crafted a documentary entitled *Tyson* (recently released on DVD). The format features Mike as a talking head interspersed with fight footage, clips of other happenings in his life, and interviews with mentor Cus D'Amato.

As a fighter, Tyson represented a perfect storm. He was a young man with prodigious physical gifts, who came out of a brutal environment wanting to hurt people. The he fell under the spell of a brilliant trainer who could virtually read his mind.

"I started believing in this old man," Tyson says of D'Amato. "He broke me down and rebuilt me. I knew that nobody physically was going to fuck with me again. That would never happen because they knew I'd fucking kill them if they fucked with me. I turned my whole life over to boxing."

The early part of the documentary establishes Tyson as a frighteningly devastating and ferocious fighter. But the seeds of self-destruction were within him and external forces helped them grow.

D'Amato died in 1985, a year before Tyson claimed the WBC portion of the heavyweight crown. Thereafter, hordes of enablers with dollar signs in their eyes looked on as Mike's conduct spiraled out of control. A knockout loss at the hands of Buster Douglas toppled Tyson from his fistic pedestal, but he remained a source of media fascination. Every misdeed and profane public outburst was reported. Then he was imprisoned for a rape that he says he didn't commit. Prison crushed his spirit.

In the ten years after his release from prison, Tyson fought sixteen times. Two of those bouts were declared "no contest." He was disqualified once for biting off part of Evander Holyfield's ear and knocked out four times. His last public act as a fighter was giving the finger to an idiot who threw a paper cup filled with Coca Cola at him as he left the ring after quitting on his stool against journeyman Kevin McBride.

Toback fashions the material at his disposal to create a sympathetic portrait of his subject. He glosses over much of Tyson's anti-social behavior, such as the return to prison in 1999 for assaulting two motorists after a traffic accident. And he repeats Mike's denial that he raped Desiree Washington; a denial voiced often enough and convincingly enough that this writer is inclined to believe that, in Tyson's mind at least, he didn't rape her.

One troubling note is Tyson's claim in the documentary that his early co-managers, Bill Cayton and Jim Jacobs, "were like slavemasters." In truth, Cayton and Jacobs did a brilliant job of advancing Tyson's ring career and maximizing his income.

Don King is referred to in the documentary as "a piece of shit." But there's no indication that Toback questioned Tyson about the role that Shelly Finkel played in managing Mike late in his ring career. Nor did Toback utilize a remarkable series of interviews that Tyson gave to Boxingtalk.com in 2004 in which Mike (fairly or unfairly) voiced anger and frustration about the role that Finkel played in his affairs.

Portions of the documentary consist of self-justifying talk on Tyson's part. At other times, he's open about his flaws. Regardless of who and what Mike is now, the person he once was is branded on his face in the form of an ever-present Maori tattoo that the whole world can see.

When Marvin Hagler and Slick Watts shaved their head, it began a trend that exists to this day. When Michael Jordan opted for a diamond stud in his ear, tens of thousands of young men followed suit. The tattoos adorning the bodies of sports stars are emulated by black and white alike. But facial tattoos haven't caught on. Despite Tyson's celebrity status, it seems that very few people want to be like this Mike.

Near the end of the documentary, Tyson acknowledges having disrespected other people for much of his life and says, "If I have any anger, it's directed at myself. I'm disappointed in myself. I just want to be a decent human being, which I know I can be."

Well and good. Still, at the close of *Tyson,* I couldn't help but think back on the words of Gerald Early, who once wrote, "Tyson is not the sum of his myths; he is the remainder. Myth tries to invest lived experience with greater meanings. But despite the stories that have proliferated around him, Tyson's life can never point to anything larger than itself, his own self-serving actions, his own madness, his own befuddlement and consternation before the revelation of his limitations. Tyson's biggest drama was, and continues to, be with himself for the salvation of himself alone."

★   ★   ★

The past few weeks have seen a stream of tributes to Alexis Arguello, who died of what appears to have been a self-inflicted gunshot wound on July 1, 2009.

Arguello was one of the great fighters of his era. He began boxing professionally in his native Nicaragua at age sixteen and won world championships in three weight divisions. "Bring me the best," he said, "and I will knock them out."

Arguello won 82 fights and defeated the likes of Ruben Olivares, Alfredo Escalera, Ruben Castillo, Ray Mancini, Cornelius Boza-Edwards, and Jose Luis Ramirez.

One man he could not beat was Aaron Pryor. Their 1982 encounter is widely regarded as one of the greatest fights ever. Pryor, at the time, had 31 wins in 31 fights with 29 knockouts. For thirteen rounds, they engaged in brutal, brilliant, stunningly violent combat as Arguello sought to wrest the 140-pound title from the champion's grasp. Then, midway through round fourteen, Pryor landed a blow that shattered Arguello's nose and brought a look of devastation to his eyes. Two dozen unanswered blows followed, sending Arguello unconscious to the canvas.

Ten months later, they fought again. And again, Pryor, indestructible, took everything that Arguello threw at him. In round ten, Alexis had reached his limit. A barrage of punches pinned him against the ropes and he went down.

This time, Arguello was in full command of his senses. He lifted his body to a sitting position and sat on the canvas, elbows resting on upraised knees, gloves crossed in front of him. He made no effort to rise and looked at referee Richard Steele with clear eyes. At the count of ten, he nodded as if to say, "That's right. In the ring, Pryor is the better man."

But what has stayed with me in the twenty-five years since then was the look of abject grief on Arguello's face. There was nothing casual about his surrender.

Even when Alexis Arguello said no mas, he did it with dignity and grace.

★　★　★

Showtime made news on July 13th with the announcement of a super-middleweight tournament called the World Boxing Classic.

Arthur Abraham, Mikkel Kessler, Carl Froch, Jermain Taylor, Andre Ward, and Andre Dirrell will engage in twelve fights. There will be three preliminary rounds, during which each fighter will face three of the other five combatants. Three points will be awarded for each victory by knock-out; two points for each victory by decision; and one point for a draw. After the preliminary rounds, the top four qualifiers will battle for supremacy in an elimination tournament.

The first fights (Taylor-Abraham, Froch-Dirrell, and Kessler-Ward) are slated to be held later this year. The finals are expected to take place in early 2011.

Abraham and Kessler are the tournament co-favorites. Each of them has one hole in his resume; the absence of a win over another elite fighter. The World Boxing Classic can rectify that.

Froch is a big strong guy who can punch. Whether that will be enough against slick boxers (Ward and Dirrell) or other big strong guys who can punch is an open issue.

Taylor has two victories over Bernard Hopkins, but lifestyle and train-ing issues have caused his career to slide downhill since then. The issue is whether he can get his act together in the short time before he faces Abraham.

Ward (who won a gold medal at the 2004 Olympics in Athens) is largely untested in the pros, as is Dirrell.

IBF 168-pound champion Lucian Bute was not invited to participate in the tournament. Many observers think that he would have been a bet-ter sixth man than Dirrell. But Andre is promoted by Gary Shaw (who seems to occupy a special place in the heart of Showtime boxing tsar Ken Hershman).

The composite record of the six tournament fighters is 161-4-1. Take Taylor out of the equation and it's 133–1 (the only loss being Kessler's defeat by decision at the hands of Joe Calzaghe).

A lot can go wrong in twenty months, and that's particularly true in boxing. Fighters get hurt; they retire. It's possible that the tournament will fall apart or not live up to expectations. But Showtime deserves credit for creating a scenario that's expected to bring twelve competitive fights to the boxing public. There are no "soft" fights in the World Boxing Classic. Each bout stands on its own merits.

A word on the place of the world sanctioning bodies in the tournament is also in order.

Carl Froch is the WBC super-middleweight beltholder. The WBC (which is hungry for sanctioning fees) has said that it will suspend its rules regarding mandatory defenses for the duration of the tournament. The WBA is expected to follow suit with regard to its beltholder, Mikkel Kessler, after Kessler makes a pre-tournament mandatory defense against Gusmyl Perdomo. Of course, as the tournament proceeds, each sanctioning body can be expected to dilute its title by introducing "interim champions," "super champions," and the like in exchange for sanctioning fees from other promotions.

Boxing fans should forget about the alphabet-soup titles that are at stake in the tournament. The winner of the World Boxing Classic will be "King of the Hill, A-number-one" in boxing's super-middleweight division. Indeed, if *Ring Magazine* wants its belts to have credibility, it will state now that the winner of the tournament will be its new super-middleweight champion.

Meanwhile, the most important thing about the World Boxing Classic is that Showtime will be televising twelve competitive fights between world-class fighters. Win or lose, each combatant is guaranteed a minimum of three fights. But he'll have to go in tough in each of them. And a real champion will be crowned at the end.

That's the way things should be in boxing. As Allan Scotto wrote recently, "Stop the silly practice of coddling fighters when they lose. You need to build your confidence? Build it in the gym. Stop wasting the precious little airtime boxing gets these days. [The soft-opponent comeback fight] does more to hurt this sport than just about anything else. It's like pitching underhand to Derek Jeter because he struck out and feels bad."

★ ★ ★

A few thoughts on the start of Showtime's "super six" 168-pound championship tournament, which began with a doubleheader on October 17th.

The concept underlying the tournament is laudable. Take six elite fighters and match them in a manner that gives the public twelve competitive fights with a champion emerging at the end. Unfortunately, the losers are becoming damaged goods.

Exhibit number one is Jermain Taylor, who has evolved into one of boxing's sadder stories.

After beating Bernard Hopkins twice, Taylor was the undisputed middleweight champion of the world. His record stood at 25-and-0 and his future was bright. Then he was talked into dumping trainer Pat Burns by enablers with their own wallets in mind. Jermain's lifestyle and training habits deteriorated thereafter. He might have wasted more talent than any fighter since Mike Tyson.

Taylor has lost four of his past five fights and been brutally knocked out three times. The most recent stoppage came at the hands of Arthur Abraham, who knocked Jermain unconscious with six seconds left in their fight. Taylor suffered a severe concussion and was taken to the hospital for overnight observation. His post-fight medical condition dictated that he not fight again.

When Taylor drops out of the tournament, there will be a feeding frenzy to fill the open slot. Whoever replaces Jermain will enter the tournament at a disadvantage because he'll have no points (and thus be tied for fourth place) entering the second round. But he'll be guaranteed two good pay-days and, if he wins both of his fights, will advance to the final four.

The other first-night loser on October 17th was Andre Dirrell, who dropped a decision to Carl Froch.

There were people who praised Dirrell's effort. Showtime commentator Gus Johnson likened him to Roy Jones Jr (which is akin to likening your average roundcard girl to Gisele Bundchen).

I thought that Andre stunk out the joint. He refused to engage for long periods of time and ran for most of the night. One can't say that he played hide-and-seek, because he didn't seek. At one juncture, he was penalized a point for excessive holding.

If a round is even with nothing happening and one guy is running away while the other guy is trying to fight, the round should go to the guy who's trying to fight. Froch won a split decision by scores of 115–112, 115–112, 113–114. He deserved it.

The irony of it all is that Dirrell's skills enabled him to hurt Froch when he threw punches with bad intentions. Too bad he didn't do it more often. He might have won.

★   ★   ★

Four year ago, Jermain Taylor looked like the future of boxing. He was young, handsome, and immensely likeable. He'd beaten Bernard Hopkins twice to become undisputed middleweight champion of the world and was getting better with every fight.

Then things went south. Jermain's most recent loss was a twelfth-round stoppage at the hands of Arthur Abraham in the opening bout of Showtime's "super six" middleweight championship tournament. After the bout, he was hospitalized for treatment of a concussion and short-term memory loss. Reliable sources report that a CT-scan conducted in Germany on the night of the fight showed that Jermain had suffered bleeding in the brain. Two subsequent MRIs in the United States indicated that the injury had healed. At least one doctor has advised Jermain that the "area of concern" in his brain should not be a factor in future fights.

Lou DiBella (Taylor's promoter) refuses to discuss the specifics of Jermain's medical condition. However, on December 11, 2009, when word came that Taylor intended to continue as a participant in the Showtime tournament, DiBella resigned as his promoter and issued a statement that read in part, "It is with a heavy heart, but strong conviction, that I will recuse myself and DiBella Entertainment as Jermain's promoter. It is out of genuine concern for him and his family that I am compelled to make this decision. It is my belief that the continuation of Jermain's career as an active fighter places him at unnecessary risk. I cannot, in conscience, remain involved given my assessment of such risk."

The view here is that Taylor should not continue as an active fighter. Showtime should examine its contracts closely to determine whether, given the circumstances, it has an obligation to televise Jermain's future fights. And the athletic commission in any jurisdiction where Taylor applies for a license to box should scrutinize his medical records.

Because Taylor changed trainers when he did, boxing never saw him at what could have been his best. That's very sad.

There might be sadder consequences if Jermain continues to fight.

★   ★   ★

Television magnifies content. That's particularly true when the content is boxing and the network televising it is HBO.

Over the years, boxing fans have come to rely on HBO's commentators and producers to give them an honest recitation of facts and informed expert opinion. That's why the November 28, 2009, *Boxing After Dark* telecast of the rematch between Lucian Bute and Librado Andrade was particularly troubling.

In the first fight between the two men, Andrade (who was far behind on points) decked Bute at 2:54 of the twelfth round. Nine seconds after he hit the deck, Bute was on his feet. At that point, Lucian had won the fight. There was subsequent confusion due to the fact that the timekeeper correctly waited until referee Marlon Wright finished his count before ringing the bell. And Wright took his time, waving Andrade back to a neutral corner at one juncture in the proceedings before continuing the count. But if the referee hadn't extended his count, the result would have been the same.

Nonetheless, on several occasions during HBO's telecast of the Bute-Andrade rematch, expert analyst Max Kellerman said that Lucian benefitted from a twenty-one-second long count. Worse, HBO showed an edited tape that made it appear as though Bute would have lost the fight but for the twenty-one-second long count. That was misleading.

One can make a tortured argument that Bute wasn't in condition to continue fighting after he rose and thus didn't properly "present" himself to the referee. That argument might hold water if the knockdown had occurred at the end of an earlier round. But this was the final round.

Here, the thoughts of Greg Sirb (former president of the Association of Boxing Commissions and executive director of the Pennsylvania State Athletic Commission) are instructive. Asked about Bute-Andrade I, Sirb says, "I can't recall a referee stopping a fight after the three-minute mark of the final round when a fighter made it to his feet within ten seconds of being knocked down. I suppose you could argue that he has the discretion to do it, but it certainly wouldn't be required of him."

Steve Smoger (one of boxing's "go to" referees for big fights) concurs, saying, "I've never heard of a referee stopping a fight after the three-minute mark of the final round under those circumstances. The fight was over when Bute got to his feet, so his condition would not have played a role in my mind."

And in any event, that wasn't the point of Kellerman's commentary. Max's commentary made it appear as though it was the twenty-one-second count that got Bute to the final bell.

Television is a "now" medium. All commentators make mistakes on the fly. But in this instance, HBO had weeks to analyze round twelve of Bute-Andrade I. Thus, some questions:

Did Max Kellerman and the producers of the Bute-Andrade II lead-in watch a tape of the entire twelfth round of Bute-Andrade I? I hope so. And if they did, why did they superimpose a twenty-one-second time clock over the action without telling viewers that fifteen of those twenty-one seconds came after the three-minute mark?

Somewhere in the process, Kellerman (as HBO's expert analyst) or someone else at HBO should have looked at the lead-in to Bute-Andrade II before it got on the air and said, "Hey, guys; this is wrong."

★   ★   ★

Like most boxing writers, I receive an endless stream of press releases. Recently, one caught my eye. It was for a celebrity boxing event to be held in Pennsylvania on July 24, 2009.

The first co-feature on the card pits "the son of boxing legend Sugar Ray Leonard" against Derik Macintosh (identified as "a guy who has never competed before, but trains on a regular basis in the hope of becoming a boxer").

Leonard, we are told, "is the same kid who was featured in the very famous commercial with his dad for 7-Up."

The release further advises that, in the co-feature, "baseball star Jose Canseco will step into the ring against 5-time World Wing-Eating champion and athlete Bill 'El Wingador' Simmons."

My first thought was, "Why Is the Pennsylvania State Athletic Commission regulating this?"

The answer is worse than that. There's no regulation at all.

Last year, the State of Pennsylvania sought an injunction against Damon Feldman, who was promoting what the state said were professional boxing contests without a license.

A judge denied the request on grounds that, in order to be a "professional" under Pennsylvania law, a fighter must compete for a purse or other prize with a value of more than fifty dollars. The judge ruled that there was no evidence in the record that any of the participants would receive anything of value in excess of fifty dollars.

But wait! Pennsylvania law also outlaws "tough guy" contests, whether or not the participants are professionals.

Here, the judge (who appears to have the brain of a brontosaurus) simply misread the law.

[Note to readers: For those of you who are untutored in dinosaurs, brontosauri were the stupid plant-eating ones].

The judge decreed that, in order for a bout to be categorized as a tough guy competition, the participants must employ multiple combat techniques, not just boxing. But the Pennsylvania statute that outlaws tough guy competitions clearly refers to boxing "OR" other techniques.

As for Damon Feldman; he's a former Philadelphia fighter, who crafted a 9-and-0 record in a four-year career that ended in 1992. His first eight opponents had a composite ledger of 8 wins against 50 losses, while his last opponent had lost 10 of 12 previous fights. Say what you will; Damon got in the ring and answered the bell multiple times.

Feldman promoted his first celebrity boxing event in 2008. He says that he now has fifty "personalities" on his roster and that this will be his tenth show. "My dream," he proclaims, "is to do a fight with Sylvester Stallone."

"I used to promote regular club fights," Feldman says. "I was licensed and everything. I wanted to be the next Russell Peltz, but I had a situation that led to some problems. If I could make money promoting regular fights, I would. But I can't, so I'm doing this."

Feldman maintains that participants in "Celebrity Boxing" don't get paid for their ring efforts and receive only a "personal appearance fee" for coming to the show.

"It's entertainment," he says. "Each fight is three one-minute rounds. Every fighter wears headgear, a mouthpiece, and eighteen-ounce gloves. You have more chance of being injured walking down the street than in one of my fights. There's a standing-eight count. I'm at ringside to make sure that everyone is doing their job. The worst thing we've had so far was a bloody nose."

As for officials; Feldman says that the Celebrity Boxing Federation (which he founded) designates the referees and judges. "The judges are mostly friends of mine," he explains. "The referee can be an actor or a movie star or a local personality. But whoever the referee is, he has to train for three days before the show so he knows what he's doing."

Celebrity Boxing exploits a misguided ruling by a state court in Pennsylvania. It appears as though the judge didn't know anything about boxing and didn't care about boxing. But a judge should be able to understand the law.

Meanwhile, Greg Sirb (executive director of the Pennsylvania State Athletic Commission) says, "The entire commission is very disheartened by this. The judge's decision leaves the door wide open to abuse by Celebrity Boxing and other promoters. It's bad for boxing. And sooner or later, someone will be badly hurt."

★　★　★

Journeyman fighter Michael Murray once observed, "Centuries ago, someone forced men to fight and called it sport."

Arturo Gatti, who died on July 11, 2009, embodied that endeavor in its purest form.

Gatti's career was notable for his refusal to accept the physical constraints that limit other fighters. He gave everything he had in every battle. His face rarely looked the same after combat as it had before. There was no quit in him; no give-up; no fold. He was pure fighter at his core.

Sooner or later, with few exceptions, even the bravest of fighters have the hope and optimism beaten out of them. For Arturo, that time came in 2007 after a knockout loss at the hands of Alfonso Gomez. "Hasta la vista, baby," he said in his dressing room following that fight. "I can't be taking this abuse anymore."

Happy endings are rare in boxing, and Arturo's was particularly sad. He lived his life outside the ring like he fought inside it; fast, dangerously, and hard. As of this writing, it appears as though his untimely death came at his own wife's hand.

So let it be said that Arturo got a fair shake from boxing, and boxing got a fair shake from Arturo. People often talked of the manner in which he fought as comprising a "human highlight reel." But he was more than that. He was loyal to the people who helped build his career. He always had a kind word for young fighters who looked up to him. Now he's gone.

People in boxing understand the loss.

★　★　★

State senator Kevin S. Parker is one of the co-sponsors of a bill currently before the New York State legislature that would legalize mixed martial arts.

On May 8, 2009, Parker was arrested by New York City police officers and charged with assault.

Parker was also arrested in 2005 after police said that he punched a traffic agent in the face. Those charges were dismissed after Parker agreed to enroll in an anger management course.

In 2006, Parker was accused of choking a staff member and smashing her glasses during an altercation in his office. No criminal charges were filed in that incident.

Some people think that Parker should be in jail. Others think that he should be in a UFC Octagon. One place where it appears he should not be is in the New York State legislature. But if he runs for reelection, it wouldn't be surprising if the people who control UFC make a significant financial contribution to his campaign.

★　★　★

The "What Were They Thinking?" Award for October goes jointly to Carlos Ortiz Jr (no relation to the fighter) and Kevin Morgan.

On October 10th, Juan Manuel Lopez and Rogers Mtagwa engaged in a thrilling twelve-round slugfest at Madison Square Garden. Lopez survived and won a unanimous decision. But for the entire twelfth round, he was virtually out on his feet, one good punch away from being knocked out. Mtagwa pursued him with abandon and outlanded him 36 to 9 (all 36 being "power punches"). Yet Ortiz and Morgan scored the round 10–9 for Mtagwa rather than 10–8.

New York State Athletic Commission chairperson Melvina Lathan is a former ring judge. "Scoring that round 10–9 was obviously incorrect," Lathan says. "That was as clear a 10–8 round as you can possibly get without a knockdown. There has been follow-up. I read them the riot act."

She should have. But the selection of better judges and better training for judges before they're assigned to fights would obviate the need for reading the riot act afterwards.

★   ★   ★

A word on Wali Muhammad (formerly known as Walter Youngblood or "Blood"); one of the people who worked behind the scenes in Muhammad Ali's training camp and was in Ali's corner from the first Ali-Frazier fight on.

Last Friday, Wali was at Portobello's (an Italian restaurant at 83 Murray Street in downtown Manhattan). He's eighty-two years old; still trim with a warm smile and sharp mind.

Wali was born in Louisiana. He has lived Harlem for most of his adult life. Sitting in Portobello's near a wall covered with photographs of fighters, he reflected on his journey thus far.

"My grandmother raised me," Wali recalled. "My mother had me at seventeen and then she was gone. When I was three, my grandmother started taking me to the fields. I'd sit on the sack and she dragged me along while she picked cotton. When I was five, I started picking cotton myself. At the end of each day, my grandmother would give me a nickel or a dime. I came north when I was fifteen. I boxed a bit. Then I got cut in a fight and the doctor said, if I fought again, it would endanger my eyesight. And I had a glass chin; that didn't help either. So I stopped boxing."

From 1948 through 1964, Wali was frequently in the employ of Sugar Ray Robinson, watching over his boxing equipment and serving as a personal aide. He was also an assistant minister to Malcolm X at the Nation of Islam mosque in Harlem. And he spent time at Sugar Ray's Café, which was a magnet for the entertainment elite.

"I met Dinah Washington [one of the most popular rhythm and blues singers of that era] at Sugar Ray's," Wali reminisced. "I got to know her quite well. Ella Fitzgerald [widely acknowledged as the greatest jazz vocalist of all time] was another friend. Ella was so sweet; a very nice woman. She gave me a pair of gold cufflinks with a small diamond in each one. I still have them. There were a lot of women. The way it was then; if you had one singer, the rest of them came after you so they could say, 'I had Dinah Washington's man.'"

"I think that, pound-for-pound, Ray Robinson was the best fighter ever." Wali continued. "And I'd have to say that Joe Louis was the best heavyweight I ever saw. Ali was a creative fighter. But Joe Louis was a scientific fighter and he could turn that right hand over so fast on the inside. If Louis could have gotten Ali against the ropes, I think he would have knocked him out."

"Joe Louis was a hero to me. It was sad when Joe got old as a fighter. It was sad when Robinson and Ali got old too, but that's the way things are in boxing. That night against Rocky Marciano, when Joe got knocked through the ropes and Ray got up from his seat and was trying to comfort him; I was sitting right there with Ray."

Wali paused for a moment before going on.

"There's so much to look back on. When Joe was getting on in years, sometimes he'd come up to Ali's training camp. I played golf with Joe Louis up there and beat him. I like to win, but just playing with Joe was special to me."

Wali joined Ali as a security man and camp assistant in 1965, prior to Ali-Liston II. Later, he became a fixture in Ali's corner. In the past, he has spoken about those times.

On Ali-Norton I (when Norton broke Ali's jaw): "During fights, Angelo [Dundee] would take the mouthpiece out, hand it to me, and I'd wash the mouthpiece. Against Norton, each round, I was taking out the mouthpiece and there was more and more blood on it. My bucket with the water and ice in it became red. In every other fight, between rounds, I'd take the mouthpiece out and put it in the bucket and there was just slobber on it. But here, after each round, I had to shake the mouthpiece to get all the blood out of it into the water."

On Ali-Foreman in Zaire: "The plan was to dance for six or seven rounds, tire Foreman out, and when he got tired, move in on him. And instead, Ali was standing in one place, taking punches. A couple of times, I asked Angelo, 'What's happening?' Angelo said, 'I don't know.' Then Foreman started slowing down."

On Ali-Frazier III in Manila: "After the fourteenth round, Ali came back to the corner and told us, 'Cut 'em off.' That's how tired he was. He wanted us to cut his gloves off. Angelo ignored him. He started wiping Ali's face, getting him ready for the fifteenth round. We sponged him down and I gave him a drink of sweetened water, honey and water, from a bottle I'd made up. I don't know if he'd have gone out for the last round or not. Ali's not a quitter; he'd never quit. But I'd never seen him exhausted like that before. Then Eddie Futch called the referee over."

"It's a wonderful feeling, being with a great man like Ali at important moments in his life," Wali said last week. "Zaire was the best. Ali against Larry Holmes was heartbreaking for me. Ali had fast hands, fast feet, and a fast mouth. That's gone now, but I have my memories."

★   ★   ★

Mary Travers (known throughout the world in an earlier tumultuous time as the iconic voice of Peter, Paul, and Mary) died of leukemia on September 16, 2009.

Music was in the lifeblood of the 1960s. The Beatles, Bob Dylan, and others changed the culture we live in. Travers (with Peter Yarrow and Paul Stookey) contributed significantly to that change with anthems like *If I Had a Hammer* and *Blowing in the Wind*.

When I began researching *Muhammad Ali: His Life and Times* in 1989, it seemed appropriate to talk with some of the other icons of "the sixties" regarding Ali's impact on society. Mary Travers was one of the people I spoke with. The thoughts she shared with me follow. They reflect her spirit and are a fitting epitaph for a wonderful woman:

"War and racism are classic problems. If they were simple to resolve, they'd be gone by now. But they're still here; they're as old as man. As we speak, there are thirty-two wars going on, and twenty-eight of them are religious conflicts. Those of us who live in the West and read history books think of religious wars as something that belong in the Middle

Ages, but they're still around. There's the bomb. We have holes in the ozone layer and all the other ecological problems on our incredible shrinking planet. And all any of us can do to help is the best we can until someone else picks up the torch and carries it along."

"Muhammad Ali held the torch high. And given the structure of what surrounded him, his accomplishments were remarkable. If he'd never done anything else with his life, his refusal to go into the United States Army would still have been of monumental importance. He stood for dignity in a culture that afforded precious little dignity to black people. And he was a hero to people who'd never had a hero before."

"To be a hero, you don't have to be the brightest kid on the block. You don't have to be the strongest kid on the block. You don't have to be the most sophisticated kid on the block. What you have to be is able to recognize the profound quality of right and wrong and want to be a constructive member of society."

"Muhammad Ali was a hero. He rejected a value system that oppressed black people, not in the intellectual arena as someone like W. E. B. Du Bois would have done, but by condemning it on moral grounds. He rejected the war, not with political sophistication, but for spiritual reasons that served him well."

"People have a tendency to be pessimistic today. The last decade had many moments of despair. The issues of the future will be issues of survival; national survival, world survival. But human beings are the inventors of hope. It's a universal spirit that runs through the centuries. And hope is cyclical. I think of Pete Seeger's song from the Bible. To everything, there's a season. A time to hope, a time to mourn. You're born and one door opens while another closes. You move from nothingness to being. Then you die and you're wherever you are."

"I think we're at the beginning of another season of hope. I can remember, when I was fifteen years old, reading Jack London and Upton Sinclair and saying to myself, 'I missed it. What an exciting time these people had, forming unions, crusading for important issues. And here I am. Eisenhower is president; Joe McCarthy is making people miserable. There will never be times like the good old days again.' And then the 1960s came along."

"This country needed Muhammad Ali in the 1960s, and I'm grateful for what he did. But the whole world needs people like him now. Being a hero isn't a permanent job. No one makes you sign up for life. But with his spirit and what he represents, he can be a force for good for many years to come."

The voice of Mary Travers will be missed in many ways.

*After the decision in Juan Diaz vs. Paulie Malignaggi was announced,
Malignaggi said, "I hate this shit." So do I.*

Texas Is Shameless

In August 2007, Paulie Malignaggi traveled to Las Vegas as a representative of Everlast at the "Magic" fashion show. Moments after his return flight to New York landed, he was taking his carry-on bag from the overhead luggage bin when another passenger recognized him.

"Hey, Paulie;" the man said. "I love you. You're a great fighter. Don't worry; Someday, you'll win a title."

Problem: Two months earlier, Malignaggi had fought twelve near-perfect rounds against Lovemore N'dou to capture the IBF 140-pound crown. Such is the visibility that attends world championships in boxing these days.

Paulie has struggled since then. He defended his title successfully against Herman Ngoudjo and in a rematch against N'dou, but looked ordinary both times. Then he relinquished the belt to fight Ricky Hatton and performed poorly against the Mancunian, suffering the second loss of his career (the first was at the hands of Miguel Cotto).

After winning a comeback fight against Chris Fernandez, Malignaggi returned to the bright lights to face Juan Diaz on HBO's *Boxing After Dark*. When Diaz-Malignaggi was scheduled, I wrote that Paulie would be going to Houston "to take on Juan Diaz, the referee, and three judges."

Malignaggi had similar concerns. The week before the August 22, 2009, fight, he made more calls to reporters than a robo-call machine in the final days of a heated political campaign.

To get the Diaz fight, Malignaggi agreed to a 138–½ pound weight limit and an eighteen-foot ring (with presumably soft padding). Both of those concessions favored Diaz. But according to Paulie, he'd been promised neutral officials for the fight.

Neutral officials were important. Texas has a reputation for hometown officiating, and Diaz is a hometown hero in Houston. Then Malignaggi learned that the referee for the fight would be Laurence Cole (the son of

Dickie Cole, who is the administrator of combat sports for the Texas Department of Licensing and Regulation). Pouring salt into the wound, the judges would be Gale Van Hoy, David Sutherland, and Raul Caiz Sr.

Van Hoy is from Texas and has a reputation in boxing circles for looking kindly on Texas fighters. Sutherland's designation (he's from neighboring Oklahoma) was also cause for concern. And Malignaggi called Caiz (who is from California) "a gofer for Golden Boy [Diaz's promoter] and a guy who's biased in favor of Mexican-American fighters."

"I understand the risks of going to the other guy's hometown," Malignaggi said. "But they're trying to make it impossible for me to win. They're doing everything to raise Juan's hand before we even fight."

The sad thing is that Paulie was right.

The history of officiating in Texas is troublesome. Laurence Cole went so far over the line in a 2006 bout between Juan Manuel Marquez and Jimrex Jaca that he was suspended for three months and fined $500 after the Association of Boxing Commissions filed a complaint regarding his performance with the Texas Ethics Commission. Prior to that, Micky Ward was deprived of a knockout victory over Jesse James Leija (of Texas) and given a loss via technical decision when the same Mr. Cole incorrectly ruled that a cut suffered by Leija had been caused by a head butt rather than a punch. The deciding vote in Leija-Ward was cast by none other than Gale Van Hoy, who ruled 49–46 in Leija's favor. The "neutral" judge (Duane Ford) had Ward ahead at the time of the stoppage.

When Rocky Juarez (another Texan) fought Chris John earlier this year, it appeared to a lot of people that the referee (Laurence Cole) manhandled John throughout the fight. Adding insult to injury, Juarez was awarded a draw, although most observers thought that John had won. Two of the judges in John-Juarez were Gale Van Hoy and Raul Caiz Sr.

These are just a few examples of the fuel that ignited Malignaggi's concern. Other Texas referees and judges have also raised eyebrows with their performance in high-profile fights.

"Dickie Cole has promised me a fair fight," Malignaggi told Max Kellerman of HBO shortly before he entered the ring to face Diaz. "Texas is not known to have many fair fights."

Kellerman was of a similar view, telling a national television audience, "They have everything stacked for Diaz."

Sutherland gave a preview of his scoring in the first televised bout of the evening, when Danny Jacobs (the fighter favored by Golden Boy) took on Ishe Smith. Jacobs won the fight. Most observers gave him six or seven rounds. Sutherland gave him all ten. At that point, one could have been forgiven for wondering whether Dickie Cole should ask Sutherland if he had the flu or cataracts or some other ailment that was impairing his vision.

Diaz-Malignaggi was a close fight. Cole warned Malignaggi several times for pushing off with his forearm, but seemed unconcerned with the low blows that Diaz threw throughout the bout. Malignaggi had a 191-to-178 edge in punches landed.

This observer scored the bout even at 114–114. Harold Lederman (HBO's "unofficial judge at ringside") had Malignaggi ahead 115–113. A poll of viewers conducted by Fightnews.com showed that roughly 60 percent of the respondents thought Paulie had won, while the remaining 40 percent were evenly divided between those who thought that Diaz had won and those who believed that the decision "could have gone either way."

Then the judges had their say. Caiz scored the fight 115–113 for Diaz. Sutherland was clearly off the mark with a 116–112 card in favor of the hometown fighter. That left Van Hoy, who scored the bout 118–110 for the hometown boy made good, Juan Diaz.

Van Hoy's score was a disgrace. "What fight was that man watching," HBO blow-by-blow commentator Bob Papa asked rhetorically. "118–110 is inexplicable."

"That was terrible," Lennox Lewis concluded.

"There's no excuse for a fighter not getting a fair shake," Kellerman added. "The marketplace spoke tonight."

The officiating in high profile fights in Texas is starting to look like the officiating in professional wrestling.

The National Football League doesn't allow hometown officiating when teams travel to the Lone Star State to play the Dallas Cowboys and Houston Texans. Major League Baseball doesn't have a separate set of standards for umpires who work home games involving the Texas Rangers and Houston Astros.

Too often, boxing countenances (and even encourages) favoritism toward hometown fighters. That's one of the reasons why the sweet science is losing the respect of the American public.

HBO, by virtue of its checkbook, is the closest thing that boxing has to an effective governing body. If HBO cares about the integrity of the fights that it televises, it will issue the following statement:

"Boxing is a great sport. A good fight is wonderful entertainment. However, it's an unsatisfying viewing experience for our subscribers when they see one thing unfold on the television screen in front of them and then the officials rule to the contrary. For that reason, HBO will no longer televise fights from jurisdictions in which we believe that fighters are not treated equally and fairly."

Things would change in a hurry if HBO took that position. Money talks.

Boxing has the greatest literary history of any sport.

Notes from the Literary Front

The thesis advanced by Mike Silver in *The Arc of Boxing* (McFarland & Company) is that boxing is a lost art and today's fighters are vastly inferior to those who plied their trade during "The Golden Age of Boxing" (which Silver identifies as spanning the years 1925 through 1955).

In the 1920s and 1930s, there were ten to twelve thousand boxers licensed at any given time in the United States. By the 1950s, that number had been cut in half. In 2006, it was 2,850.

In 2006, there were 906 fight cards in the United States, Canada, and Puerto Rico. In 1927, there were that many fight cards in New York State alone.

The gravamen of Silver's complaint is that today's fighters don't know how to fight because they don't fight often enough or against tough enough opposition to learn their craft. "Professional boxing," he writes, "has lost the grueling apprenticeship that for so many years was the foundation for the development and refinement of the boxer's art and character. No matter how much natural talent a fighter may bring to the table today, the current working environment does little to affect the realization of his full potential."

Some of Silver's complaints as they relate to boxing today are valid. He's right in bemoaning the multiple champions that exist in each weight division. Between 1925 and 1955, 173 boxers were recognized as world champions in the traditional eight weight classes. Now there are 76 "championship" slots courtesy of the WBC, WBA, IBF, and WBO in any given year.

Silver is also on solid ground in criticizing the fact that a fighter today can become a contender or even a champion without ever facing a world-class opponent. "You have guys today," he quotes Teddy Atlas as saying, "who are navigated and managed to positions instead of being developed to positions. They're not put in with fighters that are going to make them better fighters. They're consistently matched with inferior opponents. They're navigated around guys in order to get to one of these manipulated title belts on television."

Similarly, Bill Goodman (a cornerman licensed by the New York State Athletic Commission in the 1950s and '60s) declares, "The worst thing they did to boxing over the past twenty-five or thirty years was the way promoters, managers, and television magnified the cost of defeat. A fighter has to have an undefeated record or he's nothing. God forbid he should lose a fight. They might as well take him out and shoot him. This is what put the tailspin in boxing. They can't make proper matches because nobody wants to take a chance. They're all afraid of losing. One guy has a fighter he wants to move and another guy has a fighter he wants to move, but they don't want to fight each other. They'll turn the match down and get a fight with some stumblebum so they can get another win. That doesn't do any good for boxing."

Silver has a deep appreciation of the sweet science. At his best, he recounts a conversation between Benny Leonard and Ray Arcel. When the legendary trainer asked the lightweight great why he studied four-round preliminary fighters in the gym, Leonard replied, "You can never tell when one of those kids might do something by accident that I can use."

But *The Arc of Boxing* is flawed. Much of the book is devoted to long quotes from members of a "panel of experts" that Silver has put together. Some panel members are true experts. Others have suspect credentials. Their unifying attribute appears to be that they agree with the author's thesis. Ultimately, the book devolves into one long bitch about how nothing in boxing is any good anymore and hasn't been since 1955.

Expert Ted Lidsky (identified as a former amateur boxer, who was mentored by trainer Vic Zimet) proclaims, "I rarely watch fights anymore. I can't watch an entire fight. It's kind of depressing. If you watch a fight nowadays as a fan, if you can sit through an entire fight, you don't know boxing."

Mike Capriano Jr (head coach for the Camp Lejeune Marine Corps boxing team in the 1950s) opines that Roberto Duran is "overrated" and "not a top-ten all-time lightweight." Capriano then advises readers, "I love 190 pounds on a heavyweight. Who punches harder than Marciano at 190 pounds? Tami Mauriello at 190 pounds would go out and find Lennox Lewis's chin."

Right! If they ever figure out a way for Tami Mauriello to fight Lennox Lewis, I'm betting on Lennox.

Capriano also asserts, "I have no doubt that Tommy Loughran at 185 pounds could outpoint Mike Tyson."

I'll put my money on the young Tyson (and the under) in that one.

I should also note that Capriano ridicules Antonio Tarver, saying, "He really doesn't throw a left jab. He kind of sticks it out there, paws it out there."

I'm not a big Tarver fan. But if Capriano had watched more tape before forming his expert opinion, he might have discovered that Tarver is a southpaw, who jabs with his right hand.

Silver makes a good case for the proposition that the talent in boxing isn't as deep as it once was. But he tends to overlook the influx of skilled fighters from around the world today (for example, Manny Pacquiao and Juan Manuel Marquez). And at times, his "panel of experts" sounds like a pedantic Greek chorus of woe.

Rollie Hackmer (a former amateur boxer and trainer) labels Bernard Hopkins a fighter with "average boxing skill" and says that Bernard would have been nothing more than a "good journeyman" in years past.

Tony Arnold (a former fighter identified as an "archivist for one of boxing's largest film libraries") calls Hopkins "a glorified club fighter" and adds, "Fifty or sixty years ago, maybe he would have been a main event fighter in the small clubs."

"The problem," Arnold advises readers, "is the reporters don't know the difference between a third-rate club fighter and an outstanding boxer."

Count me as part of the problem. I think that Hopkins (like many fighters of the past fifty years) would have been competitive with the best in any era.

★   ★   ★

The Last Great Fight by Joe Layden details what many consider the greatest upset in boxing history; Mike Tyson's 1990 defeat at the hands of James "Buster" Douglas. The book's title is misguided. There have been other "great" fights since then. But Tyson-Douglas stands on its own as a watershed moment in boxing history and the fulcrum on which Tyson's career turned.

Prior to the fight, Layden notes, the world expected Tyson's "decon-struction of another overmatched and frightened challenger." But for one night of remarkable achievement, Douglas was the best heavyweight in the world

The early chapters of the book alternate between Tyson and Douglas. Layden summarizes Mike's early years nicely. But that material is old news unless one has arrived recently from another planet.

The early chapters on Douglas are more compelling.

"Despite his imposing physical presence," Layden writes, "Douglas is genial to the point of being disarming. There is nothing in his demeanor that suggests the hardness required of a boxer. Boxing held some appeal to him as a sport. But whatever it was that drove men like [his father and former fighter] Bill Douglas, whatever anger or animalistic instinct carried them through the battle; that was lacking in James. Though physically gifted and charming enough to talk a good game, Douglas remained ambivalent about boxing. J. D. McCauley [Douglas's co-trainer] often accompanied Douglas on training runs that became walks. When he'd grow tired of his nephew's complaining, he'd give Buster a shove in the back and exhort him to be stronger. Sometimes Buster would resume jog-ging; sometimes he wouldn't."

However, unlike most of Tyson's opponents, Douglas looked at the champion and saw, not a perfect fighting machine but a bully who could be beaten. "Most of the guys who fought Tyson lost before they got into the ring," John Russell (Douglas's other co-trainer) told Layden. "They were scared to death of the guy. He had a mystique about him. But James had no fear in him; none whatsoever. And believe me; I was looking for it."

Layden paints a compelling portrait of Douglas overcoming the fear that paralyzed so many of Tyson's opponents. And he gives readers insight into the relationship between Buster and his father, as well as the infight-ing among manager John Johnson, McCauley, and Russell.

In the end, Douglas trained seriously and fought bravely pursuant to a fight plan that was flawlessly executed except for one moment of near-fatal carelessness in round eight. Tyson, by contrast, had already begun to slip, did not take Douglas seriously, and did not train properly for the fight.

The fight itself is retold in particularly dramatic fashion. "Douglas beat Tyson in every way imaginable," Layden writes. "He appeared to gain confidence as the fight wore on, while Tyson, in a display of progressive vulnerability that would come to typify the latter stages of his career, became frustrated and ineffective."

Adding to Tyson's woes was the fact that, in Layden's words, "Tyson's support team was incompetent." As Teddy Atlas later noted, "Having Aaron Snowell and Jay Bright train Tyson was like wearing plastic thongs under an Armani suit. Those two guys couldn't train a fish to swim."

"The corner was pathetic," Jim Lampley, who was at ringside, told Layden. "You wouldn't have considered, for example, that they would come into the ring without an Enswell; without any cut material whatsoever. At that level of the sport, it's just not possible. It's like a baseball team coming onto the field without their gloves."

Layden does exceptionally good work in recounting Tyson's knockdown of Douglas in round eight. "As [referee Octavio] Meyran pried the fighters out of a clinch," he writes, "Douglas took a long look at the champion, battered and bruised, before uncoiling a big lazy left. Not a jab, really; more like a hook, but delivered with no sense of purpose. 'That was the only time I started to take notice of what I was doing,' Douglas remembered. 'I was like, damn, I'm cooking, baby. I was admiring my work, taking time to reflect. And then WHAM.'"

Douglas was on the canvas for fourteen seconds. "The count was long," Layden acknowledges. "That much is indisputable. But Douglas bore no accountability for that. He rose before the count of ten, which was all that was required of him. By all indications, he was clearheaded [listening to Meyran's count] and able to continue fighting well before he actually decided to stand up."

That said, Douglas cut things dangerously close. And the "long count" led to arrogant maneuvering by promoter Don King, (WBC president) Jose Sulaiman, and (WBA president) Gilberto Mendoza in a failed coup attempt that delayed formal recognition of Douglas's victory for two days.

Layden breaks new ground in reporting on this maneuvering. While researching his book, he spoke with Meyran who claimed that, before the fight, Sulaiman told him, "Be hard with Douglas, and be nice to Tyson."

"But I'm a professional," Meyran told Layden. "I said, 'I'm not going to do anything not legal.'"

Layden also notes that, when Douglas knocked Tyson down in round ten, Meyran treated that knockdown the same way he'd handled the earlier one; picking up the count late and starting at "one," thereby allowing fourteen seconds to elapse. The difference was that Tyson, unlike Douglas, couldn't beat the count.

In the late chapters, *The Last Great Fight* follows Douglas through the loss of his title to Evander Holyfield; his descent into obesity coupled with a near-fatal diabetic coma; and a pathetic comeback attempt that took him nowhere. In the final analysis, he was, in Larry Merchant's words, "a guy who just didn't have the desire to go as far as his talent could take him."

As for the memories that Douglas carries with him; Layden writes, "He appears neither perturbed nor overly impressed by the fact that his life will be forever defined by and measured against that single event."

"I had my moment," Douglas says. "It was a beautiful thing. Now I've moved on."

Tyson has also moved on. Layden recounts his sad decline. But one of the saddest things about Tyson's life is that all the craziness and the long drawn-out end of his ring career have obscured how good a fighter he was when he was young.

★   ★   ★

No Ordinary Joe (published by Century Books) is Joe Calzaghe's autobiography, written with Brian Doogan of the *Sunday Times*.

When an author embarks upon this type of literary venture, his editorial freedom is restricted. Thus, while Doogan has fashioned a name for himself as one of the better boxing writers in the business, *No Ordinary Joe* is the world as seen only through Calzaghe's eyes.

Still, Joe is an appealing sort. And the book (which was written before his victories over Mikkel Kessler, Bernard Hopkins, and Roy Jones) contains some interesting nuggets in his voice. Some of my favorites are:

- "I understand that in boxing the purpose is to do damage. But I can only speak for myself and say honestly that I have never wanted to seriously hurt an opponent. I'm not violent. It's just the nature of what I do. I know the argument about intent. But I'm a fighter and I can tell you what's in my mind. I have never set foot in a ring with the express intention of inflicting serious harm on my opponent."
- "It's entertaining to watch two fighters pummeling away at one another like Marvin Hagler and Tommy Hearns did in the car park at

the back of Caesars. But I don't crave to be involved in that kind of fight. When I get in the ring, I just want to beat the man in front of me and come out unscathed myself. I have no desire to come out pissing blood just so I can say that I fought in a war."

• "I'm not into being a superstar. I'm just a champion fighter. When I'm in the ring, my mind is clear and I feel more alive than I do anywhere else. The reason I fight is simple. I like to win."

• "Being a fighter is all about going against logic, going against the natural human instinct to run away from the fire."

• "Boxing is like geometry, measuring angles and space and calculating where to position yourself so that you can strike your opponent and make him miss."

• "In boxing, you need to be calm under pressure. But you also need immense heart because, one day, being able to dig deep will be your only way out."

★   ★   ★

The Lion and the Eagle by Iain Manson (SportsBooks Ltd) recounts the lives of English champion Tom Sayers and his American challenger, John Heenan, and their convergence in Farnsborough County west of London on April 17, 1860.

"All present-day pugilism," Manson writes, "is directly descended from the early English prize ring." Sayers versus Heenan marked the height of boxing in that era.

Manson leaves no stone unturned. He sets the scene on both sides of the Atlantic, where, in his words, "People were gripped by the unfolding drama as they might be by the serialized installments of a Dickens novel." In reconstructing the life of each fighter, he gives readers a full sense of time and place.

The fight itself ended in chaos without a winner being declared. By the thirty-seventh round, Heenan was fighting blind in one eye with the other eye rapidly closing, while Sayers was barely able to defend himself. At that point, the ropes were cut on one side of the ring, either to save Sayers from defeat or (if the alternative view is accepted) to save him from being strangled to death by Heenan, who was pressing the Englishman's neck against the top strand and pushing against his head with all his weight.

Manson is a good historian and a good writer. *The Lion and the Eagle* is an excellent book.

★   ★   ★

One Ring Circus (published by Schnaffer Press) is a collection of articles about the sweet science written by Katherine Dunn. All of the pieces have been previously published; the best three as part of the text of a 2005 coffee-table photo book entitled *Shadow Boxers*.

Dunn is at her best when she's writing about gritty gyms and the essence of boxing. When she turns her pen to elite champions and big fights in Las Vegas, she loses her edge. I suspect that's because she feels more at home at club fights than in glitzy hotel-casinos and has more emphathy for club fighters than superstars.

The bottom line is that Dunn writes well and writes well about boxing. Among the thoughts she offers in *One Ring Circus* are:

• "Each gym is a one-room schoolhouse. As in any other school, what counts is the teacher. Students come on their own time, after school or work. There's no extra credit, no activity bus to get them home afterwards, no college scholarship to reach for. A few have dreams of stardom; a world championship, big bucks. Most just want to hold their own on the playground or earn the respect of their family, their pals, or their mirror. They are drawn first to the toughness, wanting strength and skill to defend against the outside world."

• "It's a crapshoot for a novice walking into a gym for the first time. You want to learn to box; you need a coach to teach you. But not all coaches are created equal. An experienced fighter in a new town knows how to call around and find out who to work with. But a greenhorn rarely has a specific coach in mind. They choose a gym because they pass it on their way to work or school, or they find it in the phone book. They assume that any coach will do. Once a kid talks to a coach, he's linked to him, belongs to him. The coaches are rivals, possessive of their fighters. None of the other coaches will even pass the time of day with the kid for fear of being accused of 'buzzing' another coach's fighter; the fistic equivalent of cattle rustling. They would sooner fry than tell a kid he's accidentally picked an idiot instead of a real coach and thereby, in the first thirty seconds of his boxing career, doomed himself to failure."

• "The gym is home. For many, it's the safest place they know. A boxing gym is a place where men are allowed to be kind to one another."

★   ★   ★

Tom Cushman is known in boxing circles for his work as a reporter
with the *Philadelphia Daily News* (1966–1982) and *San Diego Tribune* (1982–
1992). *Muhammad Ali and the Greatest Heavyweight Generation* (Southeast
Missouri State University Press) is the short version of his contribution to
the literature of boxing.

The book is a collection of essays about the elite heavyweights from
Sonny Liston through Lennox Lewis with a few detours to lesser-known
Philadelphia fighters and the mob thrown in.

Cushman is a good writer. His work flows nicely from one segment
to the next. There are a few nagging factual errors, but the book is treasure
trove of personal reminiscences and anecdotes woven into context.

Cushman references Ali as, "The most prominent athlete on earth"
and "one of the great competitors of the twentieth century."

"While his meteor was ablaze," the author writes, "Muhammad Ali
defeated the four most devastating punchers of his era. Sonny Liston, Joe
Frazier, George Foreman, and Earnie Shavers, in fact, would more than
share that distinction with heavyweights of any generation."

Cushman also observes that the "defining comment" heard from
many of Ali's opponents was, "I can't believe the shots he took."

"Roll the film back to George Foreman in Africa, Joe Frazier in
Manila, to Ken Norton, Earnie Shavers, Leon Spinks, Larry Holmes,"
Cushman notes. "Those men said the same thing. Ali absorbed the type
of punishment that eventually would add to all the superlatives describing
a glittering career, the word 'tragic.' The chin that had served him so well
during the championship years eventually became his enemy, keeping him
upright when he was virtually defenseless."

Cushman's gift for metaphor is apparent in his description of Joe
Frazier as "straight ahead as a properly plowed vegetable row in one of the
fields he worked as a child."

There's poignancy in George Foreman recalling a moment after his
gold-medal performance at the 1968 Olympics. "I'd been on a local television show, and they were driving me home in a limousine" Foreman
told Cushman. "I was embarrassed for them to see where I lived. I asked to
be dropped off on a street corner several blocks away, but they wouldn't.
When they saw the house, they were more embarrassed than I was."

There's a chilling segment on the murder of Philadelphia junior-
lightweight Tyrone Everett and an entertaining remembrance of Don

King's first press conference at Madison Square Garden. "King's haircut," Cushman writes, "eventually would place the entire industry in his shade."

For humor, there's Larry Holmes (a junior-high-school dropout) saying, "I'm not the smartest guy. If I fought like I read, I'd be in trouble."

Cushman is hard on the heavyweights of the post-Ali era. Evander Holyfield is described as "a muscled-up light-heavyweight." Lennox Lewis is "a pepper-spraying pacifist."

As for Mike Tyson, Cushman writes, "Muhammad Ali, Joe Frazier, George Foreman, Larry Holmes, champions all; each brought a touch of nobility to a hard, sometimes sordid, sport. There was nothing noble about Tyson. His passage through the sport will be remembered as a parade of public embarrassments."

Those who read Cushman's book will be reminded that there was a time when fight fans didn't have to say "undisputed" before "champion" for that designation to connote the best in the world.

If Manny Pacquiao had lost to Miguel Cotto, he still would have merited serious consideration as boxing's "Fighter of the Decade." Beating Cotto sealed the deal.

Fighter of the Decade

Purists maintain that the current decade will run until December 31, 2010. Conventional wisdom holds otherwise. The Roaring Twenties encompassed the years 1920 through 1929. Popular culture dictates that The Sixties were over when 1970 began. The new millennium was celebrated as 1999 came to an end.

As the '00s draw to a close, it's time to determine who deserves recognition as "Fighter of the Decade." Four men merit consideration.

Bernard Hopkins was an unlikely candidate as the decade began. On January 15, 2000, he turned thirty-five years old. He was the IBF middleweight champion with a record of 36 wins, 2 losses, and one draw. How much longer could he go on?

A lot longer.

In the decade that followed, Hopkins fought seventeen times. On fourteen of those occasions, he emerged victorious. His biggest victories were against Felix Trinidad, Oscar De La Hoya, Antonio Tarver, Winky Wright, and Kelly Pavlik. Those aren't just names. They're challenges. He lost close decisions to Jermain Taylor on two occasions and was beaten by Joe Calzaghe.

"Bernard Hopkins," Donald Turner says, "does everything the way it should be done, in and out of the ring. Outside of his age, the only problem he has is that he's not the bravest fighter in the world. Being too brave is foolish. Not being brave enough can cost you, like it did with Hopkins against Taylor."

Meanwhile, Hopkins proclaims, "Did you ever notice, when guys fight Bernard Hopkins, they always say afterward, 'I wasn't myself in the ring tonight.' Like I don't have anything to do with it. It's like a baseball player who goes 0-for-4 and strikes out four times. Do you think maybe the pitcher had something to do with that?"

Hopkins will turn forty-five on January 15, 2010. He's the best over-forty fighter ever. "It's not about what you did yesterday," Bernard says. "You got to go into every fight with the attitude, 'My legacy starts tonight.'"

Joe Calzaghe entered the decade with a 27-and-0 mark and the WBO super-middleweight belt firmly in hand. In late 2008, at age thirty-six, he retired as an active fighter with an unblemished record of 46 wins and 32 knockouts in 46 fights.

Throughout his career, Calzaghe showed physical skills, heart, and the ability to make all necessary adjustments during a fight. He beat some good fighters (e.g. Chris Eubank, Jeff Lacy, Sakio Bika, and Mikkel Kessler) who weren't great. And he beat a once-great fighter (Roy Jones), who was well past his prime. His most impressive victory came against Hopkins.

After Calzaghe defeated Jones, Hugh McIlvanney wrote, "How can we do suitable honour to the wonderful boxing career of Joe Calzaghe while paying a decent minimum of respect to that battered old punchbag historical perspective? We could start by admitting that what was fever-ishly hailed as a triumph over a legend in Madison Square Garden looked rather more like the vandalizing of a relic. Roy Jones Jr went to the ring in New York with his once-beautiful talent blatantly burnt out. Calzaghe's only two assignments in America have confronted him with men whose aggregate age is eighty-two. The years have piled up for him too, but his undamaged looks and physical freshness testify to the benefits of having spared himself the frequent commitment to wars that has been the norm for Jones, Hopkins, and their kind."

Calzaghe doesn't pay much attention to pound-for-pound rankings and the like. He calls them "a mythical load of crap." Still, in gauging his greatness, one must question whether Joe had the inquisitors that a fighter needs to be regarded as "Fighter of the Decade."

Floyd Mayweather Jr started the millennium with 22 wins in 22 fights and the WBC 130-pound championship belt around his waist. Over the next ten years, he had eighteen fights and won all of them. In the process, he captured titles at weights as high as 147 pounds and scored notable victories over Diego Corrales, Jose Luis Castillo (twice), Zab Judah, Oscar De La Hoya, Ricky Hatton, and Juan Manuel Marquez.

Mayweather's public persona ("Money Mayweather") is a self-cre-ation. Give him credit for good marketing on that. And he has the respect of his peers. Zab Judah once remarked, "Floyd comes into every fight physically and mentally at one hundred percent."

Some observers of the boxing scene complain that Floyd runs more than he fights. But Bernard Hopkins rebuts that notion, saying, "Floyd don't run from nobody. I've seen Floyd counterpunch; I've seen Floyd move; I've seen Floyd use his speed, use his quickness. But I've never seen Floyd run."

And Mayweather himself notes, "Boxing is a beautiful sport. Boxing is art. The last time I looked, the sport was called 'boxing,' not 'toe-to-toe.'"

Still, there's a chink in Floyd's armor. His biggest wins were against smaller men moving up out of their weight class (Hatton and Marquez) and a split decision victory over a fast-fading Oscar De La Hoya. For much of the decade, he ducked the tough fights. He avoided Shane Mosley, Paul Williams, Antonio Margarito, and Miguel Cotto.

That brings us to Manny Pacquiao.

On January 1, 2000, Manny Pacquiao was twenty-one years old and virtually unknown outside of his native Philippines. During the course of the past decade, he has fought twenty-six times and become the most famous fighter in the world. His opponents in that ten-year span included Erik Morales (three times), Marco Antonio Barrera (twice), Juan Manuel Marquez (twice), Oscar De La Hoya, Ricky Hatton, and Miguel Cotto. In ten fights against these six Hall-of-Fame-caliber opponents, Pacquiao amassed eight wins against one loss and a draw.

Moreover, unlike Hopkins and Mayweather (both of whom fought many of their biggest fights against smaller men), Pacquiao has consistently challenged naturally bigger fighters. He has hurdled every major obstacle in his weight class and then some.

Unlike Mayweather and Calzaghe, Pacquiao has a less-than-perfect record for the decade. But when a fighter fights the best again and again, sometimes he loses. When Sugar Ray Robinson was young and great, he lost to Jake LaMotta. Muhammad Ali lost to Joe Frazier and Ken Norton before he got old

History judges elite fighters in large measure by their record against other elite fighters and how they perform in their most difficult challenges.

Mayweather has talked the talk. Pacquiao has walked the walk. And Manny has out-of-ring intangibles as well. In that regard, he's similar to Muhammad Ali: a great fighter, a good person, and an important symbol for his people.

"I'm just doing my job to be a good fighter," Pacquiao said after beating Miguel Cotto earlier this year.

He's doing more than that. Manny Pacquiao deserves recognition as "Fighter of the Decade."

Boxing fans today are dependent upon the Internet for in-depth informa-
tion about the sport; and in some instances, for any information at all.

The *New York Times* and Boxing

There was a time when big fights were chronicled in the *New York Times* with banner headlines in large type that stretched across the front page.

Those days are long gone. Newspapers across the country are abandoning the sweet science. Like the sport itself, writing about boxing is fading from view. But the *Times* is America's newspaper of record. Being slighted by the fabled "gray lady of journalism" cuts particularly deep.

"The *Times* is important," says publicist Fred Sternburg. "It's still the *New York Times*. If a million people buy a fight on pay-per-view, you'd think that some of the paper's readers would want to know what's going on in boxing. But you don't get that in the *Times* anymore. The *Wall Street Journal* covers boxing in greater depth now than the *Times.*"

"Do we want to be in the *New York Times?*" Lee Samuels (director of publicity for Top Rank) asks rhetorically. "Of course, we do. Coverage in the *Times* is contagious. It really gets the word out there. We make phone calls. We send them advisories on everything we do. They're always welcome at ringside. But except for the occasional big fight, we don't get any coverage at all. It hasn't been for lack of trying."

"Several years ago, we had a heavyweight championship fight at Madison Square Garden," Alan Hopper (director of publicity for Don King Productions) recalls. "The *Times* didn't cover it. Is it too much to ask that the *New York Times* cover a heavyweight championship fight at the world's most famous arena when it's a five-minute walk from their office?"

Robert Lipsyte (who covered boxing for the *Times* in the 1960s at the start of his career in sports journalism) observes, "Boxing offers an interesting window onto the world. But as far back as I can remember, the *Times* has had an editorial bias against it. And in recent years, the bias has gotten worse. When the *Times* runs anything about boxing now, it's a one-time feature story rather than ongoing coverage of the sport."

Tim Smith (the last boxing beat writer for the *Times*) has covered the sport for the *New York Daily News* since 2000. "The situation today saddens me," Smith says, "because boxing has such a rich tradition and the *Times* once covered it well. Boxing is an industry that generates more than a billion dollars in revenue each year. Why go out of your way to limit coverage of a sport that has worldwide appeal and a significant economic impact? It makes no sense to me. But someone at the *Times* has made the determination that boxing simply isn't worth their time and effort."

Indeed, the *New York Times* is one subject on which warring promoters Bob Arum and Richard Schaefer actually agree.

"The editors at the *Times* say they don't cover boxing because boxing is a dying sport," Arum states. "But the truth is that the *New York Times* is a dying elitist newspaper that has lost touch with its audience. That's one of the reasons its readership keeps shrinking and the paper is failing financially."

"I don't think it really matters," Schaefer says of the situation. "There are so many other outlets, social networks, and major online destinations like ESPN and Yahoo, which frankly have become much more relevant to the sport of boxing than the *New York Times*. All of these major newspapers are on the verge of going out of business. Obviously, they have been missing the boat. The sport of boxing has graduated into the twenty-first century. The *New York Times* has not."

The man at the center of this controversy is Tom Jolly.

Jolly is the sports editor of the *Times*; a position he has held since 2003. He's a respected editor, well-liked by the people who know him. The *Times* has two dozen fulltime reporters in its sports department. Jolly gets suggestions regarding content from many of them in addition to being on the receiving end of constant pitches from the outside.

Jolly has the final say regarding what goes in the sports section. He is not a boxing fan. He has been to one professional fight (Lennox Lewis vs. Evander Holyfield at Madison Square Garden in 1999) and watches "parts of three or four fights" on television each year.

"We try to identify the sports that matter the most to our readers," Jolly explains. "Tracking our own website and using other measures, we feel that boxing as an overall sport doesn't rise to a level of importance to our audience that would justify greater coverage."

"There are more sports vying for attention now than in the past," he continues. "Boxing has hurt itself by having so many champions. It has cut itself off from a larger fan base by putting its best fights on pay-per-view. And many of its biggest fights take place at a time that's out of our news cycle. When there's a big fight in Las Vegas, the main event doesn't start until 11:30 at night New York time."

Those are valid points, although one might note that the Olympics aren't always conveniently timed for the *Times* news cycle and still receive saturation coverage.

Jolly is on less firm footing when he says, "With sports like boxing, we look for stories that transcend the sport and are of interest to someone who's not a hardcore fan. Boxing today doesn't have a lot of stories that transcend the sport, and it doesn't have a lot of personalities who demand attention."

More on that later. But first, some statistical data.

This writer catalogued every article that appeared in the *New York Times* sports section over a one-hundred-day period. The study ran from July 1 through October 8, 2009.

The conclusion is clear.

The *New York Times* no longer covers boxing as an ongoing sport. If a fighter of importance dies, it's noted. On rare occasions, bouts are referenced. But the paper's motto—"All the News That's Fit to Print"—which is prominently displayed in the upper-lefthand corner of page one each day, doesn't extend to boxing.

During the one-hundred-day study period, articles were categorized as "full articles" or "briefs." There were seven "full" articles about boxing in the *Times* sports section and nineteen briefs. There were also four entries on the obituary page.

Thirteen of the articles dealt with the deaths of Arturo Gatti, Alexis Arguello, Vernon Forrest, and Darren Sutherland, which might lead casual readers to the conclusion that all boxers do is get murdered or commit suicide unless they're being arrested like Roger Mayweather (who was the subject of two briefs).

The most extensive boxing coverage (three of the seven full articles) dealt with women's boxing being added to the Olympics. Another full article was devoted to the recollections of a woman who grew up in the suburban Detroit house that John Roxborough (Joe Louis's manager) had previously lived in. The results of two fights were reported: Floyd Mayweather vs. Juan Manuel Marquez and (without rhyme or reason) Marco Huck vs. Victor Emilio Ramirez.

Another item considered worthy of mention by the *Times* was the fact that four officials of Mongolia's boxing team were expelled from the International Amateur Boxing Association championships for trying to bribe a referee. That occurrence took place on the same day (September 10th) that Manny Pacquiao and Miguel Cotto held a kick-off press conference at Yankee Stadium to announce their November 14th megafight. There was no mention of Pacquiao-Cotto in the *Times* the next day. Nor was there any acknowledgement of several significant fights that took place during the study period.

On July 4th, Eddie Chambers defeated Alexander Dimitrenko to become the mandatory challenger for Wladimir Klitschko's WBO crown. The next day, the *Times* didn't mention the fight. But it did report that the Kansas City Royals had acquired a thirty-three-year-old utility player named Ryan Freel from the Chicago Cubs.

On July 11, Tomasz Adamek (the best cruiserweight in the world) defended his title against Bobby Gunn at the Prudential Center in Newark. That day, the *Times* ran a feature story about mixed martial arts that covered seventy column inches. The following day, it devoted twenty-four column inches to football in France. There was no mention of Adamek-Gunn.

On July 26th, the *Times* ran a feature story about Gina Carrano (a mixed martial artist, who had a fight against Christine Santos scheduled for August 15th). On August 4th, it devoted 112 column inches (including six photos) to Carrano (who was subsequently knocked out by Santos in the first round). It's unclear why the *Times* thought that Carrano-Santos was more important than the championship fight between Timothy Bradley and Nate Campbell that took place in the same time frame.

On August 16 (the day after Roy Jones vs. Jeff Lacy and Nonito Donaire vs. Rafael Conception), there wasn't one word about either fight in the *Times*. But the *paper* found space for a news brief reporting that Bordeaux had beaten Sochaux in a French soccer league game.

Juan Diaz vs. Paulie Malignaggi took place on August 22nd. That day, the *Times* reported the qualifying times for the Sharpie 500 in Bristol, Tennessee. Not one word on Diaz-Malignaggi. On August 23rd, the *Times* reported the result of every match in the Solheim Cup golf competition in Sugar Grove, Illinois, and the results of every game in the Little League World Series. Not one word on the outcome of Diaz-Malignaggi.

On August 26th, there was a fight card at B.B. King's (three blocks from the *Times* offices). On the day of the fights, the *Times* found space to announce that Gary Rizza had been named trainer by Guilford College; Jay Myers was the new women's assistant soccer coach at Manhattan College; Mark Paluszak was the new men's and women's golf coach at Otterbein College, and Peachy Trader had resigned as women's basketball coach at Thiel College. But there was no mention of that night's fights.

On August 27th, the *Times* reported that Scott Fitzgerald had been named assistant sports information director at Goucher College; Steve Bintz was the new men's and women's assistant volleyball coach at Pfeiffer College; and Catherine Barry was the new assistant field hockey coach at Union College. No fight results from B.B. King's were reported.

Also on August 27th, Bob Arum held a press conference at Madison Square Garden to announce an October 10th MSG card featuring Juan Manuel Lopez and Yuriorkis Gamboa. The next day, the *Times* didn't mention it. But it did report the result of every match contested at the Pilot Pen tennis tournament in New Haven, Connecticut.

Nor was there any mention in the *Times* of Vitali Klitschko's September 26th WBC heavyweight title defense against Chris Arreola.

The only staff-written article that the *Times* devoted to professional boxing as an ongoing sport during the one-hundred-day study period was a July 14th piece on Showtime's "super six" super-middleweight tournament.

So what sports did the *Times* cover during the period in question?

Certain events (Wimbledon and the U.S Open in tennis; the British Open and PGA in golf) received saturation coverage. So did the Tour de France. In fact, the *Times* ran seventy-eight articles about cycling during the one-hundred-day study period (three times as many as it devoted to boxing).

Baseball (which was in season the entire one hundred days) was the dominant sport in terms of coverage. The *Times* ran 1,173 pieces (490 full stories and 683 briefs) about America's national pastime. The National Football League, despite not starting its season until early September, was in second place (164 full stories and 416 briefs).

Boxing was far down the list.

During the study period, there were feature stories in the *Times* sports section about the hockey program at the University of Nebraska-Omaha;

a rodeo participant named Lee Ray, who ranks twenty-second among team-roping heelers on the National Rodeo Tour; rugby in Colorado; lumberjacking; APBA (a baseball board game played with dice); the Moose Moss Aquatic Center in Moultrie, Georgia; the Professional Windsurfer Association Slalom World Cup in Turkey; the Meadowcreek High School football team in Norcross, Georgia; and trout fishing in Calgary.

Each of these articles was longer than anything the *Times* ran about professional boxing.

The *Times* also reported match-by-match tennis results from the ECM Open in Prague; the Mercedes Open in Stuttgart; the Catella Swedish Open in Bastad; the Internazionali Femminil di Tennis Di Palermo in Sicily; the Slovenia Open in Portoroz; the Nuernberger Gastein in Austria; the Guangzhou Women's Open in China; the Open de Moselle in Metz; the ATP BRC Open Romania in Bucharest; the Tashkent Open in Uzbekistan; the Toray Pan Pacific Open in Tokyo; the PTT Thailand Open in Bangkok; and the Proton Malaysian Open in Kuala Lumpur.

Given this data, is it too much to ask that the *Times* devote some agate type and one-inch "briefs" to the results of major fights?

In some ways, the lack of boxing coverage at the *Times* has become a self-fulfilling prophesy. The paper's readers care less about the sport because the *Times* gives them less reason to care.

In dismissing boxing, the *Times* is ignoring the growth of the ever-expanding Hispanic market.

And most significantly, at present, the *Times* couldn't cover complex boxing issues on short notice if it wanted to. Tim Smith left the paper nine years ago. Richard Sandomir is an excellent journalist, but his primary beat is the interaction between sports and television. It has been many years since he made regular stops on the boxing tour.

Tom Jolly has built his staff around versatile journalists who can report with authority on a variety of subjects. But he doesn't have a "go to" person on staff who is grounded in the sport and business of boxing.

As for the future; the *Times* is planning to cover Pacquiao-Cotto. The paper has assigned Greg Bishop (a respected writer whose area of expertise is football) to report on Pacquiao's iconic status in the Philippines and on the fight itself.

But that's only one event. More importantly, the *Times* should reconsider the belief that "boxing today doesn't have a lot of stories that transcend the sport, and it doesn't have a lot of personalities who demand attention."

One doesn't have to look beyond New York to find personalities and stories that *Times* readers could appreciate.

Start with John Duddy. The movie-star-handsome Irishman came to New York in 2003 to pursue his ring career. Since then, he has fashioned a 27 and 1 record with 17 knockouts and fought at Madison Square Garden eight times.

Transcend boxing?

On January 30, 1972 (a day known as "Bloody Sunday"), fourteen unarmed demonstrators were shot to death by British soldiers during a civil rights march in Northern Ireland. One of the dead was seventeen-year-old John Francis Duddy. His nephew is now a symbol of reconciliation.

"He was my uncle," the fighter says. "That's my history, and there's nothing I can do about it. His name was John Francis Duddy, and my name is John Francis Duddy. He was a fighter and I'm a fighter, but I didn't become a fighter because he was a fighter. My father never talked at length about my uncle when I was growing up. It wasn't a political home. We were taught to treat people with respect regardless of race, creed, or color. My uncle's death was a tragedy, but it happened years before I was born."

Then there's Paulie Malignaggi, also from New York. Parts of Paulie's childhood were like scenes from a horror movie. Malignaggi has style and he never shuts up. Every time he enters the ring, he's like a man with a penknife facing an opponent armed with an AK-47. That because Paulie can't punch (only five knockouts in twenty-nine fights). But he can box his ass off. He's a former IBF junior-welterweight champion who's reaching for the brass ring again.

On August 22nd, as noted earlier, Malignaggi journeyed to Houston to fight hometown hero Juan Diaz. Before the fight, Paulie told everyone who would listen that the referee and judges were going to rob him. Given past history, he had reason to mistrust the Texas Department of Licensing and Regulation (which would oversee the fight). Sure enough . . .

And don't forget twenty-two-year-old Danny Jacobs; an 18-and-0 middleweight with an ingratiating personality, who's one of the most-promising prospects in boxing. Jacobs might fizzle out and fall short of the mark. Or he might be the best fighter to come out of New York since Mike Tyson and Riddick Bowe.

The *New York Times* is a great newspaper and a treasured American institution. But it could, and should, do a better job of covering boxing.

I revisted HBO with this article in late September.

HBO and Boxing: At a Crossroads

HBO and boxing are at a crossroads. The first draft of the network's overall budget for 2010 was presented in July. It called for a $15,000,000 reduction for HBO Sports; a cut in excess of 20 percent. Then, during the first week of September, Michael Lombardo (president of HBO's programming group and West Coast operations) further signaled senior management's displeasure with the status quo by instructing HBO Sports president Ross Greenburg to cut several million dollars from the budget for the last quarter of 2009.

The key players in the drama that's unfolding are HBO CEO Bill Nelson, co-president Richard Plepler, and Lombardo. Sources say that these three men have been frustrated by the absence of a coherent overall plan for boxing at HBO. Plepler (who has an extensive background in public relations) is said to have taken particular notice of the publicity that Showtime received when it announced its 168-pound championship tournament. He wonders why HBO Sports, with a far larger budget, has stirred so little media interest in its own boxing programming.

At an early stage of the budget discussions, the powers-that-be asked Greenburg for a comprehensive plan that outlines his vision for the future of boxing at HBO. In making their request, they told him that simply saying HBO intends to buy better, more competitive fights in the future doesn't constitute a plan. That's what HBO should have been doing all along. They want a plan.

During the week of September 21st, Greenburg and his staff rehearsed the presentation of their case for restoration of the cuts from next year's budget. That presentation was made to Nelson, Plepler, and Lombardo on Thursday, September 24th. Sources say that senior vice president for sports operations and pay-per-view Mark Taffet, HBO Sports senior vice president Kery Davis, HBO Sports executive producer Rick Bernstein, and HBO Sports senior vice president and chief financial officer Barbara Thomas were also present.

"It's surprising how short the meeting was," says a source with knowledge of the gathering. "It lasted less than thirty minutes. Ross was the presenter on behalf of HBO Sports, but he didn't fight the cuts. He knows he has problems with senior management. His main concern right now seems to be not making waves."

HBO's budget will be finalized by Bill Nelson in late October or early November. Then it will be presented to Time Warner CEO Jeff Bewkes for approval. Nelson, Plepler, and Lombardo are unlikely to tell Greenburg where to cut $15,000,000 from his 2010 budget. That will be his decision. But if the $15,000,000 cut stands, most of it is expected to come out of boxing. There will be lower license fees, fewer fights, and, most likely, layoffs. It's possible that *Boxing After Dark* will be discontinued.

"The problem," one source says, "is that any plan Ross puts forward will be met with skepticism because, when it comes to boxing, his biggest initiatives have failed. His plan to hitch HBO's wagon to Golden Boy and the Golden Boy output deal have been a disaster. And the idea of anointing Victor Ortiz, Alfredo Angulo, James Kirkland, Robert Guerrero, and Chris Arreola as HBO's stars of the future doesn't look so good."

For some of Greenburg's bosses, the lasting symbol of the network's relationship with Golden Boy is a $100,000 party that HBO had planned for the night of Oscar De La Hoya vs. Stevie Forbes. A few days before the fight, HBO Special Events realized that the list of attendees was devoid of big names and cancelled the party.

"Ross has lost a great deal of credibility with senior management because of his dealings with Golden Boy," a source says. "It goes back to when he convinced them to invest heavily in the license fee and marketing for De La Hoya-Forbes on the premise that it would be a big event. It wasn't. Now Ross goes into the meetings and tries to sell boxing. And they tell him, 'Ross, look at the ratings.' For $15,000,000, Mike Lombardo can develop two new series and maybe deliver the next *Sex and the City* or *The Sopranos*."

The future of boxing at HBO is more contingent now than at any time since former HBO Sports president Seth Abraham took over the reins more than two decades ago. With that in mind, let's look at what HBO has done in boxing this year, starting with its flagship offering.

HBO World Championship Boxing got off to a good start in 2009. It's first two shows were Antonio Margarito vs. Shane Mosley on January

24th and a February 28th doubleheader with Juan Manuel Marquez vs. Juan Diaz and Chris John against Rocky Juarez. Everybody understood going in that those were likely to be exciting fights.

Then, on April 11th, HBO televised Paul Williams vs. Winky Wright and Chris Arreola against Jameel McCline. Williams is near the top of most "pound-for-pound" lists. Wright is thirty-seven years old and has won one fight since 2005. Williams won eleven of twelve rounds (all twelve on one judge's card).

As for Arreola-McCline, HBO was grooming Chris for a title shot (more on that later). Jameel is thirty-eight years old and has lost four of his last five fights. In fact, McCline had retired from boxing and taken a fulltime job when he was seduced back into the ring to fight Arreola for one last paycheck. He fought scared and bailed out in the fourth round.

Then things got worse. On May 9th, *HBO World Championship Boxing* paired the rematch between Chad Dawson and Antonio Tarver with a tape-delay of Manny Pacquiao's second-round knockout of Ricky Hatton. Neither bout, it was suggested afterward, was "live."

Greenburg's decision to spend $3,200,000 plus production and marketing costs on Dawson-Tarver II left a lot of people shaking their heads. Their first fight (on Showtime) had been twelve rounds of tedium that engendered a paid attendance of 911 (a true emergency number). The only reason they were fighting again was that Tarver exercised a rematch clause in his contract.

Dawson-Tarver II typified much of what's wrong with the decision-making process at HBO Sports. It was summer stock on a Broadway budget. According to records filed with the Nevada State Athletic Commission, 1,426 tickets were sold. The live gate receipts totaled a meager $170,280. Something is very wrong when a network pays a license fee that's nineteen times the live gate for a fight that can't sell out a small hotel venue.

At the start of the telecast, HBO boxing analyst Max Kellerman called Dawson-Tarver II "a fight that no one really wants to see." After the bout, he labeled Dawson a B-plus fighter in a C division." It's unclear why HBO paid $3,200,000 (plus marketing and production costs) for a fight between a B-plus fighter and a past-his-prime forty-year-old in a C division.

Significantly, HBO's ratings went down during the telecast. Subscribers turned on the television to watch a week-old tape of Pacquiao-

Hatton. When Dawson-Tarver II began, they didn't just stop paying attention. They switched to another channel or turned off their sets.

Afterward, Dan Rafael of ESPN.com wrote, "Nickelodeon is supposed to be for reruns, not HBO's *World Championship Boxing*. But that's what we got when the network, often with a budget shortfall, wasted a $3.2 million license fee for a rematch it did not need to do and nobody wanted to see. What a shame it poured all that money down a drain when it could have used it far more wisely. Alas, we got a fight that provided no fireworks and went virtually exactly as everyone predicted it would go."

To make matters worse, two weeks earlier, Showtime had televised a fight-of-the-year candidate in Carl Froch vs. Jermain Taylor. HBO had turned down Froch-Taylor twice; the first time in favor of a dreary encounter between Taylor and Jeff Lacy in November 2008, the second time in favor of Dawson-Tarver II. Showtime paid $900,000 less for Froch-Taylor than HBO paid for the Dawson-Tarver rematch.

World Championship Boxing rebounded on June 13th with an entertaining match-up between Miguel Cotto and Joshua Clottey. Here, it's worth noting that HBO paid a $2,650,000 license fee for Cotto-Clottey, and the fight engendered a live gate of approximately $1,700,000. That's a multiple of 1.56. Compare that with the multiple on Dawson-Tarver II.

Then, having overspent on Dawson-Tarver II and several other fights, HBO Sports ran into budget problems and took *World Championship Boxing* off the air for fifteen-weeks. It returned on September 26th with a less-than-scintillating offering. Chris Arreola against Vitali Klitschko was paired with a tape-delay telecast of Floyd Mayweather Jr vs. Juan Manuel Marquez.

Arreola is an entertaining overweight club fighter, who might someday develop his potential but had never fought, let alone beaten, a world-class fighter. There was nothing in his record to suggest that he was a credible challenger for Klitschko's WBC belt.

He wasn't. Arreola fought with honor but was badly outclassed from the opening bell. There was never a moment when the outcome was in doubt. Klitschko turned him into a human bobblehead doll and outlanded him 301 to 86. Chris's corner called a halt to the beating after ten ugly rounds.

Fighters gain credibility by virtue of the fact that they fight on HBO. But HBO loses credibility when it markets a fighter as more than he really is and the truth is subsequently revealed by the fighter's ring performance.

Why did HBO put so much time, money, and effort into building Arreola as a paper challenger?

It would be nice to think that the powers that be at HBO Sports know something that the rest of the boxing world doesn't know. But too often, it appears as though boxing people know things that the people running HBO Sports don't.

The next fight scheduled for *HBO World Championship Boxing* is a November 7th rematch between Chad Dawson and Glen Johnson. Their first encounter (on Showtime) was entertaining. But Dawson won 116–112 on all three judges' scorecards. Johnson is forty years old, and the result is unlikely to be different the second time around.

HBO is paying a reported $2,000,000 for Dawson-Johnson II. The opening bout that evening will pit Alfredo Angulo against Harry Joe Yorgey. Yorgey is not what people used to think of as an "HBO-quality fighter."

Where HBO Pay-Per-View is concerned, the network deserves credit for cutting back on the number of events it schedules. There were eight pay-per-view cards in 2008. That shortchanged HBO's regular subscribers and led to the belief in some circles that, if a fight was "only" on *World Championship Boxing,* it wasn't a big fight. Also, several of HBO's 2008 pay-per-view offerings revolved around relatively insignificant fights. That led to confusion in branding.

By contrast, there have been two HBO Pay-Per-View cards in 2009 (Pacquiao-Hatton and Mayweather-Marquez) with one more (Pacquiao-Cotto) slated for November 14th. That's a step in the right direction.

The early reports are that Mayweather-Marquez (like Pacquiao-Hatton) did exceedingly well in terms of pay-per-view buys. More significantly, the buy rate for Mayweather-Marquez swamped a competing show that UFC offered on the same night. That's a testament to the marketing power of HBO's *24/7* series and, on a broader note, good news for boxing.

Unfortunately, *Boxing After Dark* (the third component of HBO's boxing programming) has fallen short of the mark in 2009.

BAD began the year with a good fight between Andre Berto and Luis Collazo on January 17th. Then came a Valentine's Day tripleheader: Alfredo Angulo vs. Cosme Rivera, Sergio Martinez vs. Kermit Cintron, and Nate Campbell vs. Ali Funeka.

Angulo-Rivera was a predictably horrible fight that should never have been televised. It came about because Ricardo Mayorga pulled out of the bout and HBO was unable to prevail upon the promoters of record to find a satisfactory replacement. That being the case, the network should have cancelled the fight and saved the license fee. Instead, it opted for Rivera as Angulo's opponent.

On fight night, Angulo (who is being marketed by HBO as a rising star) weighed 165 pounds. Rivera (a faded journeyman) weighed 150. That's a differential of two weight classes. Their encounter was a brutal beating rather than an athletic competition.

Martinez-Cintron was a bad styles match-up that had the crowd booing through six rounds, two minutes, and fifty seconds. Then Martinez knocked Cintron out with what the cameras showed was a punch and Kermit claimed was a head butt. Referee Frank Santore was sufficiently confused that, after deliberating for several minutes (which gave Cintron time to recover), he decided to preside over a de facto five-round rematch. Ultimately, the fight was declared a draw.

Nate Campbell vs. Ali Funeka (the final televised bout of the evening) dragged on sufficiently long that, on the east coast, *Boxing After Dark* became *Boxing Long After Midnight*.

The next *Boxing After Dark* telecast was also problematic. On March 7th, HBO televised a triple-header featuring three Golden Boy fighters that the network was marketing as future stars. In each instance, the "house fighter" had been developed by another promoter and lured away by Golden Boy with the promise of dates on HBO and a signing bonus that was underwritten by HBO dollars.

At the start of the telecast, blow-by-blow commentator Bob Papa proclaimed, "These are all highly competitive match-ups." That simply wasn't true. Robert Guerrero (developed by Dan Goossen prior to jumping ship for Golden Boy) was a 10-to-1 favorite over Daud Yordan in a fight that ended in a two-round "no contest" when Guerrero bailed out after suffering a cut from an accidental head butt. Victor Ortiz, a 5-to-1 favorite (previously with Top Rank), stopped Mike Arnaoutis in round two of a bout in which Arnaoutis landed a total of three punches. Then James Kirkland (developed by Gary Shaw) steamrollered Joel Julio, who quit on his stool after six rounds. Going in, Kirkland-Julio had looked like a more competitive fight than it turned out to be. No blame to HBO on that one. The other two match-ups weren't HBO-quality fights.

On April 25th, *Boxing After Dark* televised Juan Manuel Lopez vs. Gary Penalosa and Lamont Peterson vs. Willie Blain. Lopez is a legitimate champion. He's one of the most exciting young fighters in boxing and has superstar potential, so it's understandable that HBO okayed the match-up as a way of introducing him to its subscribers despite the 8-to-1 odds. Peterson was a 7-to-1 favorite over Blain in a bout that was far less viewer-friendly.

On May 30th, Andre Berto won a lackluster decision over Juan Urango, who was fighting out of his weight class to pick up *Boxing After Dark* dollars. On the same card, Alfredo Angulo was exposed when he lost a unanimous decision to Kermit Cintron.

Then Victor Ortiz was undressed when he quit in the sixth round of a June 27th *Boxing After Dark* bout against Marcos Maidana.

"They [HBO] gave their dates to one promoter, whose stable has now been wiped out," Bob Arum observed afterward. "They would love to give us dates, but they can't. They've committed dates to Golden Boy, who now has no fighters except retreads to put in. It was the wrong decision when they made it and now it's coming home to roost."

On August 22nd, *Boxing After Dark* was headlined by a good fight between Juan Diaz and Paulie Malignaggi (more on that later). The undercard saw the return of Robert Guerrero (who's a lot less exciting to watch than Juan Manuel Lopez) against a very ordinary Malcolm Klassen and Danny Jacobs (a good young prospect) against battleworn Ishe Smith.

The key to the August 22nd card (and many others that HBO has televised this year) is that it was promoted by Golden Boy.

"You're not getting the best boxing available on HBO," Kevin Iole of Yahoo.com wrote afterward. "You're getting the best boxing Golden Boy can deliver. There's a significant difference."

The Golden Boy output deal (which runs through 2011) is a millstone around HBO's neck. The next *Boxing After Dark* show of 2009 is slated for November 28th. At present, it looks as though viewers will see a rematch of last year's encounter between Lucian Bute and Librado Andrade. It will be the third rematch of a Showtime fight that HBO has televised this year.

Why Bute-Andrade (for which HBO will pay a reported $550,000 more than Showtime paid)? Andrade is a Golden Boy fighter, and Golden

Boy has the date. Ali Funeka vs. Joan Guzman will round out the card.

There's also talk that, despite its budget problems, HBO will add a December 12th *Boxing After Dark* date to its schedule. The names initially floated were Victor Ortiz, Robert Guerrero, and Jorge Linares (who Golden Boy signed recently with the promise of HBO dates; a promise that no other promoter can make). Now a rematch between Juan Diaz (another Golden Boy fighter) and Paulie Malignaggi is likely.

In the ring, one mistake can get a fighter knocked out. In programming, the damage from mistakes is incremental, but it adds up blow by blow. The current situation at HBO is a natural consequence of errors in judgment that people in the boxing community have been talking about for years.

Sixteen months ago, Bob Arum declared, "If I was in charge of boxing at HBO, the core of my programming would be twelve big shows a year. If they want to do *Boxing After Dark,* fine. But the key would be twelve big shows a year. Go back to being the network that puts on great fights that everyone wants to see and everyone talks about. That's how to make people enthusiastic about HBO like they used to be and how to make new fans for boxing."

That's still sound advice. HBO's plans for the future should be predicated on televising the biggest and best fights possible once a month on *HBO World Championship Boxing.* And the network should hold Golden Boy to the same standard that it holds everyone else. Let Golden Boy develop fighters the way Top Rank does. Then put them on HBO.

HBO's announcing teams are still a problem that has to be fixed.

Also, "There's a lot of fat in HBO's budget," one knowledgeable industry veteran says. "They're overstaffed and they overspend. The license fees are still excessive for some of their fights. They could cut production costs by twenty to twenty-five percent and the audience would never know it. Staff salaries [as opposed to salaries paid to talent] aren't set against the sports department budget, but they factor into the overall financial picture. And it's a mystery what some of these guys on staff do."

"HBO's economic model is all wrong," another industry insider says. "Right now, HBO, and HBO alone, determines the value of fighters and fights, and they're way off-target a lot of the time. HBO decided that Dawson-Tarver II was worth $3,200,000 and Dawson-Johnson II is worth $2,000,000. But if you look at ratings and ticket sales, those numbers are ridiculous. The public, not HBO, should create the value."

The biggest obstacle that HBO faces in rebuilding its boxing franchise is that not enough people there have in-depth knowledge of the business and sport of boxing. One HBO employee notes, "Ross hasn't been able to put together a plan for boxing that works because he doesn't know the business the way Seth [Abraham] did; he has no one on staff who knows the fighters the way Lou [DiBella] did; and there are times when he lets his personal feelings get in the way of sound business judgment."

Bob Arum builds on that theme, saying, "To do the job right in any business, but particularly in boxing, you have to be on the ground. And these guys aren't on the ground. When it comes to boxing, Ross has no feel for the job. The most knowledgeable person he has on his staff is [Mark] Taffet. Taffet is a politician, but at least he's a bright politician. Some of the people over there are morons."

"Ross has been in the business for thirty years," a longtime HBO employee offers. "Richard Schaefer had no experience of any kind in boxing until he hooked up with Oscar. So what happens? Schaefer outnegotiates Ross and winds up with a pile of dates, and HBO winds up with a few good fights and some garbage. Has Ross figured out yet that the Golden Boy output deal was a dumb thing to do? If he hasn't, it doesn't speak well for the future."

"Right now, Ross is just throwing stuff against the wall and hoping that something sticks," the speaker continues. "The problem with that is, when you throw stuff against a wall, you usually get a mess."

HBO Sports has to go in a new direction insofar as its boxing programming is concerned. Its goals should be to (a) reestablish the almost mystical aura that once attached to HBO Sports; (b) recreate the buzz that surrounded HBO fights in the 1990s; and following logically from these two points (c) increase ratings.

So let's get specific. Here are some concrete steps that HBO Sports can take to revive its boxing program.

(1) HBO should focus its choice of fights and the marketing of these fights on the issue of "WHO'S #1?'"

Forget about champions. The world sanctioning organizations have made a mockery of the term. And forget about the *Ring Magazine* belts. The *Ring* is owned by a promoter. And even if it operates in good faith, its championship-belt rules don't work in today's world. That's evident from the number of *Ring* titles that are currently "vacant" and the fact that Carlos Baldomir was *Ring*'s welterweight "champion" in 2006 despite the fact that there were a half-dozen welterweights who were better than he was.

HBO should identify the most credible rankings possible. That might mean convening its own "panel of experts." It could involve compiling composite rankings based on the work of others. Then, when feasible, it should match the #1 fighter in a given weight class against the top-ranked available challenger.

"WHO'S #1" works for college football and college basketball. It works for tennis and golf. It can work for boxing.

(2) One of HBO's most satisfying offerings during the past decade was the 2001 middleweight championship tournament with Bernard Hopkins, Felix Trinidad, William Joppy, and Keith Holmes. Given the network's economic clout, it could orchestrate similar tournaments in various weight divisions today.

There's a lot to admire about Showtime's 168-pound tournament. It guarantees fans twelve bouts between elite fighters. But the Showtime tournament will take too long to unfold. There won't be a winner until 2011.

HBO should televise a series of four-man elimination tournaments. Some of these tournaments could crown the #1 fighter in the world in a given weight class. Another tournament could identify the #1 American heavyweight.

Where young fighters are concerned, HBO should take *Boxing After Dark* back to its roots. Make it about young fighters in crossroads fights. Match the best young prospects against the best young prospects in four-man elimination tournaments. Don't televise Danny Jacobs against Ishe Smith in a fight where everyone knows that HBO wants Jacobs to win and, if Smith wins, it's back to the drawing board. Match Jacobs against another good young middleweight on the rise. That way, no matter who wins, there's a star in the making.

Given today's economic realities, promoters and fighters will line up to participate in these mini-tournaments because they have nowhere else to go. Even with its impending budget cutbacks, HBO has far and away the biggest checkbook in boxing and is the final arbiter of which big fights are made.

But (and this is a big "but") for the tournaments to work, the matches will have to be made by people who know boxing and aren't swayed by the entreaties of particular promoters or managers.

(3) Boxing is HBO's signature sport; plain and simple. Everything else that HBO Sports gives its subscribers is available elsewhere. If the network plans to stay in boxing, it should introduce a low-budget magazine show that probes, investigates, and addresses serious issues in boxing.

(4) HBO boxing has gotten stale. It's doing the same thing over and over again. Creative thinking is in order. For example, "rivalry weekends."

Paulie Malignaggi had some pointed things to say about the officiating in Texas after he fought Juan Diaz. A lot of people agreed with him. How about a New York versus Texas fight card? Malignaggi (New York) vs. Diaz (Texas); Danny Jacobs (New York) vs. TBA from Texas; and so on down through the off-television preliminary fights.

Also, instead of pretending that nothing has changed, HBO should relaunch its boxing program. It should tell the boxing community, the boxing media, and boxing fans (most notably, its subscribers) that this isn't just a paint job or new graphics over the same old product. It should declare loud and clear, "We've listened to you and, like a good fighter, we've made adjustments."

One thing HBO should NOT do is key its entire boxing program for 2010 to a possible Pacquiao-Mayweather fight. One big pay-per-view extravaganza isn't the solution to what ails HBO Sports. De La Hoya vs. Mayweather was styled as "the fight to save boxing." It did remarkable pay-per-view numbers and made a lot of money for those involved. But the status of boxing in the United States and the fortunes of HBO Sports have continued to decline since then.

Meanwhile, there are several more issues that require attention. The first revolves around HBO's role in boxing and its moral obligation, if any, to the sport.

At present, HBO is the only real power in boxing in the United States. By virtue of its checkbook, it's the closest thing that boxing has to an effective governing body.

HBO can't carry boxing on its shoulders, and it shouldn't be expected to. Nor is it HBO's job to clean up boxing. But it is HBO's job to provide satisfying viewing to its paying subscribers. And it makes no sense for HBO to underwrite conduct that tarnishes the product that's at the core of HBO Sports.

The issue crystallized when Paulie Malignaggi journeyed to Texas to fight Juan Diaz on August 22nd.

Hometown decisions are all too common in boxing. But in recent years, Texas has become known for particularly biased officiating in big fights. That fact was not lost on Malignaggi, who had significant reservations about fighting Diaz in Houston. But given the parameters of the deal that Golden Boy (Diaz's promoter) and HBO were offering, he had no choice.

It was a close fight. To the extent that Laurence Cole's refereeing was a factor, his actions shaded toward Diaz. Most observers thought that Malignaggi won.

"I was a little nervous while I was waiting for the decision," Paulie recalls. "But I was confident I'd won the fight. Then they announced the judges' scores. And when they got to 118–110, I said to myself, 'This is crazy; neither of us won ten rounds; the fight was closer than that.' But as strange as it might sound, when they announced 118–110, I figured I'd gotten the decision because not even a blind person could have given ten rounds to Diaz."

"Then they announced that Diaz was the winner," Malignaggi continues. "My heart dropped. And the next thing was, this rage started rising inside me. I have no beef with Juan. It was an honest fight between two honest fighters. He fought as hard as he could. But before the fight happened, I told the media that they were going to rob me and I was right. I've watched a tape of the fight several times. I have it scored 7-4-1 in my favor, so call it 7–5 for me. Could someone have scored the fight even? I won't question their competence or integrity if they did that. But the judges' scores were ridiculous, and it's no accident that they were ridiculous in favor of Juan Diaz."

In the aftermath of Diaz-Malignaggi, there was a firestorm of protest. Ross Greenburg was moved to say, "These kinds of things are terrible for the sport. They have to stop."

But in many respects, the buck stops with HBO.

In his post-fight commentary, Max Kellerman said in part, "Let me preface this by saying everyone deserves a fair shake and there's no excuse for a fighter not getting a fair shake under any circumstances. However, the marketplace spoke tonight. Paulie Malignaggi has not been able to cultivate the kind of following that Juan Diaz has been able to here in Houston. So, for that reason, Juan Diaz winds up with the powerful promoter and the hometown decision, if you consider this a hometown decision. So even though every fighter always deserves a fair shake, I think here the marketplace spoke and Juan Diaz gets the nod."

What Kellerman left unsaid is that HBO is the marketplace. That fact is evident in every fight it buys. Look at Chad Dawson. Earlier this year, Mike Criscio (Dawson's manager) told Mitch Abramson of the *New York Daily News*, "Having a title doesn't mean anything these days, because it's about the money and fighting on a network. We're basically at the mercy of HBO," To that, Gary Shaw (Dawson's promoter) added, "They don't have some of the power; they have all of it."

The question now is how HBO will use its power. Diaz-Malignaggi is about more than one bad decision. It's about the integrity of boxing and HBO's role in the marketplace.

Were the powers that be at HBO actually surprised by what happened in Texas? If so, they haven't been paying attention to the fights they've televised in recent years from the Lone Star State.

Is HBO intent on righting a wrong and using its economic might to forge a Diaz-Malignaggi rematch with neutral officials or is it just trying to ride out the storm? Sources say that HBO, Golden Boy, and Team Malignaggi have reached an agreement for a December 12th rematch on *Boxing After Dark* subject to Diaz's approval. Let's hope it happens. If so, a tip of the hat to all involved.

There are also serious questions regarding the means by which HBO Sports is constructing its schedule for December and beyond. Here, a bit of history is in order.

HBO is hoping to televise Kelly Pavlik vs. Paul Williams on December 5th. The fight has been on and off the boards because of a nagging staph infection that has troubled Pavlik for months.

That scheduling decision put Greenburg at odds with Golden Boy CEO Richard Schaefer, who says that Ross had promised him December 5th for a Shane Mosley fight. Regardless, Schaefer agreed to shift gears and promote Mosley vs. Joshua Clottey on December 26th. Contracts were negotiated and put in final form. Then, before they could be signed, Greenburg said that Mosley's next fight should be moved to January 30, 2010 (which HBO had previously promised to Golden Boy for Bernard Hopkins).

The shuffling and re-shuffling led Schaefer to declare, "I am very disappointed, angry, and upset about the lack of respect that has been shown [by HBO] to Shane Mosley and Bernard Hopkins, and I am not going to tolerate that any longer. To string people along is the wrong way."

That earned a riposte from a rival promoter, who declared, "Right now, for ten seconds, Ross and Kery [Davis] are treating Golden Boy like they treat everyone else, and Richard is throwing a shit-fit. Welcome to the club."

Meanwhile, things were getting dicey on another front. Greenburg decided that the most logical opponent for Mosley to fight on January 30th would be Andre Berto. The problem was that Berto's promoter (Lou DiBella) was in discussions with Gary Shaw about Andre fighting Timothy Bradley (one of Shaw's fighters) as part of a two-fight deal for Berto on Showtime.

On Monday, September 14th, Berto (who was visiting in New York) found his way to HBO's offices, where he met with Luis Barragan (director of programming for HBO Sports) and Kery Davis. The conversation touched on Berto's future. That, in and of itself, was of questionable propriety, since the meeting is said to have occurred without the knowledge of Al Haymon (Berto's manager) or DiBella (Berto's promoter). After the meeting, Davis spoke with Haymon and told him that it had taken place. But that was only part of the story. Berto had a second meeting at HBO on Tuesday; this one with Ross Greenburg.

A network executive's job is to buy programming; not to meet with fighters and discuss possible fights in the absence of their manager and promoter.

DiBella was not aware that the Greenburg-Berto meeting was going to take place. Haymon told DiBella afterward that he was also unaware that it would happen.

Berto describes his September 15th meeting with Greenburg as "a meet and greet type of thing that didn't last longer than ten minutes."

Ray Stallone (HBO's vice president for sports publicity and media relations) says, "Andre Berto had a meet and greet with Ross at HBO that lasted for ten minutes."

The similarity of these statements reminds one of the coordinated response one hears when a high-profile politician is caught with his hand in the cookie jar.

Other sources (who spoke with Greenburg and Berto) elaborate, saying that Greenburg told Berto he should fight Shane Mosley on HBO in

January; that HBO would put more money into the pot than had been previously offered for the fight; and that, if Berto beat Mosley, he could become a crossover star.

Greenburg might have thought that he was meeting with Berto in confidence. If so, he failed to convey that message with sufficient clarity to Andre, who went out and tweeted to the world.

DiBella learned about the Greenburg-Berto meeting on September 16th, when Rick Reeno (who broke the story on Boxingscene.com) telephoned him and asked for comment. One of Reeno's associates had read about the get-together in Berto's "tweets."

In recent months, there has been increasing talk among promoters about filing a lawsuit against HBO that would allege conspiracy in restraint of trade, tortious interference with contract, and other violations of law.

"A lawsuit might make it difficult to get dates on HBO," says one promoter. "But why worry about burning the bridge when you're not allowed on the bridge?"

Consideration has also been given to filing a complaint with the Justice Department, asking that the government investigate allegations that HBO Sports is acting as an unlicensed promoter in violation of federal law and (more seriously) engaging in anti-competitive conduct. The latter allegation would move beyond boxing and touch upon corporate-wide issues such as the relationship between Time Warner (HBO's parent company), Time Warner Cable, and In Demand (the conduit through which virtually all cable-TV pay-per-view telecasts flow to cable system operators).

Antitrust is an issue with the potential to dwarf all other problems that HBO Sports has at the moment.

"If I'm Bill Nelson" one industry insider says," I call Ross into my office and ask, 'Did this meeting with Andre Berto really happen? And if so, what in the world were you thinking?' Ross did the same thing when he met with Winky Wright, and he wound up giving dates to Gary Shaw [Wright's promoter] to bail himself out. Everybody makes mistakes. Ross's problem is that he doesn't learn from them."

"Lou should be happy about this," adds another industry veteran. "If he doesn't die of a heart attack, he'll get a good settlement out of it. And what makes it really crazy is, you know that HBO would dump Mosley-

Berto in a second if they could make Mayweather-Mosley. But that's Ross. His attitude is, 'We're HBO; we can do whatever we want.' People are getting angry."

Meanwhile, the hole that HBO Sports finds itself in keeps getting deeper. Ironically, the network is now looking to Bob Arum (not Golden Boy) to salvage the year with Pacquiao-Cotto and Pavlik-Williams.

As for what comes after that; the thoughts of someone who has sat opposite HBO at the negotiating table for years are instructive. "We look at boxing as the be all and end all," he says. "But boxing is a tiny cog in the Time Warner machine. If things keep going poorly at HBO Sports, they might simply replace it with a new part."

If HBO were to go out of the boxing business, the short-term effects would be disastrous for a handful of elite fighters and promoters. But other sports in the United States get along fine without HBO.

Boxing is growing increasingly popular in other parts of the world. But in the United States, it's being strangled by a bottleneck in the pipeline that's supposed to bring the sport's most compelling fights to its followers but doesn't. By way of analogy; Howard Stern lost much of his audience when he left terrestrial radio for Sirius. The move isolated him from the general public. Boxing has lost much of its relevance for a similar reason. Its best fights exist in isolation on premium cable television networks and pay-per-view.

Thus, in the long run, HBO's disengagement might actually be good for boxing. It would force promoters to be promoters again, spur ingenuity in the marketplace, and maybe even get the sport back on broadcast television.

Let the chips fall where they may.

There are a lot of chips.

Round 4
Non-Combatants

The most conventional thing about David Diamante is his hair. An explanation follows.

A Diamante in the Rough

One night next month, moments before the opening bell, ring announcer David Diamante will take the microphone for one of the many fight cards he works in the New York metropolitan area.

Diamante is tall and slender with a gaunt face, aquiline nose, and piercing blue eyes. His voice is a gift and he uses it well. The tip-off that something is very different about him is his hair; dreadlocks that extend well below his waist and, unbraided, would reach to the floor. He started growing them in 1988 and hasn't cut them since, although he acknowledges, "The longer ones break off from time to time."

"I'm not a stupid guy," Diamante says. "I know I could cut my hair and make more money. But I'm not motivated by money and, right now, I like my hair the way it is. Maybe I'll wake up one morning and cut it because I want to. I'm a different kind of guy."

Adding to the self-description, Diamante explains, "I'm multi-layered. I see a lot of different sides on each issue. I love life. I'm spiritual. I'm a dreamer. I'm a rebel. I swim upstream. There's a fire that burns inside me. I love breaking the mold. My life has been an incredible journey. I'm into adventure and other cultures. I love traveling. I've been to dozens of countries all over the world. I like motorcycles. I'm into cigars. I live on the edge. I'm a perfectionist. If I'm going to do something, I want to do it well."

"But I've been through some dark times," he continues. "It's a sordid history. I've done crazy things and seen worse. I've been in jail for drug and drinking-related stuff. I've seen people stabbed in the heart and get their heads bashed open with baseball bats. One time, I saw a guy get shot point blank in the head. He was lying on the curb. He was alive but he was dying and his brains were coming out of his head. I had nightmares about that for a long time."

Diamante was born in Baltimore in 1971. His father grew up poor and put himself through law school. David's mother was a teacher and now works in his father's law office.

"My father and I don't get along, but I have a lot of respect for him," Diamante says. "He has a strong moral code and lives by it. Growing up, I had a lot of family issues; particularly with my dad. I did a lot of drugs from sixth grade on. I was self-medicating, but you don't have the perspective to understand things like that when you're young. For a while, it was a blast. Then things got nasty. I was running with a real bad group of guys that you could have called a gang. I did a lot of fighting and was suspended from school lots of times. There was this rage inside me."

Diamante graduated from high school in 1989. At the urging of his grandparents, he went into rehab when he was twenty. "Talking with one of the counselors," he recalls, "I had a moment of clarity when the stupidity of what I was doing to myself hit me. The problem was, when I got out of rehab, I was homeless with nowhere to go. I remember sitting down on the curb outside a liquor store with six cans of soda. A can of Coke, a can of grape soda, root beer, Sprite, orange soda, and ginger ale. I mixed them together, drank them, got sick to my stomach, and slept in the park that night, hating my life."

Three days later, he met a girl at a punk rock concert.

"She was really cool," David remembers. "Great looking, rode a motorcycle. I had the shakes and explained to her that it was because I'd been clean for three days and my body was adjusting. She told me she understood because she'd gone through the same thing and had been clean for two years. I was hoping we could hang out together but she had to go to a Narcotics Anonymous meeting, so I went with her. I walked into this room, and I saw all these guys in the meeting who were like the people I'd hung out with. Guys with tattoos and motorcycle helmets. I was like, 'Wow; there are cool people who are sober.'"

Diamante felt he had to get out of the Washington, D.C., area to stay clean. There were too many negative associations in his old neighborhood, so he went to California. He thought he'd live in Los Angeles, but wound up in San Francisco. He had a relapse. "My life was a mess and I was worse," he recalls. Then he returned to Narcotics Anonymous.

"I got clean for good when I was twenty-one," David says. "December 4th is my clean date. I've been clean for more than sixteen years. I don't do drugs anymore. I don't drink at all."

Journeying through life, Diamante has worked as a fry cook, dish-washer, stock boy, and bike messenger. He has tossed pizza, been a DJ, and put in time as a bouncer at more than a few strip clubs in California. Closer to the arts, he started playing drums in fifth grade and has been a member of several punk rock bands. In recent years, his main gig was emceeing at Scores East (an upscale adult club in New York).

"Scores was an interesting place," Diamante says. "I worked there three nights a week from seven at night till about 5:30 in the morning. I fronted for the club and orchestrated what happened on the nights when I was on. I ran the rotations, talked to the patrons, and played music the whole night. I love naked women; I love playing music; and the money was good. So it was a win-win-win situation."

Scores lost its liquor license and closed at the end of 2008. As for what he'll do next, David notes, "I have some stuff brewing, but no final word yet." The sweet science will benefit if ring announcing is part of his future.

Diamante has never boxed competitively. But he started sparring in his late twenties while living in East Oakland and still spends time in the gym. He got into ring announcing about five years ago.

"Watching television," David explains, "I'd see guys like Ed Derian, Mark Beiro, Michael Buffer, and Jimmy Lennon. I liked them a lot. I believe in doing what I want to do, so I approached Justin Blair [who runs amateur fights at the Church Street Gym in Manhattan] and asked if I could do one of their shows. He said yes, and they've been using me ever since."

Diamante has worked about twenty pro cards. Three shows stand out in his mind.

In September 2005, David was the ring announcer for Jimmy Lange vs. Perry Ballard at George Mason University in Virginia. "I went to school there for a while," he says, "so that night was special for me." Seventeen months later, he hit the big-time with an HBO *Boxing After Dark* tripleheader: Paulie Malignaggi vs. Edner Cherry, Sechew Powell vs. Ishe Smith, and Andre Berto vs. Norberto Bravo. That was followed by James Moore against J. C. Candelo in March 2008 at Madison Square Garden.

"There's no school for ring announcing," Diamante says of his craft. "It's on the job training. You learn as you go. My style as an announcer is traditional out of respect for the sport. I never lose sight of the fact that it's not about me; it's about the fighters. If I get nervous before a fight, I remind myself that I'm not the guy in the corner. These guys go into the ring and risk their lives. I watch these guys fight and I'm in awe."

"But I've always been a showman," David continues. "I understand what goes into the experience when someone goes to a live event. It's about the fights but it's not only about the fights. A good ring announcer can rev up the crowd and even the fighters and change the experience for everyone."

As for his own personal journey, Diamante says, "I did a lot of work on myself to get to where I am in my life. Now my thing is, I try to come nice and show respect for people. But give me my respect and don't cross the line. If you cross the line, there might be a problem." He pauses to reflect; then adds, "I am who I am, and I'm doing the best I can. To come out of everything I've gone through, to have my health and the life I have now is a blessing."

The public-at-large doesn't know his name. But Seth Abraham was a key player in shaping the business of boxing as it exists today.

Seth Abraham: Then and Now

HBO is the dominant player in boxing today. It wasn't always that way. In the mid-1980s, the broadcast television networks (ABC, CBS, and NBC) ruled the ring. The man most responsible for upending that hierarchy was Seth Abraham, the architect of HBO's boxing program.

Abraham was born on August 20, 1947. Conspiracy theorists might note that he has the same birthday as Don King (although King was born sixteen years earlier). Seth was also born in the same hospital as Bob Arum.

Abraham's parents were lawyers, who met when they were students at Brooklyn Law School. Freida Braun Abraham was the school's first woman graduate and had the second highest grade-point average in the Class of 1931. Irving Abraham had to settle for a grade-point average in the top ten.

In 1951, when Seth was four, his mother died of cancer. "I remember a darkness descending on our home," he says. "They didn't know how to treat cancer in those days. My mother spent a lot of time at home in bed, which was where she died [in November 1951]. I have only isolated memories of her, but I remember the day she died vividly."

"The one bright spot that summer," Seth reminisces, "was that we lived around the corner from Ebbetts Field and my father started taking me to baseball games. I remember my first game very well. It was a Saturday afternoon. The Dodgers won; my father let me have a sip of his Schaefer beer; and the entire experience was spectacular. That afternoon, I fell in love with baseball completely."

Abraham attended Midwood High School in Brooklyn, where, in his words, he "straddled the worlds of jockdom and make-believe intellectualism." He was sports editor and then editor-in-chief of *The Midwood Argus* (the school newspaper) and had "middle-of-the-road" grades.

"I wouldn't say that I was a juvenile delinquent," Seth recalls. "I was never in trouble with the law, but I was in trouble in school all the time. In junior high school, once, I brought in a book called *World's Most Famous Nudes* and passed it around the class. Anyone who opened it up got an electric shock. I wound up in the dean's office for that one. I invented headaches and toothaches to stay home when I was young and cut class in high school a lot."

He was also a good enough baseball player (a lefthanded hitter, who played first base and centerfield) to receive a baseball scholarship to the University of Toledo.

And good enough to have tryouts with both the Philadelphia Phillies and St. Louis Cardinals.

"But I did very poorly at the tryouts," Seth acknowledges. "I was a good college ballplayer, but there's a world of difference between a college fastball and a major league fastball and a greater difference between a college curveball and a major league curveball."

Abraham graduated from Toledo in 1968 and enrolled at Boston University, where he received a master's degree in journalism in 1969. While in graduate school, he worked as a stringer for the Boston bureau of the *New York Times*. Then he took a job as a writer covering education and the United States Supreme Court for *Facts On File* (a news reference magazine based in New York). From there, he went to Hill & Knowlton (a public relations agency), where his primary responsibilities involved publicizing Gillette's involvement with Major League Baseball on behalf of Gillette.

In 1975, Bowie Kuhn (the commissioner of Major League Baseball) offered Abraham a public relations job, but it was a lateral move and he turned it down. Several months later, a more desirable position opened up; this one as a special assistant to the president of Major League Baseball Promotions. The job involved interacting with companies (such as Gillette) that had ongoing relationships with Major League Baseball. It was a step up the corporate ladder and reunited Seth with a childhood love.

While at Major League Baseball, he also found love of a different kind; marrying Lynn Rubenstein in 1977 after a five-year courtship.

"Lynn is really smart," Seth says. "Book smart; common sense smart; IQ smart. She's my best friend and the person I trust most. It would be an understatement to say that she's the reason for a lot of the success I've had in my life."

In 1978, David Meister (who had been director of radio and television for Major League Baseball) left the national pastime to become head of the sports group for a small cable company called Home Box Office. Meister asked Abraham to join him. "But I had pipe-dreams that someday I might be commissioner of Major League Baseball," Seth recalls, "so I turned him down."

Then Michael Fuchs (HBO's vice president for original programming) recruited Abraham more aggressively. Seth succumbed and, the day after Labor Day 1978, began working at HBO. His first assignment involved handling negotiations with on-air sports talent, which at the time included Curt Gowdy, Merle Harmon, Len Dawson, Marty Glickman, Don Dunphy, and Larry Merchant.

"I had the ignominious distinction of firing Don Dunphy," Seth says. "I replaced him with Spencer Ross and added Ray Leonard to the telecasts. That was the first broadcast team I put together."

Then Abraham started making deals for fights, although he admits, "I had no boxing experience and didn't know what I was doing. One of the first fights I bought was a fight from Bob Arum that didn't exist. Once Bob had a guarantee from me, he went out and tried to make the fight and couldn't."

In 1982, NBC tried to lure Abraham away from HBO with an offer to become head of programming for NBC Sports.

"HBO was still a small company," Seth remembers. "And the NBC offer came with a much higher salary than I was making at HBO. I discussed it with Michael [Fuchs], and he told me, 'I can't match the money. But I promise you, if you stay at HBO, as my career goes up, yours will go up too.'"

Abraham stayed, and Fuchs made good on his promise. Eventually, Michael became chairman of HBO and Seth was named president of HBO Sports. Following a 1989 corporate merger, his title was changed to president of Time Warner Sports.

"I've been fortunate," Seth says, "in that, for most of my professional life, I've had great bosses. They were fabulous mentors. I was at HBO for twenty-four years; seventeen of them working for Michael. Unquestionably, he had the greatest impact on my life of anyone I've ever worked with."

Under Abraham's guidance, HBO became *the* star-maker in boxing. A nine-page profile by Richard Hoffer that ran in the January 15, 1990, issue of *Sports Illustrated* declared, "Abraham quietly guides boxing's most important division and he negotiates the Tyson fights you will see on TV for some time to come. He helps decide who will be the next Sugar Ray Leonard and, for that matter, when and whom the old one will fight. He controls, to a large degree, the colorful business of boxing."

Fuchs goes further, saying, "Seth was one of the pioneers who built the modern HBO. He embraced the idea that HBO had to be different from what the broadcast networks were doing. He made boxing an anchor for HBO Sports, and everything else we did in sports spread from that. His signature, more than anyone else's, exists on HBO Sports to this day."

Meanwhile, Abraham loved what he was doing. "I like responsibility," he says. "I always wanted to be the man at bat with the bases loaded in the bottom of the ninth inning and the game on the line. I've always enjoyed showmanship. It factors into everything I do. That's why I wear a boutonniere [a flower in the buttonhole of his lapel]. And I loved the game, negotiating with people like Don King and Bob Arum. It was like playing chess. Sometimes I won and sometimes I lost, but I always enjoyed it."

Abraham became known internally at HBO for a management style that brought a wide range of people into the decision-making process.

"Leadership is about consensus," he says. "If you're the boss, everybody knows that you're in charge and that you have the final vote. But you don't effectively manage an organization by fiat or by ignoring the opinions of the people you've chosen to work with you."

And he was a champion of editorial integrity, insisting that the network's commentators be allowed to speak honestly without fear or favor with regard to the events that they covered.

When Mike Tyson's contract with HBO came up for renewal, Abraham had a choice: dump boxing analyst Larry Merchant to placate Tyson and Don King (who were aggravated by on-air criticism from Merchant) or lose Tyson (the greatest draw in the history of HBO). Seth stood by his commentator, losing Tyson but preserving his network's editorial integrity.

Looking back on that time, Merchant says, "Seth is the kind of executive that I'd want to be if I wanted to be an executive. He was ambitious but not bloodless. He was a visionary and a good administrator. He had an appreciation for talent, whether it was the guys behind the microphones or the suits behind the desks, and he let them do their job."

"And unlike some executives," Merchant continues, "Seth was able to separate the personal from the professional. He understood that, in the end, it's what comes over the television screen that matters, and he was always willing to put aside personal differences in the interest of improving the end product. There was a real family feeling at HBO Sports in those days, and Seth was responsible for a lot of that."

In autumn 2000, Abraham left Time Warner Sports for a new challenge as executive vice president and chief operating officer of Madison Square Garden.

The first six months went well. Seth reported directly to MSG president and CEO Dave Checketts, who he'd enjoyed working with on HBO-MSG matters in the past. The middleweight championship tournament (won by Bernard Hopkins) was put into place. Other initiatives were planned. Then Checketts was fired by James Dolan (president and CEO of Cablevision, the Garden's parent company). In addition to his other titles, Dolan became president and CEO of Madison Square Garden.

Dolan is an impulsive man. That put him at odds with Abraham's modus operandi. Seth recalls, "No matter how difficult negotiating with Don King and Bob Arum might have been, there was always some floor of civility and logic. You could expect that, ultimately, facts and rational thought would carry the day. And none of that was in play at the Garden with Jim. It wasn't about facts; it wasn't about logic or being thoughtful. It was always about what Jim wanted."

"Jim is a zealot when it comes to the Knicks, Rangers, Radio City Music Hall, and the Rockettes," Abraham continues. "They aren't toys for him. He takes his responsibilities very seriously. But zealotry can lead to very difficult emotions, and sometimes his passion is out of control. Jim's two favorite words are 'I want.' And I struggled with that. Every day, I rode a rollercoaster based on his emotions. I couldn't predict what might happen. I couldn't protect against it. Every day was suspenseful because I didn't know what to expect from my boss."

"It ended peacefully," Seth recounts. "In April 2003, I went to Jim and said, 'You don't need an executive like me. You need somebody who will be an administrator for you and implement what you want.' Jim asked me to think about it. For a few months, things got better. But then the problems started up again. In September, I told Jim that I wanted to proceed with the divorce. The papers were signed in January 2004, and I left in February."

In 2005, Abraham formed Starship SA; a one-man consulting company through which he addresses issues that involve sports marketing, promotion, and communication on a global basis.

"I'll think of a concept," Seth explains. "Then I sit down with a yellow pad and work on the idea. It could take a day, a week, a month. When I'm confident that I have it right, I ask myself, 'Which company would be interested in this idea?' and I go to my Rolodex. Having been in the sports and entertainment business since 1972, I have access to an extraordinary group of men and women. My Rolodex is my greatest asset. I arrange for a meeting to present my idea. No one has ever turned me down for a meeting. Then the idea rises or falls on its own merits. On occasion, clients approach me. But as often as not, I initiate the contact."

Comcast was Abraham's first client. He went to them and said, "You should be licensing sports libraries for video-on-demand. These are the libraries. Here's how you can program them. I can set up meetings with the copyright-holders." That led to a deal between Comcast and Top Rank, and later to a relationship whereby Seth represented Top Rank and Main Events jointly with regard to their libraries.

Abraham has also done consulting work for Anshutz Entertainment Group (owners of the Staples Center and 02 Dome). The New York Jets retained him for advice regarding their television programming and ways to monetize their new stadium. He has advised several start-up companies and worked with New York City deputy mayor Dan Doctoroff on a pro bono basis in an effort to bring the 2012 Olympics to New York.

"I don't bill on an hourly basis," Seth says, outlining the parameters of his work. "The way I set up each deal is, I'm hired for three months at an agreed-upon fee. At the end of three months, we can renew or not renew for another three-month cycle. I work an average of twenty hours a week and generally have several clients at any given time. The business is structured in a way that gives me maximum flexibility and freedom to travel and do whatever else I want to do. Having worked in corporations for more than thirty years, there's something giddy for me in being able to come and go as I choose."

Coming and going as he chooses means more time for hobbies.

Abraham is a collector. He collects antique fountain pens ("I have about a hundred") and wrist-watches ("fifty to seventy-five").

He also has a huge collection of sports memorabilia that includes five World Series rings and approximately 150 autographed baseballs signed by the likes of Babe Ruth, Hank Aaron, Ted Williams, Willie Mays, and Mickey Mantle (not to mention Ronald Reagan, Bill Clinton, Gerald Ford, Henry Kissinger, Ted Kennedy, and Al Gore).

Where boxing memorabilia is concerned, Seth enumerates, "Sugar Ray Leonard gave me the robe he wore in the first fight I did with him at HBO. Shane Mosley gave me the shoes he wore when he beat Oscar De La Hoya at the Staples Center in my next-to-last HBO fight. I have one signed glove worn by each fighter in Hagler-Hearns and lot of Mike Tyson stuff."

But the collection that's dearest to Abraham's heart is a group of letters from Abraham Lincoln and six Civil War generals: Ulysses S. Grant, William Tecumseh Sherman, Abner Doubleday, A. P. Hill, Robert Rodes, and Stonewall Jackson.

"The Jackson letter is the prize of my collection," Seth says. "He died early in the war and wrote very few letters."

The most notable general absent from the collection is Robert E. Lee. "He's very expensive," Seth explains. "And it's a seller's market. A note in his hand can easily cost $75,000. Maybe someday . . ."

Abraham now spends a lot of time reading. There are three thousand books in his home library, including four hundred volumes on the Civil War.

"I walk home from work every day and sit in a chair and read from three to six in the afternoon," he says. "I read a book a week; mostly history, biography, and politics; not much fiction."

He plays in two full-court basketball games each week; one on Saturday at the McBurney YMCA that starts at 7:30 AM and runs until ten o'clock; the other at Dalton High School on Monday evening. "I'm the second-oldest player in each game," he says. "And I take them very seriously."

Also, for the past two spring semesters, Abraham has taught a once-a-week course in sports administration and management issues at Washington University in St. Louis (his daughter's alma mater).

"I love what I'm doing," Seth says, reflecting on his life today. "It would be very difficult for me to return to a fulltime corporate environment. After more than thirty years, I have time for friendships that I let atrophy for the sake of my career. I can pursue my interests and do what I want to do with my family when I want to do it. I'm very content."

"You know; I have breakfast with [New York City mayor] Michael Bloomberg several times a year," Abraham says in closing. "At one of those breakfasts about a year ago, Michael said to me, 'You're wasting yourself; you could have another career.' But I see things differently. I don't consider what I'm doing now to be wasting myself. I'm not wasting time; I'm enjoying it."

Ricardo Jimenez is one of the many people behind the scenes who make boxing work.

Ricardo Jimenez

Another big fight week is here. All eyes are about to focus on Manny Pacquiao and Miguel Cotto. Through it all, a soft-spoken man with a round face and neatly groomed walrus mustache will be in the background, quietly doing his job.

Ricardo Jimenez is Top Rank's interface between the English- and Spanish-speaking people of the boxing world.

"I worked with Ricardo before I was at Top Rank," says company vice president Carl Moretti. "I thought I knew how nice he is and how good he is at what he does. Now that I'm with Top Rank, I feel those things even more strongly."

"Ricardo is a great person with a big heart," adds Lee Samuels (Top Rank's director of publicity). "I'm so glad he's on our team."

"The media loves him," Bob Arum proclaims. "The fighters love him. I love him. He's Mexican, but the Puerto Ricans love him. He's a great great guy."

"Ricardo is promiscuous," observes Top Rank matchmaker Bruce Trampler. "He falls in love with all the fighters he works with and they all fall in love with him. Most people have no idea how active he is with the fighters behind the scenes. He's like an uncle to these guys. They all defer to him. He's honest; he's loyal. It's a situation where the job is perfect for the man and the man is perfect for the job."

And then there's the competition. In the back-stabbing world of professional boxing, what do other publicists say about Jimenez?

Fred Sternburg: "Ricardo knows what the media needs and wants. He knows what sells. He's completely dependable. He's always there. He never gets ruffled. I'd say I'm his biggest fan, but I'm sure you can find a lot of people who would say that."

Ed Keenan: "This is a crazy business. There are times when people are screaming and yelling and going in ten different directions. But Ricardo always has everything together."

Alan Hopper: "Boxing is filled with bullies and people who have way too much testosterone. Ricardo is the antithesis of that. He's one of the nicest people I've met in my life, in or out of boxing."

Ricardo Jimenez was born in Chihuahua, Mexico, on November 28, 1955. His father worked in a shoe repair shop owned by Ricardo's grandfather. When Ricardo was ten, his oldest brother finished high school and wanted to go to college.

"Two things were important in my family," Jimenez says. "Sports and education. But my father couldn't afford the tuition; so he moved to Los Angeles to work in a shoe factory, where he could make more money and send money home for my brother's tuition. Then he became a foreman in the factory and brought the rest of us to Los Angeles. I was in fifth grade. I didn't speak English. So in school, I sat with the fifth-grade kids in math, history, and science. But in reading and writing, I had to sit with the second-grade kids for two hours every day."

Ricardo graduated from high school and took a job in the mailroom at an insurance company. He also enrolled at Cal State-Fullerton University, where he registered for night courses. Eventually, he was placed in charge of the mailroom. In 1983, he graduated from college.

Three years later, opportunity knocked. *La Opinión,* which is sold throughout southern California, is the leading daily Spanish-language newspaper in the United States. In 1986, the paper sent two of its five sports reporters to Mexico to cover the World Cup. That left a void at home, and Jimenez was hired on a temporary basis.

Ricardo's English was flawless by then. His Spanish was another matter. "I spoke Spanish well," he says. "Writing was a different game because my schoolwork had been in English. Everybody in the sports department took me under their wing, and the copy editors helped me a lot."

After three months, *La Opinión* offered Jimenez a permanent job. The "Anglo" sports (football, basketball, and tennis) became his turf. He was the paper's go-to guy for the Los Angeles Lakers and Oakland Raiders. He covered ten straight Super Bowls. In 1997, he was named acting sports editor and became the paper's boxing writer. One year later, "acting" was removed from his title.

Good things happened to Jimenez at *La Opinión.* He enjoyed his work. He learned at lot. He met a woman who was a reporter for the metro section and would ultimately become his wife. They were married in 1998 and have two daughters (Alejandria, age ten; and Elizabeth, eight).

"But the paper began to change," Ricardo says. "The sports staff was cut. More and more editorial decisions were made based on the budget instead of what news was important. I got tired of working so hard and not being able to cover sports the way I thought we should. It wasn't fun anymore."

In November 1999, Jimenez traveled to Las Vegas to cover a WBO super-flyweight title bout that was co-promoted by Top Rank. On the day of the weigh-in, Lee Samuels asked him, "Do you know anyone we can hire to help with publicity on the Spanish shows?"

"How about me?" Ricardo suggested.

"Would you leave the newspaper?"

"Yes."

"And Lee said nothing," Jimenez remembers. "Then, right after Christmas, I resigned from the paper. I had to slow down. I'd had enough. It was time to do something else. I told myself, 'I'll manage a McDonald's franchise if I have to.' I just wasn't happy there anymore."

A few days later, Samuels telephoned.

"I heard you quit."

"Yes."

"Can you fly to Las Vegas this afternoon and meet with Bob? We'll have a ticket waiting for you at LAX [Los Angeles International Airport]."

"I flew to Las Vegas that afternoon," Jimenez recalls. "The first thing Bob said to me was, 'This is not an interview. There's a job here for you. I just want to know what happened at the newspaper; why you left.' I told him how I loved writing and loved sports; but things at the paper had gotten so I was worrying more about business than writing and sports. He offered me a job that day."

Jimenez joined Top Rank on January 15, 2000. The company had a monthly show on Univision and was about to add a monthly show on Direct TV. The first fight card that he worked was a January 22, 2000, match-up between Julio Alvarez and Israel Cardona. One month later, he was assigned to Marco Antonio Barrera's camp during the build-up to Barrera-Morales I.

"Since then, it has been one fight after another," Ricardo says. "My job is primarily public relations. Anything from Top Rank that comes out in Spanish, I write. I deal with scheduling for all of Top Rank's Hispanic fighters. I set up interviews. I translate for them. I get them to the TV fighter meetings."

But it's more than that. Jimenez is the face of Top Rank for the company's Hispanic fighters. If they need tickets, they go to him. If they need hotel rooms or an airport pick-up for a family member or girlfriend, they go to him. Whatever it is, they go to Ricardo.

"I love what I do," Jimenez says. "I love boxing. I've been watching fights since I was a kid. The travel gets to me sometimes; especially being away from my family. But I really enjoy the relationships I have with the fighters. It's all worthwhile when they thank me after a fight for what we've done together. I love it when their kids come up and hug me. And Top Rank is such a good company to work for. Lee is the best. Lee taught me most of what I know about my job. And it all starts with Bob. Bob knows that not every fight will be a home run, but he treats every fight like it can be. He expects everyone at Top Rank to be professional and do their job. But he lets us do our job and shows appreciation when we do."

The fighters that Jimenez has worked with since joining Top Rank include Erik Morales, Jose Luis Castillo, Jorge Arce, Julio Cesar Chavez Jr, Juan Manuel Lopez, Antonio Margarito, and dozens of lesser-known warriors. Then there's Miguel Cotto, who occupies a special place in Ricardo's heart.

"I'd never been to Puerto Rico until I went with Bob after the 2000 Olympics to announce the signing of Miguel Cotto, Ivan Calderon, Ruben Fuchu, and Edwin Algarin," Jimenez recalls. "I still remember; Bob gathered all four fighters together before the press conference and told them, 'If you do your job, we'll do our job.'"

Two of the four fighters did their job; the other two couldn't. Ricardo views the matter from his own personal perspective when he says, "To see Miguel Cotto grow from the day we signed him to where he is now brings great joy to me."

And when two of Top Rank's Hispanic fighters face off against one another?

"That can be hard," Jimenez acknowledges. "Cotto-Margarito was very difficult for me. Cotto is my guy and Margarito is my guy. I worked with Cotto for that fight, and Lee worked with Margarito. Before the fight, I thought it would be okay for me. Then they started fighting. The first six rounds, I was all right because Miguel was winning and neither guy was getting hurt. After that, it got hard to watch. I walked to the back of the arena and watched it from there. I just wanted it to be over. I was happy for Tony that he won because I know how hard he worked, but I felt worse for Miguel. I've never watched a tape of that fight. I don't think I ever will. I saw it once. I don't want to see it again. Then the handwraps became an issue. I'm disappointed over that more than anything else."

Jimenez treats everyone in the media with respect, whether they write for a major metropolitan daily or a small Internet site. He's unfailingly courteous and always returns telephone calls. Whenever possible, he facilitates requests for information and access. Because of his newspaper background, he understands what writers need.

"Ricardo goes above and beyond the call of duty," says Tom Gerbasi (one of boxing's pioneering Internet writers). "He always tries to help you and he's the best translator out there. We've all had the experience of asking a fighter a question and the fighter rambles on in Spanish for thirty seconds and then the translator says, 'He feels strong.' Ricardo gives you everything the fighter says. I know that because my wife is Puerto Rican. She listened to one of my tapes and told me, 'This guy translated every single word.' Ricardo is one of the best in the business; any business."

But is Ricardo Jimenez too good?

"I know I'm supposed to learn English," says former junior-bantamweight champion Jorge Arce. "But Ricardo is so good, why bother?"

My friendship with Artie Curry started with words between us at a time when we had a cordial relationship but had yet to become friends. In early 1999, we were sitting together after a press conference. I made a flippant remark about Artie "baby-sitting" fighters for HBO. And Artie went off on me, saying that I was being disrespectful of him and disrespectful of the fighters he worked with. He was angry. And he was right. When he stopped berating me long enough to take a breath, I told him, "It was a stupid thing for me to say. I apologize. I was wrong." Artie looked at me open-mouthed. Then he hugged me. From that moment on, we were friends.

Arthur Curry: His Life and Legacy

A lot of people liked Arthur Curry. Almost everyone else loved him.

Artie's mind was filled with wonderful thoughts and his feelings were founded on love. He was about giving. He enjoyed doing things for people and took care to never hurt anyone. He was a man of integrity who radiated truth. He spoke his mind and didn't hide his feelings. "Being real," he called it. But he was always kind.

Given the childhood that Artie endured, it would have been easy, even natural, for him to grow into a bitter angry man. But he fought back from an ugly start, never used his origins as a crutch, and spent his adult years teaching people about character by the example of his conduct. He was the embodiment of the idea that the reward one gets for being good in life is that one takes pleasure in being good.

Arthur Sheppard (which was Artie's name as a child) was born in Harlem on February 18, 1960. His life began in a single-parent home with his mother and two older sisters. A younger brother was born in 1962.

"I have no idea what my mother did," Artie said ten years ago, reflecting on his early childhood. "She was just a lady I saw from time to time."

When Artie was four, he and his siblings were placed in separate foster care facilities. Two years later, his natural mother was brutally murdered. Not long after that, his father (who Artie met once in his life) drank himself to death.

For thirteen years, Artie was shuttled from home to home. Later, he recalled, "I was in group homes; I lived with families; I stayed with friends. There was a lot of pain. But one thing I remember was, every summer, the foster agency sent us to a summer camp, where they had arts and crafts, chess, canoeing, activities like that. Each year, that camp gave me a vision of hope; a belief that life could be better than what I was going through. So even at a young age, I felt there was a better way."

Years later, Artie was asked, "Why are you so happy all the time?"

"Because I cried so much as a child," he answered.

Artie's life changed dramatically when he was seventeen years old and scheduled to be discharged from foster care within a year. A jazz singer named Edward Curry and his wife Lise (a small-business administrator) wanted to adopt a newborn child. The Currys were an interracial couple (Lise is white). An agency supervisor who had previously worked with Artie asked if they would consider taking him in as a boarder.

"This man believed in Artie and didn't want him out on the streets or living with the wrong people," Lise explains. "We didn't have it in mind to take in a young man that age. My husband said, 'Okay; we'll spend some time with him and then decide whether to do it with him or an infant.' And I told my husband, 'No. This is someone who has been treated so badly in his life. He doesn't need another rejection. If we meet him, it's to take him.'"

The Currys agreed to take Artie in as a boarder. On the day that the arrangement was finalized, they treated him to a celebratory lunch before bringing him home.

"We sat down in the restaurant," Lise remembers. "Artie looked at the menu but he was reluctant to order. I told him, 'You can have anything you want,' and he said, 'I'll have what you have.' I tried to tell him differently; that he could make his own choices. Then I realized that he couldn't read the menu. Seventeen years old and he couldn't read or write. He had so many needs, and the challenge that my husband and I faced was to motivate him to fill those needs without destroying his self-esteem."

The Currys lived in a meticulously kept three-bedroom row-house in the East Flatbush section of Brooklyn.

"We had been married for ten years when Artie arrived," Lise recalls. "And there were adjustments to be made. Edward had always been the center of my life. Now he was sharing me; not with a child, but with an adult man. Artie was eager to please, but he wouldn't do a song-and-dance to please us. They locked horns from time to time."

But Artie never took the good things in his new life for granted, no matter how small or commonplace they might have been. And later, he spoke of the gratitude he felt, saying, "For the first time in my life, there was someone who had confidence in me and believed in me. I experienced love for the first time, and everything changed. Without my new parents, I don't know what would have happened to me. Before them, I'd been in constant pain. I'd always felt that I had an inner beauty, but I'd never had a foundation to build on. There was so much I had to make up for, and they opened a whole new world for me."

At Lise and Edward's urging, Artie took adult education courses at Kingsborough Community College. There, he met Isaac Daniel ("Frisco"), who would be his friend for the next three decades.

Frisco is now a security guard on Wall Street and runs a youth basketball league. "Artie was such a good friend," he says with a smile. "Whatever was going on in our lives, he always kept things between us so simple. Sometimes he'd tell me, 'Damn, you got a good job, Frisco. If I wasn't working at what I do, I'd want to do what you do. I'd just walk around the building like you do and look at pretty women all day.'"

After Artie developed basic reading and writing skills, he enrolled in an art class at Fashion Institute of Technology. "He doodled artistically all the time, and I saw that he had talent," Lise says. "No one had told him that before. He did well at FIT and that built his confidence even more."

Then, when Artie turned twenty-one, he asked Edward and Lise if he could change his name to Curry and if they would legally adopt him. "That was important," he said later. "It erased a lot of negatives. I wanted to honor my parents and I was proud to be a Curry."

The legalities were concluded at Surrogate's Court in Brooklyn. The judge told Artie that he'd once presided over the adoption of a forty-year-old nun but that Artie was the second-oldest person to receive the honor. Then, following standard procedure, he gave Artie a lollipop.

At age twenty, Artie took a job in the mailroom at the media conglomerate then known as Time-Life. Co-workers from that era remember him as a soft-spoken young man with a warm smile, a big cuddly bear with no claws. In July 1980, he met another of the people who would change his life.

Curt Viebranz was a newly minted MBA who had just began work at a fledgling cable company called HBO that was part of the Time-Life empire.

"Artie ran a cart up and down the hall, delivering the mail," Viebranz recalls. "We both liked talking with people. So when he finished his deliveries, he'd come back to my office and we'd talk. People ask 'how are you doing' all the time. Artie really wanted to know. But we also talked about where he was in his life and what he thought he could be. He was eager to better himself. At some point, he wanted to do more than deliver mail."

"I liked Artie," Curt continues. "He was such a nice guy and there was a magnetism about him. After he'd been delivering mail for a while, he decided to interview for a job in creative services at HBO. I knew Mary Dickey, who was doing the hiring, put in a word for him, and he got the job."

"Artie had taken a few courses at FIT, so he had a bit of an art background," Dickey says, picking up the saga. "Curt thought that creative services would be a good place for him to take an entry-level job as a first step on a career path. One of the things we assigned him to do was create camera-ready mechanicals. This was before everything was done on computers. It was very precise deadline-oriented work, and Artie did it extremely conscientiously. In some ways, he was like a big kid, but he took his responsibilities seriously."

A big kid. The phrase rang true.

"If you put Artie with a group of children," Viebranz says, "an hour later, he was the recreation director." And Dickey recounts a moment that spoke volumes about the kind of person Artie was.

One day, Mary brought her son (who was four years old) to the office. "John disappeared with Artie," she reminisces. "And by the end of the day, John absolutely adored him. On the way home, I asked what they'd done together, and John told me that Artie had taken him around and introduced him to some of his friends, which meant just about everyone in the building."

Two of Artie's "friends" made a particularly favorable impression on John. One was a woman who worked in the cafeteria. Her job was to take used trays off a conveyor belt, dump the garbage, and hand the trays to a man who washed them (John was fascinated by the conveyor belt). The other friend was someone whose job wasn't as much fun as taking trays off a conveyor belt, but he was "very nice." John identified him as a man named Michael Fuchs.

That was Artie's world. He knew everyone in the cafeteria on a first-name basis. Michael Fuchs was the chairman and chief executive officer of HBO.

"Artie was special," Dickey says. "He made you feel good about yourself. He respected boundaries, but he was always willing to reach across boundaries to shake hands. He never demeaned people. Everywhere he went, he left something positive behind. There was a light in him that shone on everybody he met. People say that I played a key role in Artie's life, but he played a key role in my life too."

Then a problem arose. Potentially, a big one. Computers were making many jobs in creative services obsolete. And at the same time, HBO was experiencing a budget squeeze.

"Artie was on the list of people to be let go," Viebranz remembers. "Mary and I agreed that justice would not be served if that happened. So I went to Michael Fuchs, and he said, 'You're right; let's keep the guy.' It's remarkable, really. Michael was a relatively new CEO. He had so many fish to fry. But not only did he keep Artie; he took the time to look after him and find a place for him at HBO Sports."

Seth Abraham (then president of HBO Sports) continues the narrative.

"The sports department was very small when Artie started working there," Abraham says. "It was nothing like what it became later on, and we didn't really have a job for Artie. But there was always work to be done in production, and I asked Ross [executive producer Ross Greenburg] to find something for Artie to do. Ross had a view of what he wanted his staff to be, and Artie didn't fit the mold. The work Ross gave him was menial and largely unfulfilling. But it was an opportunity and Artie made the most of it."

Brien McDonald (who now produces *Friday Night Fights* for ESPN) remembers those times.

"I met Artie his first day on the job at HBO Sports," McDonald recalls. "I was a production assistant. Artie had been assigned to work for me. He had no television or production experience, and I had to figure out what he'd do. We didn't get along at first. We met for the first time in the hallway. Artie seemed very defensive and let me know who he was and who he knew. I was like, 'I don't know who you are. I just know you've been hired and you've got a job to do and I have to show you how to do it.' We left mad at each other. Later on, I started to understand the sort of person he was. We worked closely together and a real friendship developed. At one point, Artie apologized for that first day. We both remembered it. He told me that he'd been apprehensive and nervous about starting in a new job and he knew that he'd come on too strong. I wish there were more people like Artie sprinkled around the world. I'm sure there are some, but not enough."

Artie's primary responsibility in sports production involved clipping newspaper articles. HBO subscribed to newspapers from around the country. His job was to clip items that related to boxing. Then, when the network licensed the rights to televise a fight, he'd gather the relevant articles together and put them in a production folder. Over time, he developed a system that co-workers recall as being organized and very neat. But he didn't want to clip articles for the rest of his life.

"Artie never complained," Seth Abraham says. "But after a while, I could see that he wasn't happy. Lou [HBO Sports vice president Lou DiBella] and I talked about it. Lou was HBO's point person on boxing at the time. And we decided that, with Artie's people skills, he was the ideal person to interface with the fighters. He could represent our position to them and, at the same time, explain their needs to HBO. So we moved Artie from production to the business side of things. He began reporting to Lou instead of Ross. And very quickly, he created a totally unique role for himself."

"Seth never gave Artie anything that he didn't deserve one hundred percent," DiBella adds. "And that's not a knock on Seth, who understood how good Artie was and could be. That's an expression of admiration for Artie. Anyone who spent any time at all with him knew he was special unless they were a moron. Artie brought out the best in everyone, even the creeps."

In 1996, Artie assumed the newly created position of "manager, HBO sports talent relations." His primary responsibility was described in the corporate manual as "building and maintaining relationships with boxers, support staff, and entourage."

"I had great teachers," he later acknowledged. One of them was Janet Indelli, who worked directly for Abraham and, in Artie's words, "taught me a lot about responsibility and accountability" and how to best make his spirit thrive in a corporate environment.

Indelli, for her part, recalls how, when she and HBO production coordinator Tami Cotel broke up with their respective boyfriends, Artie helped them through those trying crying times.

"I can see it's going to be long summer for both of us," Artie told Janet. Later, he observed, "It's a good thing that you and Tami didn't break up at the same time. It might have been too much for me to handle."

"When you were talking with Artie," Indelli says, "you always felt that, in that moment, no one else mattered to him. He wasn't one of those people who's always looking over your shoulder to see if there's someone better to talk with."

In the ensuing years, Artie became part of the fabric of HBO. He had a love affair with the entire company because of the many wonderful people he met there and the opportunities that HBO gave him.

That love was returned in full. The era now thought of as the Golden Age of HBO Sports was also a golden age for Artie. He came into his own when Seth Abraham gave him the responsibility of dealing directly with HBO's fighters. He had found the place where he was meant to be.

There was a special spirit at HBO Sports in the 1990s. The people who were there, particularly those involved with boxing, were a tightly knit group and Artie was very much a part of that. It seemed as though someone was always in his office; an eighteen-year-old who had just started in the mailroom or an executive vice president.

"Artie was good for the morale of everyone at HBO," says Larry Merchant. "I thought of him as a cross between a regular guy, a revered religious figure, and a comic-book action hero. Every time you left him, you felt good about having been in his presence. He could get a smile from anyone."

Dave Itskowitch (now chief operating officer for Golden Boy Promotions) recalls, "I was twenty-two years old and clueless when I started working at HBO. Artie took me under his wing. Once a week, I'd sit in his office and we'd talk for an hour. It was like therapy for me. If I was stressed, he'd calm me down. If I was sad, he'd cheer me up. I asked myself sometimes, 'What did I do to deserve this kind of love?' And after a while, I realized that was Artie. There was no bad in him."

Jon Crystal met Artie in 1992, when he was a summer intern at

HBO. The following year, he began working for the network on a full-time basis. He's now a producer for HBO Sports.

"Artie was more than a hug and a handshake," Crystal says. "He was much deeper than that. You'd talk with Artie about some problem you were having. And a few days later, he'd call and say, 'I haven't forgotten what we talked about. I'm still thinking on it.'"

"There was so much life in him," Crystal continues. "He met my mother for the first time at a screening for an HBO documentary on Arthur Ashe. In a very nice way, he looked her over from top to bottom and said, 'Damn! I'm glad I'm not Ray Charles or Stevie Wonder.' Artie might have been a foster-care child, but he was the one who adopted people on a weekly basis. Whatever the hierarchy at HBO, we all reported to Artie."

Thomas Odelfelt, another producer at HBO Sports, says, "You didn't need to know Artie well to know what a warm people person he was. My office was two doors down from his. It was probably the most traveled corridor at HBO. Everyone would come by to see Artie. I'm surprised they didn't have to change the carpet on a regular basis."

"Years ago, we had a hockey team at HBO," Odelfelt continues. "We played late at night. I was on the team. We were terrible; we lost every game. I mentioned it to Artie. And the next Tuesday night, eleven-thirty, we're on the ice at Chelsea Piers. The game's ready to begin. I look up and there's Artie. Every time I was on the ice, I heard, 'Thomas, bomaye! Thomas, bomaye!' [patterned on the chant 'Ali, bomaye' shouted in Zaire]. Artie had nicknames for everyone. From that night on, he called me 'Gretzky.'"

"Artie was goodness," says Ray Stallone (HBO vice president for sports publicity). "You couldn't meet a nicer person. There wasn't a bad bone in his body."

Artie could relate to anyone, whether it was Reggie (who shined shoes in the office) or the most powerful corporate executives.

Seth Abraham recalls, "Artie understood that people like Jeff Bewkes [HBO's CEO in the 1990s, now CEO and chairman of Time Warner], Lou, and I were his bosses. But he was never a sycophant. He straddled the line between deference and friendship perfectly. There was no sense of self-importance about him. He did things quietly and never bragged about his role. People trusted Artie."

"Artie was one of the kindest people I've ever met," says Mark Taffet (HBO senior vice president, sports operations and pay-per-view). "And he saw the big picture in life. He asked me once how my son was doing in school. I told him, 'Great; his grades are good.' And Artie said, 'No. How is he doing in school?'"

As Artie's career progressed, he became a symbol for all of the young men and women in low-level positions at HBO. He stood for the proposition that, since he'd made it, maybe they could make it too. But his reach extended far beyond the walls of Time Warner.

"You couldn't be in boxing and not know Artie Curry," Bob Arum observes.

Newcomers to the boxing scene were warmly greeted. Artie would take it upon himself to find out who they were, introduce himself, and make them feel at home. There were no pretensions. He didn't push himself on people. But he could always find a common thread that enabled him to bond with anyone of any race, creed, color, or station in life.

There were a lot of things that Artie didn't like about boxing. The shady side of the business and the brutality of the sport were in conflict with his nature. Frisco, who shared similar values, recalls, "In all the years that Artie and I were friends, we never went to a fight together. He asked me lots of times, but I didn't want to see guys hitting each other. That's not my thing."

But Artie loved fighters. Their struggle reminded him of his own.

Artie described his role at HBO Sports as follows: "I'm the hands-on guy with the fighters. Whatever they need, I'm there for them. Part of it is entertainment; taking them to ballgames, shooting pool. But it's also listening to them, helping them. I've been a fighter all my life, so I understand these guys. I'm real with people all the time, so the people who know me trust me. That's the strength of my position."

Larry Merchant later observed, "Artie took that job and made it his own. The fighters depended on Artie. Men who were fighting the next night would call him at one o'clock in the morning for inspiration."

"Artie was the most consistent person I met in boxing," says George Foreman. "The thing that bothers boxers more than anything else is fair-weather friends. Artie was the same with you whether you were on top of the world or down-and-out. If a boxer was down, Artie still treated him like he was bigtime. Come to think of it; Artie treated everyone like they were bigtime."

"Artie could always turn a negative into a positive," Foreman continues. "If you were down about something, just getting a call from Artie would lift you up. He was always thinking about other people. If he asked me for something, it was always for someone else. Artie would text me from time to time and say, 'George; so-and-so is down. Why don't you give him a call.' Even after I retired from HBO, Artie kept me working. People cared about Artie because he cared about them. And the more you spoke with Artie, the more depth you found. He was very important to me, and I'm not just saying that because he's gone. Artie was one of my heroes."

When Roy Jones was HBO's flagship fighter, Artie was the network's primary pipeline to Jones. Ten years ago, Roy declared, "Artie Curry is one of the best friends a person could have. He does his job. He's a true professional, but he's a whole lot more than that. Sometimes, when it feels like the whole world is against me, Artie will say, 'Look, brother; keep your head high; do what's right and everything will be okay.' And he tells me what he thinks is right, whether or not he agrees with me, which is the way friends should be. Artie is never this way today and another way tomorrow. There's no slippin' and slidin', no games; just straight-up real honesty. The man is family. Artie Curry is a blessing to me."

"The dude was cool," Jones says today, elaborating on that theme. "If a person was down, Artie would bend over and pick him up. He was the one guy at HBO that, no matter what, the fighters could go to. He was always there for me, and he was always there for a lot of other people too. You didn't have to call Artie when there was a problem. He'd call you."

"The bosses at HBO say we're a team," Roy continues. "But they don't always treat you like teammates. Artie was with you every step of the way. It's not like, when there was a problem, he favored one side over the other. That's not the way he was. He just wanted everyone to see the other side's point of view and help everyone get along."

Tony Walker (director of affiliate relations for HBO-PPV) recalls a day when Lennox Lewis became aggravated during an HBO production shoot. "Lennox was at his peak as heavyweight champion," Walker remembers. "And he's a big guy, very physical. He got up to leave. Artie stood right in front of him and said, 'No, brother; this is one you've got to do.' And Lennox did it."

"Oh, yeah; I remember that," Lennox says with a smile. "HBO had some people getting me ready for an interview and there was a problem.

It was a question of my hair and how to present me. Some people aren't known for tact. I talked to Artie. You could always talk with Artie. And right away, he was on the phone saying, 'Send someone who knows how to do black hair.'"

"Artie helped a lot of fighters, including me, adjust to HBO and learn how to deal with things that came up along the way," Lennox notes. "People are complex; people have different personalities. And Artie could always bridge the gap. He'd say, 'Maybe you aren't making your point right. Let's try it a different way.'"

Ronnie Shields was one of Artie's closest friends in boxing. They often had three-way telephone conversations with Jolene Mizzone of Main Events that lasted for hours.

"I met Artie in 1988," Shields recalls. "We just hit it off. A lot of people and Artie just hit it off. He was fun to be with, but he had a serious side too. He'd tell you stuff that you didn't want to hear but he thought you should know. And almost always, he was right."

"There'd be situations all the time" Shields continues, "where a fighter wouldn't want to do something and HBO would want him to do it. And the fighter would say, 'If Artie asks me to do it, I'll do it.' So Artie would come down and sit with the fighter. But he wouldn't just say, 'I want you to do it.' He'd explain how, 'This isn't only for HBO. It will get you exposure that will make you bigger and get you more money down the road.' And if you heard that from Artie, you knew it was true. He never acted like he was special, but he was. He wanted to make people happy. That was his joy. Whenever I spent time with Artie, I walked away with a smile."

"I have two older sisters," says Shane Mosley. "Artie was like my big brother. When I was younger, he gave me advice about how to conduct myself around HBO staff, how to dress, things like that. If I had a question about anything—life, boxing, whatever—I'd go to Artie. He'd give me his honest opinion, and then he'd do his best to see that things worked out right. He used to tell me, 'Don't forget where you came from.' He was big on that. And he always told me how lucky I am that my mother and father are still in my life; that I should always remember how special that is."

"We talked about boxing sometimes," says Winky Wright. "But it was more about life; making sure I didn't mess myself up. If a fighter did something out of place, Artie would tell him because he cared about us as people, not just as fighters. And it wasn't just the fighters. Artie showed respect for the little people in boxing; the ones that the suits at HBO don't even know their name. That's the way he was with people. Artie showed respect for everyone."

"Every now and then," says Mark Breland, "Artie would talk with me about what he went through when he was young. But he never dwelled on it. He was about now and the future and the good things in his life. One time, he saw me; I was walking around with my head down. Artie took one look and asked, 'What's the matter, brother.' I told him, and he started talking to me about life. 'Things aren't as bad as you think they are. There's people that care about you. There's no problem that you can't overcome.' Artie had a way of making you feel good. And I was like, 'Wow; I can deal with this thing.' He was always so nice."

"Artie came to my house in Arkansas," says Jermain Taylor. "He had this old music that we were listening to. The Temptations, Four Tops, Supremes; stuff like that. Artie got up and did a few dance steps. He was a better person than he was a dancer. But I remember thinking; not that many people at his level take the time to come to your home. Artie made you feel special."

"Artie had no enemies," says Oscar De La Hoya. "And in boxing, to have no enemies, you have to be special. One time, he asked me if I'd go out on a double-date with him. He told me that, if I said 'yes,' he could get any woman he wanted to go out with him that night. But whether I was up or down in my career, he treated me the same. And when I was down in my life, he was there for me."

One of Artie's closest friends was Brian Adams. They met in 1994, three years before Brian embarked on a ring career that saw him compile a record of 17 wins against 4 losses with 8 knockouts and 1 KO by. Adams now runs the Golden Gloves for the *New York Daily News*. Artie called him "my little brother." Brian's nickname for Artie was "The Wise One."

"Artie didn't care about what he got," Adams says. "It was all about what he could give to you. Some people call to see how you're doing when they need something. With Artie, it was the opposite. He'd call to see what he could do for you. He didn't like it when someone came to him with their hand out. But if he saw that you were in need, he'd help you."

Other people in Artie's position might have tried to build financially on the friendships that they'd developed with elite fighters. They would have made side deals to steer fighters to a particular promoter or, more ambitiously, tried to establish their own promotional company.

Artie wasn't like that. He was content with his life the way it was. He had a passion for backgammon and the New York Knicks. He also liked playing basketball. One of his fondest memories involved a pick-up game in which he was guarded by Roy Jones.

"Roy was on me," Artie recalled. "But he wasn't guarding me that tight. I put two shots in from the outside and, after the second one, he moved in on me. I got the ball again, put up a jump shot . . . swish! Roy shook his head, smiled at me, and said 'dang!' I loved that moment."

"Every memory I have of Artie is special," Roy says in response. "Sometimes Artie would call me at three o'clock in the morning. He knew I was up then. He'd tell me, 'Hey, Jones; I got someone who wants to say "what's up." ' Then whoever it was would get on the phone and they'd be asking, 'Is this really Roy Jones?' But because it was Artie who made the call, they'd know it was me."

Those who knew Artie best also know that he was a "neat freak." One of his proudest moments came when he bought a two-bedroom apartment with a large terrace in the Williamsburg section of Brooklyn with a view overlooking the Manhattan skyline. Once a week, a housekeeper came in to clean the apartment. After she left, Artie would go around, moving everything an inch here or an inch there so it was exactly the way it had been before.

"Artie always said the best way to keep things is to take care of them," Frisco recalls. "But sometimes he was a bit much. Once, when a girl was staying with him for a weekend, he called me and said, 'Frisco, she moved the rug in the bathroom when she took a shower and didn't put it back.' I told him, 'Hang in there, buddy. You can make it to Monday.' "

Lise Curry has similar memories and says, "Artie would have women as guests and call me and complain about the mess they were making. I'd say, 'How much mess can one person make in a weekend?' And he'd tell me, 'She's never coming back.' "

Carmine Gangone owns and operates Carmine's Pizzeria on Graham Avenue in Brooklyn. He and Artie met in 1996 and became friends. Often, after work, Artie would visit a small bar owned by Jimmy Glenn. He'd have a glass of wine, talk with Jimmy, and take the subway home. Then he'd stop by Carmine's, which was a few blocks from his apartment.

"We'd sit and talk," Carmine remembers. "Hours would go by. After a while, everyone in the restaurant—the waiters, the busboys, the other customers—knew him. Artie talked with the old Italian guys, the young hip-hop guys, everyone. When he came by, it was like a movie star coming in."

"But he did have this thing about neatness," Carmine acknowledges. "Last year, he gave a party on his terrace so we could see the fireworks on the 4th of July. And the whole time, Artie was walking around with a big plastic bag, asking, 'Are you done with that beer yet? Throw the can in here.' You couldn't even finish your beer. And he kept saying, 'Damn! You guys are messy.'"

Artie also liked "downtime." There were occasions when he just wanted to be alone. That was true whether he was in his apartment or surrounded by people. Once, he journeyed to Easton, Pennsylvania, for Larry Holmes's fiftieth birthday party. It was a festive occasion with boxing personalities sprinkled throughout the crowd. For the entire night, Artie sat on a stool at the end of the bar, alone, with a glass of wine. He was content, thinking and observing, having a good time.

Some people thought of Artie as innocent. He wasn't. There was an innocence about him, but he also had a way with women and enjoyed their company in many ways. He was engaged twice; once in his mid-thirties (they lived together) and briefly, years later, a second time.

"Artie liked his privacy and he liked his own space," Brian Adams says. "I think that's one of the reasons he never got married. He had his own life and his own rhythm. He wasn't ready for marriage yet."

But he wanted, someday, to have children.

"Artie loved being around children," Brien McDonald remembers. "And children knew instinctively that he was warm and safe and good. He definitely wanted to be a father someday, but it was important to him that he not have children out of wedlock. When he had children, he wanted to be a father to them in every sense of the word. In his mind, that also meant being a good husband."

Thus, Artie's friends were his family. He was a good listener. People confided in him and he always kept the confidence. He accepted his friends the way they were and didn't try to change them. He was constantly sending text messages ("If you love someone, you have to let them know you care about them," he said). And he very quietly sent walking-around money to people who were down on their luck. An envelope would arrive in the mail with a note that made it sound as though the recipient was doing Artie a favor by taking the money rather than the other way around.

Artie didn't send store-bought cards to commemorate occasions. He'd draw one. He was also a bit of a musician. On birthdays, he'd telephone, play *Happy Birthday* on the harmonica, and then sing it.

"Family wasn't about DNA to Artie," says Lou DiBella. "It was about loyalty and love."

Of all Artie's friends, no one was closer to him than Pam Waring (now manager of promotions for HBO Sports).

Pam began work at HBO in 1985 as a secretary in the finance department. She met Artie shortly after she transferred to building maintenance. In 1989, she took a job as a secretary in the sports department. That same year, she and her husband (Kenny) adopted a seventeen-day-old baby who they named Kevin.

Pam remembers a time when she, Kenny, and Kevin were with Artie and Roy Jones. Kevin had just done well on a difficult test, and Artie was proud of him.

"Tell Roy what you got," Artie prompted.

"Eighty-five," Kevin responded.

"Eighty-five," Roy said. "The only time I saw an eighty-five was on a speeding ticket."

"Kevin talked with Artie on the phone all the time," Pam remembers. "If there was something that, for whatever reason, he didn't feel comfortable talking about with Kenny or me, he talked with Artie."

Artie, in turn, was thankful that Kevin was in his life. "It gives me a chance to do things I never got to do when I was growing up," he said.

Over the years, Artie and Pam forged a relationship akin to the bonds between a brother and sister. "He didn't cook," she says, "so he came to our house for home-cooked meals all the time. Sundays, he'd come over and watch ballgames on television with Kenny and Kevin. He never had that family setting when he was growing up and he loved being part of a family."

"I always felt safe when I was with Artie," Pam continues. "When I was on the road at fights for HBO, I didn't have to worry about being a woman alone in a strange town because Artie was there to take care of me. We'd eat all our meals together and go sight-seeing together. It got so Kenny started calling Artie my road-husband."

But Artie lived in the real world. And no matter how harmonious an environment he tried to create, inevitably there were problems.

In early 2000, Lou DiBella left HBO to pursue a career in boxing promotion. Later that year, Seth Abraham departed to become executive vice president and chief operating officer of Madison Square Garden. Ross Greenburg was promoted to the top position at HBO Sports. Kery Davis assumed DiBella's duties.

Seth had been a father figure to Artie. Lou was akin to a big brother. Artie had suffered more than his share of abandonment during his life, and their leaving added to the hurt.

George Foreman recalls, "The only time I saw Artie down was when Seth Abraham left HBO. Artie loved Seth and he wasn't sure what it would be like for him after Seth was gone. That was the one time I gave Artie advice. I told him, 'You've made something of yourself at HBO. People at HBO love you. Don't give all that up because one person isn't there anymore.'"

Abraham and DiBella understood Artie's gifts. They'd created a role for him as a liaison between HBO and its fighters, and Artie had performed masterfully. But after their departure, he began to feel marginalized. There was a new attitude at HBO Sports: "We're paying the fighters a lot of money. They should be happy and do what we want them to do."

Carmine Gangone recalls, "Artie said that things changed for him when Seth Abraham left. Some of what he did was taken away from him and he understood that he was never going to be treated by the new guys the way he wanted to be treated."

One incident spoke volumes. In April 2001, when Lennox Lewis fought Hasim Rahman in South Africa, Artie was on the list of HBO personnel slated to meet Nelson Mandela. Then, at the last minute, he was bumped in favor of Kery Davis's wife. The incident upset him and left him feeling that he was devalued in the eyes of the people who ran HBO Sports.

"Artie was so sad and hurt," one of his co-workers remembers.

"There was nobody in the world he wanted to meet more than Nelson Mandela. It wasn't that he wanted to tell people, 'Guess who I met.' Nelson Mandela had deep meaning to Artie; it was almost spiritual. And something that he had been promised, something important, was taken away from him."

"This wouldn't have happened a year ago," Artie said.

More of Artie's responsibilities were given to others. He was excluded from the meetings that the HBO announcing team and key production personnel held with fighters on the day before each fight. A new generation of boxers didn't know him as well as previous generations had. "He was a bigshot who didn't act like a bigshot," says Paulie Malignaggi. "I wish I'd gotten to know him better."

On May 3, 2008, Artie underwent knee-replacement surgery at Beth Israel Hospital in New York. He had a fear of doctors and hospitals but told Ronnie Shields, "I got to do it because I'm tired of limping."

Frisco recalls, "Artie said to me that, when he was in the hospital, none of the bosses in the sports department called to see if he was okay. That told him a lot."

There was more to come. On May 28, 2008, Ross Greenburg held a staff meeting. He was upset about leaks to the media (and this writer in particular) and told the dozen-or-so people in attendance that he was going to find out who the "moles" were and "destroy" them. Thereafter, according to sources at HBO, he ordered that the office computers and BlackBerries of five people be seized and searched.

Some of the targets of the searches didn't seem to fit the profile of people likely to leak information to the media. Their inclusion on the list gave rise to speculation that a secondary purpose of the investigation might have been Greenburg's desire to learn what people were saying internally about him.

A search of Artie's computer and BlackBerry failed to reveal any improper leaking of information. However, there was an email in which Artie referred to Ross as an "asshole."

On September 19, 2008, Greenburg called Artie into his office and confronted him with the email. Artie disliked confrontation. But in the face of assault, he would stand his ground. Later, in a moment of anger, he told a friend, "I'm glad they found it. I'm tired of the way Ross is treating me, and I'm tired of pretending one thing and feeling another."

Still, Artie felt pressure that he hadn't felt before. And because he was unaware that the computers and BlackBerries of other HBO personnel had been searched, he felt like even more of a target and alone.

Then Artie was confronted with an allegation that he had misappropriated HBO property. Eventually, it was determined that his FedEx account number had been compromised by a third party. But he was subjected to the indignity of being required to explain why he'd sent caps, T-shirts, and other HBO paraphernalia to various people in the boxing industry.

"The HBO family is getting a little dysfunctional," he said.

Finally, in spring 2009, Artie was told that, in the future as a cost-cutting measure, HBO would only send him to four out-of-town fights a year.

Respect was enormously important to Artie. Respecting other people and being respected. Now he felt that his boss wanted him to quit and was humiliating him in the process.

"The hurt ran deep," Frisco says. "Artie was so proud to be at HBO. There were so many people there that he loved. And to have one or two people treat him with such disrespect; that bothered him a lot."

But the hurt was offset by the bonds that Artie shared with countless co-workers and friends. And at one point during his difficulties, he received a telephone call from Time Warner chairman and CEO Jeff Bewkes, who, in Artie's words, "just called to say hello." Whether by design or chance, that call lifted his spirits considerably.

On Thursday, April 2nd, after what he regarded as an unsatisfactory meeting with Kery Davis to discuss his future, Artie left the office and went across the street to Bryant Park. There, he called several friends to discuss his situation at HBO. He was at peace with himself and completely comfortable with who he was.

"They will never break my spirit," he said.

On the afternoon of Saturday, April 4th, Artie and Brian Adams went to see the Yankees play the Chicago Cubs in an exhibition game at the new Yankee Stadium. That night, they partied together. On Sunday morning, Brian received the final text message that he would ever receive from his friend. Sent at 7:56 AM, it read in full, "Everything happens for a reason, my young brother."

Later that morning, Artie had breakfast with Carmine Gangone at Carmine's Pizzeria. On Sunday night, he and Frisco had dinner together.

"After dinner, we sat in the park for about an hour-and-a-half," Frisco remembers. "Artie didn't say much. He was more quiet than usual, but there were times when Artie liked quiet. You know how it is with a good friend. You can be together and not talk, but you're happy just sitting together, knowing the other person is there."

The last thing that Artie said to Frisco in the park was, "Do you remember the days when we just had a dollar in our pocket and how happy we were?"

Frisco drove Artie home. Later that evening, Artie telephoned him and said, "I took some medicine for a foot fungus that's bothering me and I'm having a bad reaction. I'll never take this medicine again."

On Monday, Frisco called Artie at 7:00 AM. "I asked how was he doing," Frisco says. "Artie told me, 'I'm okay. I'm starting to feel like myself again.' But he was breathing hard. And in the back of my mind, I was wondering, 'Why are you breathing hard if you're okay?' So I called him again two hours later and he told me, really, he was starting to feel better, so that was all right."

At 8:40 PM, shortly before the start of the NCAA basketball championship game between North Carolina and Michigan State, Frisco sent Artie a text message that read, "I hope you're OK, brother. Love you."

"After the game, I texted Artie two or three more times," Frisco says. "But he didn't answer. I figured maybe he was sleeping. On Tuesday, when I still didn't hear from him, I started to get nervous. I called and texted and said, 'Just text me that you're okay.' Then I thought, 'Well, maybe he just wants to be alone.' But on Tuesday night, I was worrying a lot. On Wednesday, I asked some people if they had heard or seen Artie since Monday, and everyone said no. Carmine and Brian said the same thing, so I went by Artie's place and spoke to the landlord. He lived on the same floor as Artie, and I begged him to open the door. The landlord said, 'I can't let you in.' I said, 'I don't have to go in. You go in and tell me. All I have to know is if my friend is okay.' I was praying that maybe Artie fell and broke his leg and couldn't move or he was so sick that he couldn't call but we could get him to the hospital and he'd be all right."

The landlord entered Artie's apartment. Artie was lying in bed. Nothing seemed out of the ordinary except for a glass that had fallen onto the floor. Artie looked to be sleeping. He was dead.

Frisco couldn't bring himself to call Pam Waring. Instead, he called Carmine, Artie's mother, and Marvelle Southerland (a friend of Artie's at HBO). Eventually, Brian Adams called the Warings.

Carmine, Brian, and Lise Curry came to the apartment.

Brian looked at Artie and said to himself, "This isn't happening. It's not real."

Lise refused to believe that Artie was dead until a police officer told her that it was true.

"I cried like a baby," Frisco says. "I couldn't stop. I sat there, looking at Artie till two o'clock in the morning; thinking about all the years we spent together, looking over him the way so many times he looked over me. Then they took his body away and I followed the ambulance to the morgue. I don't know why. I guess I just wanted to make sure he got there safely."

Artie's death sent a wave of grief through the boxing community. The news hit particularly hard at HBO, where he'd touched so many lives. Artie was proud of having worked at HBO; and to many, he was the heart and soul of HBO Sports.

On the first *World Championship Boxing* telecast after Artie's death, Larry Merchant addressed the tragedy and began his remarks with the words "a good man died young." He ended in tears. Jim Lampley was also unable to maintain his composure.

On May 13th, the HBO community came together at Madison Square Garden for a memorial service. Jeff Bewkes and Bill Nelson (the current chairman and CEO of HBO) were among those who addressed the gathering.

Now Artie's friends are reaching out to each other to share memories. There's a void where he stood, but his mantra ("peace and love, brother; peace and love, sister") lingers in the mind.

Jon Crystal speaks for many when he says, "It seems like, in death, the outpouring of love has done justice to Artie. And I'm very happy about that. It's not often that an actual one-of-a-kind person comes into your life. We don't meet many people like Artie. There aren't many people like Artie."

Artie considered himself spiritual, not religious. He didn't adhere to the rituals and teachings of any one denomination.

"But Artie had God in his heart," Roy Jones affirms. "He was an angel that God sent to heal souls."

"Artie is what religion is all about," says George Foreman. "He was a walking Sunday school lesson. He treated people the way he wanted to be treated. The Golden Rule."

"Artie opened up his arms and his heart to every person he met," says Jolene Mizzone. "He gave me a positive mindset and changed how I feel about life."

"Artie was music," says Dave Itskowitch. "Right now, I just feel like I haven't seen him for a while. But he'll always be with me."

"Artie was a miracle," says Lou DiBella. "He conquered a childhood that was full of unimaginably bad things and turned himself into the person he wanted to be. My life is better because I knew Artie."

And Jim Lampley reminisces, "Several years ago, I asked Artie why he thought we were such good friends. We came from such different worlds. Artie said, 'Soul,'—sometimes he called me soul—he said, 'Soul; real knows real. It's as simple as that.' I'll go to my grave thinking that, coming from Artie, that's the highest compliment anyone has ever paid to me."

"The best memorial I can think of," says Mary Dickey, "would be if we all tried to be a little more like Artie."

The beauty of morals is that each person can control his or her own destiny. We're all at the mercy of external forces. Our personal lives and jobs are dependent in varying degree upon the will of others. Morality is the one area where every person is endowed with absolute power to be the person that he or she wants to be.

Artie Curry understood that principle and made the most of it. He was more than a nice guy. He was an extraordinary spirit who never stopped trying to help other people the way a few special people had helped him find his way.

Reflecting on their thirty-two-year friendship, Frisco says, "Artie's birthday was on February 18th and mine was February 24th. Every year, we celebrated our birthdays together. Next year was going to be fifty for Artie. That would have been a big one."

Frisco smiles.

"Artie loved it that he did things his way. I know, if he was here, he'd tell everyone, 'Don't feel sorry for me because I had a great life.' I keep saying that to myself so I'll feel better. But I'm hurting because he's gone."